THE READERS' ADVISORY GUIDE TO
GENRE BLENDS
FOR CHILDREN AND YOUNG ADULTS

ALA READERS' ADVISORY SERIES

The Readers' Advisory Guide to Genre Blends
for Children and Young Adults

The Readers' Advisory Guide to Horror, Third Edition

The Readers' Advisory Guide to Genre Fiction,
Third Edition

The Readers' Advisory Guide to Teen Literature

The Readers' Advisory Guide to Graphic Novels,
Second Edition

The Readers' Advisory Guide to Genre Blends

The Readers' Advisory Guide to Historical Fiction

The Readers' Advisory Guide to Mystery, Second
Edition

The Readers' Advisory Guide to Street Literature

The Readers' Advisory Handbook

Serving Boys through Readers' Advisory

Research-Based Readers' Advisory

Serving Teens through Readers' Advisory

The Readers' Advisory Guide to Nonfiction

Romance Readers' Advisory

Short Story Readers' Advisory

THE READERS' ADVISORY GUIDE TO
GENRE BLENDS
FOR CHILDREN AND YOUNG ADULTS

Pauline Dewan and Meagan Lacy

CHICAGO | 2022

Pauline Dewan is a liaison librarian at Wilfrid Laurier University in Canada. Coauthor of the book *Connecting Children with Classics* (2018), she has also published "Survival of the Fittest: The Evolution of the Children's Survival Novel" and "More than Child's Play: The Scaffolding Role of Toys, Games, and Play in Children's Literature." She served for five years on a province-wide readers' advisory committee and won a RUSA Reference Service Press Award for her article "Reading Matters in the Academic Library: Taking the Lead from Public Librarians." She received her MLIS from Western University (Canada) and PhD in English literature from York University (Canada).

Meagan Lacy is chief librarian at Stella & Charles Guttman Community College, CUNY. In addition to coauthoring *Connecting Children with Classics* (2018) with Pauline, she received the Emerging Scholar Award for her article "Portraits of Children of Alcoholics: Stories that Hope to Hope," published in *Children's Literature in Education*. She received her MLIS at the University of Washington and her MA in English at Indiana University at Indianapolis. She is currently completing her MFA in creative writing at City College, CUNY.

© 2022 by Pauline Dewan and Meagan Lacy

Extensive effort has gone into ensuring the reliability of the information in this book; however, the publisher makes no warranty, express or implied, with respect to the material contained herein.

ISBN: 978-0-8389-4990-0 (paper)

Library of Congress Cataloging-in-Publication Data
Names: Dewan, Pauline, author. | Lacy, Meagan, author.
Title: The readers' advisory guide to genre blends for children and young adults / Pauline Dewan and Meagan Lacy.
Description: Chicago : ALA Editions, 2022. | Series: ALA readers' advisory series | Includes bibliographical references and indexes. | Summary: "This helpful guide orients readers' advisory staff, educators, and collection development librarians with a hand-picked selection of hybrid genres and novels published since 2000"—Provided by publisher.
Identifiers: LCCN 2021062001 | ISBN 9780838949900 (paperback)
Subjects: LCSH: Fiction in libraries—United States. | Readers' advisory services—United States. | Reading interests—United States. | Fiction genres. | Children's stories. | Young adult fiction. | Fiction—Bibliography.
Classification: LCC Z711.5 .D49 2022 | DDC 025.2/780883—dc23/eng/20220120
LC record available at https://lccn.loc.gov/2021062001

Cover image © info@nextmars.com/Adobe Stock. Text design in the Palatino and Univers typefaces.

♾ This paper meets the requirements of ANSI/NISO Z39.48-1992 (Permanence of Paper).

Printed in the United States of America
26 25 24 23 22   5 4 3 2 1

ALA Editions purchases fund advocacy, awareness, and accreditation programs for library professionals worldwide.

Contents

Series Introduction, by Joyce Saricks and Neal Wyatt   *vii*
Acknowledgments   *ix*

Part I: Foundations

1 Genre Blends   *3*
Their Emergence, Appeal, and Special Considerations

2 Reader Appeals and Book Appeals   *13*
Doorways into the RA Conversation

Part II: Annotations

3 Graphic Novels for Children and Young Adults   *23*

4 Historical Fantasies for Children and Young Adults   *43*

5 Historical Mysteries for Children and Young Adults   *65*

6 Magical Realism for Children and Young Adults   *85*

7 Steampunk Fiction for Children and Young Adults   *109*

8 Verse Novels for Children and Young Adults   *131*

Subject/Theme/Appeals Index   *155*
Coping with Challenges Index   *181*
Author/Title Index   *199*

Series Introduction

Joyce Saricks and Neal Wyatt

SERIES EDITORS

In a library world in which finding answers to readers' advisory (RA) questions is often considered one of our most daunting service challenges, library staff need guides that are supportive, accessible, and immediately useful. The titles in this series are designed to be just that. They help advisors become familiar with fiction genres and nonfiction subjects, especially those they don't personally read. They provide ready-made lists of "need to know" elements such as key authors and read-alikes, as well as tips on how to keep up with trends and important new authors and titles.

Written by librarians with years of RA experience who are also enthusiasts of the genre or subject, the titles in this series of practical guides emphasize an appreciation of the topic, focusing on the elements and features fans enjoy, so advisors unfamiliar with the topics can readily appreciate why they are so popular.

Because this series values the fundamental concepts of readers' advisory work and its potential to serve readers, viewers, and listeners in whatever future space libraries inhabit, the focus of each book is on appeal and how appeal crosses genre, subject, and format, especially to include audio and video as well as Graphic Novels. Thus, each guide emphasizes the importance of whole-collection readers' advisory and explores ways to make suggestions that include novels, nonfiction, and multimedia, as well as how to incorporate whole-collection elements into displays and book lists.

Each guide includes sections designed to help librarians in their RA duties, be that daily work or occasional interactions. Topics covered in each volume include:

- The appeal of the genre or subject and information on subgenres and types so that librarians might understand the scope of the topic and how it relates to other genres and subjects. A brief history is also included, giving advisors context and highlighting beloved classic titles.

- Descriptions of key authors and titles with explanations of why they're important: why advisors should be familiar with them and

vii

why they should be kept in our collections. Entries for read-alikes accompany these lists, allowing advisors to move from identifying a key author to helping patrons find new authors to enjoy.

- Information on how to conduct the RA conversation so that advisors can learn the tools and skills needed to develop deeper connections between their collections and their communities of readers, listeners, and viewers.

- An introduction to the genre or subject designed to get staff up to speed. Turn to this section to get a quick overview of the genre or subject.

- Resources and techniques for keeping up to date and understanding new developments in the genre or subject. This section will both aid staff already familiar with the genre or subject, plus familiarize those not yet in the know.

- Tips for marketing collections and lists of resources and awards round out the tools that staff need to be successful working with their community.

As readers who just happen to be readers' advisors, we hope the guides in this series lead to longer to-be-read, -watched, and -listened-to piles. Our goal is that the series helps those new to RA feel supported, less at sea; and, for advisors who have been at this a while, that it provides new ideas or new ways of looking at foundational concepts. Most of all, we hope this series helps all advisors feel excited and eager to help patrons find their next great title. So dig in, explore, learn, and enjoy the almost alchemical process of connecting title and reader.

Acknowledgments

We would like to express our heartfelt gratitude to our series editors, Joyce Saricks and Neal Wyatt. They offered us tireless support and insightful advice every step of the way. We would also like to thank our gracious editor, Jamie Santoro. She made writing this book easy. We have so appreciated the care and expert guidance of these three unparalleled editors.

Part I

Foundations

1

Genre Blends
Their Emergence, Appeal, and Special Considerations

Emergence of Genre Blends

Novels for children and teens are not written in a vacuum. They reflect the ideas, trends, and beliefs current at the time of writing. As ideas about young people have changed, so too have the novels written for them and the genres that are popular.

During the Middle Ages and even up until the eighteenth century, belief in original sin predisposed adults to view children as depraved creatures who needed taming and spiritual guidance.[1] Children were considered adults-in-training, who around the age of seven could begin gradual entry into the adult work world.[2] Not surprisingly, genres for children were religious and educational: catechisms, ABCs with moral verses, elementary textbooks called primers, and books of courtesy describing the manners and customs of polite society.[3]

But by the mid-eighteenth century, a gradual secularization of attitudes initiated other changes. "Some people began to see childhood," Hugh Cunningham points out, "not as a preparation for something else, whether adulthood or heaven, but as a life to be valued in its own right."[4] Novels were now written for them and featured children as protagonists—a change indicative of their elevated status. Although books for children expanded exponentially at this time, they were still pious in tone and overtly didactic. Authors known as the Rational Moralists dispensed information in the guise of Realistic Fiction. The Sunday School Moralists also wrote "realistic" stories, written to persuade children of the importance of religion. Children often read adult fiction, especially Adventure stories such as *Robinson Crusoe* and *Gulliver's Travels*. By the nineteenth century, cheap editions of books expanded readership for both adults and children. During the 1820s, "penny dreadfuls" emerged. Although these mass-produced, sensational stories were not initially written for children, they were eagerly read by them.

It was not until the second half of the nineteenth century that many of the genres we are familiar with today emerged. The golden age of children's literature lasted until World War I, introducing such genres as Fantasy, Adventure, Family Stories, Animal Tales, School Stories, and Desert Island novels. Adventure stories were mainly narratives of empire building written for boys, although girls eagerly read them, too. Girls were expected to read domestic novels of family life. With the twentieth century, Science Fiction gained in popularity; Mystery novels flourished with Nancy Drew and the Hardy Boys; and the grim "New Realism" of the 1970s introduced issues previously considered unsuitable for young readers.[5]

Except for the New Realism books, many pre-twenty-first-century novels depict a world in which problems exist but are solvable. Children are mostly white, able, and middle class. Although adults in these earlier novels cause problems for children, most play a supportive role.

Novelists' understanding of the needs and psychology of youth has continued to develop, resulting in an increasingly perceptive literature. With the turn of the twenty-first century, novels for young people routinely depict life that is more aligned with their actual experience of it. New genres have emerged, constituting one of the fastest-growing areas of fiction for children and teens. Genre blends, which are also known as hybrid genres or cross-genres, combine two genres into a single merged category. We use the term *genre blends* in this book to emphasize the intermingling of categories, a union that produces something original. Genre blends emerged later than single genres and have provided authors with new opportunities for writing.

Genre blends extend traditional boundaries. Many genre-blend novels challenge accepted ideas, avoiding a "homogeneous, one-voiced, and 'one-discoursed' worldview."[6] These twenty-first-century genres allow for innovative possibilities and ideas.

Public librarians, school librarians, teachers, and anyone who buys books or offers readers' advisory suggestions should learn about these emerging genres. Although Megan M. McArdle has written a readers' advisory book about genre blends for adults, no one has yet written about genre blends for children and teens.[7]

The Wide Appeal of Genre Blends

Genres provide a way of classifying the immense range of fiction that exists. As Sarah Worth and Sean McBratnie observe, genres are useful for making category distinctions and facilitating choice for readers: "Genre is not merely dictated by subject or theme or content, but it helps readers to know how to interpret, evaluate, and how to properly manage expectations of a text. If I am anticipating a Horror Fiction and end up reading a Psychological Thriller, I am bound to be disappointed and think that the work was not as successful as I might have anticipated otherwise."[8] Genre also acts as an appeal element for readers. Books in each genre contain features that readers look for because they know they like them. Those who love Science Fiction, for example, understand that books in this category will take place in an imagined future and contain elements such as scientific and technological marvels, space travel, and life on other planets. Not all novels in this genre will appeal to every Science Fiction fan, but readers can expect to find many choices that will.

Genre blends are not necessarily better or worse than single genres. Every genre appeals to the fans who enjoy its characteristic features. What a genre blend does, however, is extend the range of categories and thereby choices from which to select. We discuss six genre blends in this book, each embodying a unique set of characteristics and appeal elements.

By the very fact that a blended genre combines two categories, it potentially attracts a wider audience than does a single genre. Readers interested in Mysteries, for example, and those interested in Historical Fiction might both be interested in Historical Mysteries. And since each of the two genres in a blend has its own set of appeals, the combination of the two increases the number of ways a novel can attract readers.

In the classroom, genre blends might appeal to students who are bored with traditional genres. Teachers looking for a curricular tie-in novel about Victorian London, for instance, might attract more interest with a Steampunk novel or Historical Fantasy than with a Historical Novel.

When two genres are blended together, they can produce a unique and sometimes unconventional result. Like mash-ups, the union of two forms creates something new and transformed. Although there are many conventional genre-blend novels, there are certainly numerous books that offer something different. Readers who are attracted to novels that are original, untraditional, or out of the ordinary will find many examples in genre-blend categories. Those who are bored with single genres and anyone who just wants a change may find one of the genre-blend categories suited to their tastes. Genre blends are also a good way for readers to try out a single genre they would not normally choose. A Steampunk novel, for instance, might entice readers to consider a Historical Novel or a work of Science Fiction.

Shelf Placement and Findability

No matter how wonderful a book is, it does not matter if readers can't find it. All fiction suffers from the problem of discoverability, and genre blends are no exception.

The majority of books that sit on a library bookshelf do so with the spine facing outward. Consider the fact that even the widest spine is less than a couple of inches. That is very little product to capture a reader's attention. Now think about how many books fit on a shelf, how many shelves a bookcase holds, and how many bookcases sit side by side, forming endless aisles of the same product. Once books are shelved, they become all but invisible—true needles in a library haystack. The larger the library, the more problematic discoverability can be. These challenges make marketing and promotion of books especially important.

Next, consider the arrangement of books on the shelf. Although many public and school libraries classify their nonfiction, fewer do their fiction, preferring instead to arrange it alphabetically by author. Research has shown that one of the primary ways children find books is by browsing.[9] Yet alphabetical arrangements of books hinder browsing. As Sandra Bojanowski and Shelley Kwiecien have said of their alphabetically arranged fiction, "It felt like the refrigerator, stove, and sink were in separate rooms. You can still cook a meal but not easily."[10] According to Scholastic's latest study of reading, 89% of six-to-seventeen-year-olds say that their favorite book is the one they choose themselves.[11] However, 42% of them have trouble finding a book they like. Infrequent readers have greater difficulties; 59% report problems finding a good book to read.

Moreover, there are too many books to browse in most fiction areas. Although readers love large libraries with lots of choice, too much choice is overwhelming. When Sheena Iyengar and Mark Lepper studied store customers, they found that "an extensive array of options can at first seem highly appealing to consumers, yet can reduce their subsequent motivation to purchase the product."[12]

Marketing and Promoting Genre Blends

Shelf Considerations

Consequently, the first way to promote genre blends is to reconsider those shelves. Arranging books by genre is a first step in creating a more manageable browsing experience. Libraries that have done so believe that it is a more intuitive and user-friendly system for children and teens.[13] Arranging books by genre has also boosted their circulation statistics.[14]

However, books that do not fall easily into a category are problematic for genre-classified arrangements. Because genre blends straddle two genres, they may seem especially problematic. A book can sit in only one spot on a shelf unless a library purchases multiple copies. Some genre blends seem to naturally warrant their own space on a shelf; Graphic Novels are the most obvious example, followed by Verse Novels. Although each of these genres is a blend of two categories, their status as a unique genre is more obvious than genre blends such as Historical Mysteries that can be considered a subset of a parent genre. We would recommend, however, that every genre blend merits its own space in a genre-arranged collection, separate and distinct from other genres. Just as Mystery stories appeal to some readers, so, too, do books of Magical Realism or Historical Fantasies. It is convenient for readers to find all these books together on a shelf.

Although libraries use front-facing books to draw attention to selected items, expanding the number of front-facing books would be beneficial. A front-facing book captures customers' attention in two ways. The very fact that it faces a different way than the other books makes it stand out. But, just as important, it makes the book cover visible. These covers are designed by skilled illustrators and designers to entice buyers. In addition, the illustration, fonts, and colors work together to present a visual cue to the content. Although many libraries have limited shelf space, rigorous deselection can clear added space, which in turn will highlight the books that remain.

Tempting Reluctant Readers

Promotional efforts should be directed toward non–library users, nonreaders, and reluctant readers, not just committed library users and readers. A Pew study of public libraries found that an astonishing 19% of American adults have never visited a public library. As children and teens, then, they never entered a library door.[15] In a survey of 1,700 sixth-grade students, comments such as "Nothing usually makes me want to read" and "It stinks and I don't like to read anyway" indicate the negative feelings that some children harbor toward reading.[16] These young people might possibly enjoy a genre-blend novel as something different than their past experience with reading. However, they must first be tempted to pick one up. Retailers pay attention to visual merchandising—the art of presenting products in a way that makes them appear irresistible to shoppers.[17] Creating attractive library spaces could make the experience of choosing books a more positive one.

Using posters that promote the actual reading experience can be another effective strategy. "Clever advertisers promote their products and services," observe Rachel Van Riel, Olive Fowler, and Anne Downes, "by helping consumers imagine themselves using them."[18] Look for a poster of a child or teen immersed in reading a genre-blend novel, or create a collage of photos of readers lost in a good genre-blend book.

Book and Whole-Collection Displays

Some genre blends are not as well-known as long-standing single genres — readers may not be familiar with Steampunk or Verse Novels, for example. Book displays are proven methods of attracting customers and an effective way of highlighting genre blends. Many children and teens enter a library hoping to find a book that appeals to them. They are not sure just what they want but believe they will recognize it when they see it. Giving them a manageable number of books in an attractively laid-out display helps solve the problem of too much choice. Some of these readers will be curious about an unfamiliar genre that attracts their attention in a display.

Although the main content of a genre-blend display will be the novels themselves, additional items can also spark interest. Consider a whole-collection display on a genre-blend theme. A Steampunk display, for example, could include nonfiction books about the Industrial Revolution, Victorian inventors, or the history of flight. Historical Mysteries could contain Sherlock Holmes videos or books of actual historical criminals such as Jack the Ripper. Verse Novel displays about sensitive subjects could include videos on the same theme or nonfiction works that explore the topic in depth. These whole-collection displays work well because many genre-blend novels inspire readers to want to know more about the book's subject matter. Consider placing three sets of bookmarks or annotated book lists in the midst of the display to provide fiction, nonfiction, and video suggestions. These bookmarks and reading lists will raise readers' awareness of the many items available.

But it is not always enough to create an attractive display — retail studies suggest the importance of a display's location. Tony Morgan identifies platinum, gold, silver, and bronze zones in a store layout, observing that platinum areas attract the most attention.[19] These are high-traffic areas, visible to shoppers. The library consultant Rachel Van Riel observes that libraries don't always make the most of their "platinum" areas, using them instead for such things as self-service kiosks, hold shelves, and copy machines.[20] High-traffic platinum areas are an obvious choice for a book display.

Whenever customers must wait for any reason, they have time to look around. Retailers take advantage of lineups at cash registers to highlight products. Studies have shown that sales of point-of-purchase products are higher than products in other locations in a store.[21] In fact, displays in any location where customers are not preoccupied with task-focused behavior capture people's attention.[22] A genre-blend display located near a circulation desk is an ideal opportunity to attract the notice of readers.

One Oregon public library created permanent shelf displays, placing them at the beginning of the author-arranged children's fiction section. Inspired by readers' advisory conversations with children, the library decided to create "staff picks by genre." Readers' advisors found that because they personally selected the books and kept the shelves filled, the books had high appeal and circulated well.[23] If such an arrangement were used for Magical Realism books, for instance, readers who have never read one would see the display before getting to the regular shelves. The right location makes books visible to readers—books that might otherwise remain buried in the collection.

Online Marketing

Increasingly, the library door that many middle and high school readers enter is the virtual one. As e-book collections continue to grow, many young people choose books from the library website and apps. Consequently, an impactful homepage that periodically highlights a genre blend would attract readers to these books. A slider with a selection of striking book covers whets readers' appetites and gives them a taste of what is to come. Visual cues such as book covers work better than long blogs or wordy discussions. Social media platforms like Pinterest or Instagram are especially suited to the display of book covers. Young people listen to their peers, so providing an interactive catalog that allows readers to provide feedback is also an effective strategy.

How to Stay Up to Date

Keeping up with the ever-expanding volume of books is becoming a Herculean task. Also problematic is the number of customers who expect librarians to know every book they mention. When *Library Journal* surveyed readers' advisors, they found that "the biggest cause of RA angst is keeping up with books and genres, a problem cited by 21% of the librarians. Almost as many, at 17%, noted discomfort with unfamiliar genres." Moreover, when asked how confident readers' advisors are with different age groups, they indicated greater self-assurance with adults (72%) than children (58%) or young adults (51%).[24] Keeping up with genre blends for youth indeed appears to be daunting.

Certainly, readers' advisors cannot know every new book; but they can still become knowledgeable about a genre. Creating a personal reading plan can be empowering. Reading a few books in an unfamiliar genre gives readers' advisors a feel for the category as a whole. A plan might specify dedicating a year to a specific genre blend before moving on to another. Keeping a journal and jotting down a few notes, especially about appeal factors, comes in handy when working with readers. Librarians who enjoy reading for pleasure would probably not find this onerous. Keeping track of books read in a platform such as Goodreads or Library Thing is motivating for many people.

Although there is no shortage of online resources about single genres, there are far fewer about genre blends. The database Novelist is an excellent resource for all genre blends. Searching for a specific one, then reordering results by the most recent publications, will alert readers' advisors to new books in a genre. Since Goodreads's lists are populated by users, they indicate which books are most popular with readers. For resources on each of the genre blends, see the list at the end of the book.

What to Expect in This Book

For each of the six genre blends, we provide descriptions of twenty or so novels and a list of approximately twenty more. If a favorite novel is not included in our book, it is not because it is without merit; we could not include all the many wonderful genre-blend novels that have been written because of space limitations. We kept the following criteria in mind as we selected novels for each chapter:

- The storyline and characters must be compelling.
- The novel must have been positively reviewed. Many of the books we chose had starred reviews.
- A novel must not be dated, especially in terms of language. We bypassed fiction that children or teens of today would not enjoy.
- We chose a range of books with characters of different races, abilities, ethnicities, and religions in order to bring more visibility to minority voices and stories.
- We included novels with male protagonists as well as female ones.
- We chose some books for children and some for teens.

Most of the children's novels we selected are written for middle schoolers. We did not find many genre-blend novels for younger children.

Each of our annotations introduces the storyline and focuses on what distinguishes the book—the features that make it so appealing. We are especially interested in matching the right reader with the right book, so each annotation discusses what type of reader would like each book.

We also provide two read-alikes for each novel. These titles are not necessarily confined to books in the same genre. We believe that any novel can lead readers in unexpected directions and introduce them to unfamiliar genres.

We also believe that the more doorways into books that readers' advisors have at their disposal, the greater the likelihood they can find a good match between a reader and a book. Following each annotation, we identify:

- challenges that the main character faces, such as bullying or poor body image
- book-centered appeal elements, such as fast pace or strong female characters
- themes or subjects, such as child labor or weapons of mass destruction

The next chapter discusses these doorways in greater detail.

NOTES

1. Colin Heywood, *A History of Childhood: Children and Childhood in the West from Medieval to Modern Times* (Cambridge, UK: Polity Press, 2001), 171.
2. Hugh Cunningham, *Children and Childhood in Western Society Since 1500* (Abingdon, UK: Routledge, 2005), 81.
3. Patricia Demers and Gordon Moyles, eds. *From Instruction to Delight: An Anthology of Children's Literature to 1850* (Toronto: Oxford University Press, 1982), 1.
4. Cunningham, *Children and Childhood*, 58.
5. Anyone interested in the history of children's literature will find Peter Hunt's *Children's Literature: An Illustrated History* (Oxford: Oxford University Press, 1995) as well as Seth Lerer's *Children's Literature: A Reader History from Aesop to Harry Potter* (Chicago: University of Chicago Press, 2008) informative and engaging.
6. Christin Galster, "Hybrid Genres," in *Routledge Encyclopedia of Narrative Theory*, ed. Manfred Jahn and Marie-Laure Ryan (London: Routledge, Taylor & Francis, 2010).
7. Megan M. McArdle, *The Readers' Advisory Guide to Genre Blends* (Chicago: ALA Editions, 2015).
8. Sarah E. Worth and Sean McBratnie, "In Defense of Genre Blending," *Aesthetic Investigations* 1, no. 1 (2015): 41.
9. Joan Bessman Taylor, Andrea Hora, and Karla Steege, "Self-Selecting Books in a Children's Fiction Collection Arranged by Genre," *Journal of Librarianship and Information Science* 51, no. 3 (2017):858; Syahranah A. Raqi and A. N. Zainab, "Observing Strategies Used by Children When Selecting Books to Browse, Read or Borrow," *Journal of Educational Media & Library Sciences* 45, no. 4 (2008): 499.
10. Sandra Bojanowski and Shelley Kwiecien, "One Library's Experience," *Knowledge Quest* 42, no. 2 (2013): 20.
11. Scholastic, *Kids & Family Reading Report: Finding Their Story*, 7th ed., 2019, https://www.scholastic.com/readingreport/home.html.

12. Sheena S. Iyengar and Mark R. Lepper, "When Choice Is Demotivating: Can One Desire Too Much of a Good Thing?," *Journal of Personality and Social Psychology* 79, no. 6 (2000): 997, https://doi.org/10.1037/0022-3514.79.6.995.

13. See, for example, Taylor, Hora, and Steege, "Self-Selecting Books in a Children's Fiction Collection"; Sue Kimmel and Krystal Lancaster, "Where Are the Books about Trains? A Case Study Exploring Reorganization of the Children's Section in a Small Public Library," *New Review of Children's Literature and Librarianship* 25, no. 1 (2020): 1–13, https://doi.org/10.1080/13614541.2020.1774267; Valerie Nesset, "A Look at Classification and Indexing for Elementary School Children: Who Are We Really Serving?," *Indexer* 34, no. 3 (2016): 1–4; and Andrew K. Shenton, "The Role of 'Reactive Classification' in Relation to Fiction Collections in School Libraries," *New Review of Children's Literature and Librarianship* 12, no. 2 (2006): 127–46, https://doi.org/10.1080/13614540600982892. For an entire issue devoted to classification challenges in public and school libraries, see *Knowledge Quest* 42, no. 2 (2013).

14. Steven Engelfried, "Rethinking Shelving: Making Your Children's Collections User-Friendly," *Oregon Association Quarterly* 22, no. 3 (2016): 5–9; Julie Hembree, "Ready! Set! Soar! Rearranging Your Fiction Collection by Genre," *Knowledge Quest* 42, no. 2 (2013): 62–65.

15. John B. Horrigan, *Libraries 2016: Trends in Visiting Public Libraries Have Steadied, and Many Americans Have High Expectations for What Their Local Libraries Should Offer* (Pew Research Center, 2016), http://www.pewinternet.org/2016/09/09/libraries-2016/.

16. Gay Ivey and Karen Broaddus, "'Just Plain Reading': A Survey of What Makes Students Want to Read in Middle School Classrooms," *Reading Research Quarterly* 36, no. 4 (2001): 362.

17. Claus Ebster and Marian Graus, *Store Design and Visual Merchandising: Creating Store Space That Encourages Buying* (New York: Business Expert Press, 2011), 77.

18. Rachel Van Riel, Olive Fowler, and Anne Downes, *The Reader-Friendly Library Service* (Newcastle upon Tyne, UK: Society of Chief Librarians, 2008), 10.

19. Tony Morgan, *Visual Merchandising: Window and In-Store Displays for Retail* (London: Laurence King, 2008), 117.

20. Rachel Van Riel, "All Set to Change: Challenging Traditional Practice in Library Design" (conference presentation, Ontario Library Association's Super Conference, Toronto, ON, February 1, 2017).

21. Deborah L. Vence, "Point of Purchase Displays," *Marketing News* 41, no. 18 (2007): 8.

22. Paco Underhill, *Why We Buy: The Science of Shopping* (New York: Simon & Schuster, 2009), 71.

23. Engelfried, "Rethinking Shelving," 8.

24. Henrietta Thorton-Verma and Meredith Schwartz, "The State of Readers' Advisory," *Library Journal*, February 3, 2014, https://www.libraryjournal.com/?detailStory=the-state-of-readers-advisory.

2

Reader Appeals and Book Appeals

Doorways into the RA Conversation

R eaders' advisory (RA), as we recognize it today, exists in large thanks to Joyce Saricks and Nancy Brown and their book, *Readers' Advisory Service in the Public Library*. Before their book's publication in 1989, readers' advisory had received little professional attention and few resources existed. Although the origins of readers' advisory could be traced back to the early twentieth century, these programs focused on readers' self-development and continuing education—not pleasure reading. While in the second half of the century this prescriptive approach fell out of fashion, so did readers' advisory, so that, in the early 1980s, when Saricks and Brown began administering their newly created readers' advisory department, they basically had to build a program from scratch. Their framework, in other words, arose out of the desire to be more patron oriented and responsive to leisure reading needs, and also because their "readers asked for answers neither had a clue how to provide."[1]

Through trial and error, the authors quickly discovered that extensive knowledge of popular works did not always help them recommend titles to their patrons. Rather, it was often more helpful to ask readers about previous books they had enjoyed and to listen for features that either contributed to them enjoying (or not enjoying) one book over another. They called these elements the book's "appeal," and they served as the foundation of their readers' advisory framework.

Described in the most recent edition, the appeal framework includes questions pertaining to a book's pacing; characterization; storyline; and frame, which is a term that encompasses a book's setting, atmosphere, background, and tone.[2] Saricks provides questions that readers' advisors can use to uncover a book's appeal as well as a list of keywords that she considers useful vocabulary for generating conversation with readers.[3] For example, readers who like a "page-turner," or "a book they can't put down," are referring to a book's "pacing" and are likely looking for a title with a satisfying conclusion rather than one that is ambiguous or open-ended. Similarly, some readers like intimate, first-person accounts, or "character-driven" novels, while others prefer stories that place characters at a distance. Such differences refer to a novel's treatment of "characterization."

Although Saricks's framework was created with the adult reader in mind, identifying book-related appeal elements can help librarians, teachers, and parents suggest titles for children and young adults as well. These descriptors provide context about a title—"a feel for the book"[4]—that may not be captured fully by a summary or synopsis. For example, obviously, a young reader who may be interested in stories about the Middle Ages won't connect with *every* book set during this time period. Other preferences about book-related appeals will narrow down suggestions. For example, does the reader like "romance" or "survival stories"? Narratives that are "character-driven" or that contain "multiple perspectives"?

Matching readers to titles will also depend on the reader's *mood*. For instance, one day a reader may be in the mood for something slow and ruminative; on another day, the same reader might want an easy distraction or a book that is faster paced. In other words, *the reader*, not just the book, must also be considered in order to provide meaningful reading advice. Experienced readers' advisors know this intuitively. However, RA handbooks, such as this one, are often arranged by book-related characteristics, which can give the impression that matching the reader to the book is simply a matter of information retrieval: the librarian listens for keywords about a reader's book-related preferences and then searches the index for corresponding titles.[5] But approaching readers' advisory as if it were just another reference question will likely lead to mediocre patron interactions. As David Beard and Kate Vo Thi-Beard argue, excessive "focus on the book as object"—that is, on book-related appeals—overemphasizes *what* readers read instead of *why* they read.[6]

And yet, getting at the "why" of reading is especially important when suggesting titles to children. Unlike readers' advisory for adults, the goal is usually not only to point them to books they will enjoy but also to help them discover the pleasures of reading so that they develop a love of books and enjoy all the benefits associated with a lifelong reading habit.

CHAPTER 2 | Reader Appeals and Book Appeals

Put simply, reading is key to human flourishing. Avid reading has been linked to creativity,[7] academic achievement,[8] and, by extension, job opportunities. Literary reading has also been linked to empathy[9] and virtues such as compassion and tolerance—traits that are sorely needed in today's polarized political environment.

Unfortunately, studies into children's reading behavior also suggest that children's attitudes toward recreational and academic reading tend to grow more negative over time, especially for those least-able readers. To mitigate against this trend, reading researchers repeatedly suggest giving children autonomy—that is, the freedom to make choices about their reading.[10] As Stephen Krashen explains, "free voluntary reading," or "reading because you want to," is critical to reading development, as it lays down the groundwork needed to achieve higher levels of reading proficiency.[11] Such proficiency is all the more necessary in the face of today's complex literacy demands. News headlines, job applications, advertisements, medical prescriptions, voting ballots—the world is immersed in texts. A lack of literacy skills, including reading literacy, writing literacy, and information literacy, may mean not only lost opportunity but also disenfranchisement.

Given this understanding about children's reading development, it's reasonable to conclude that the more we know about a child's background and interests, the more able we are to match them with appealing choices that might encourage a lifelong reading habit. For this reason, each entry in our handbook addresses both book-related and reader-driven appeal elements. In other words, users will find information about key book-related features (its "feel," in the tradition of the Saricks framework) as well as aspects of it that might resonate with a reader's particular situation, personal needs, or mood at the moment (that is, reader-driven appeal).

While we also admit that it is impossible to predict *every* way a reader might connect to a particular book, these annotations at least offer some guidance about potential audiences. Furthermore, we want to acknowledge the reality that many libraries simply cannot afford to employ a children's or young adult librarian, so this guide also offers a means for those who may lack background or subject expertise to identify core collections and promote titles that will also appeal to their child and young adult patrons.

Genre Blends: Definitions and Annotations

Each chapter begins with a definition and description of the genre blend. These introductions are written to provide users with enough context to understand how the genre blend developed and how it is evolving. By identifying key characteristics, users can also begin to imagine and anticipate potential audiences.

Following the introductions are the annotations. The annotations are divided into two sections: "Sure Bets" and "More Excellent Genre Blends." "Sure Bets" are popular titles that have wide appeal and that also best demonstrate the genre blend's characteristics. These are the novels we encourage librarians and teachers to read in order to become more familiar with the genre's conventions. The "More Excellent Genre Blends" section contains annotations that also have timeless appeal but whose audiences may be smaller and more specific.

Each annotation is written with two purposes: (1) to summarize and "sell" the book to potential readers, and (2) to critically evaluate the title's merits in terms of potential reader appeal and/or pedagogical appeal.

The first paragraph is generally a summary written as a book talk. It is intended to give enough information to pique a reader's interest but without spoiling the ending. Librarians can use this summary language when booktalking or when creating a display or promotional materials for their library.

That said, the critical evaluation—found primarily in the last paragraph of the annotation—often does give away the ending. This analysis is intended to help librarians, teachers, and parents understand how the title might appeal to a particular reader (for example, considering curiosity or mood) and, for teachers specifically, how it might relate to their curriculum or classroom instruction.

Finally, next to the title of each novel, we have indicated grade-level ranges so users can quickly identify a title's general audience (that is, elementary, middle, or young adult), plus symbols to indicate whether a title is available as an audiobook (🎧) or as part of a larger series (📚).

For Those Coping with (Challenges)

In order to connect children with books, it is also helpful to consider what motivates readers to read in the first place. For this understanding, Catherine Sheldrick Ross's research on avid readers sheds some light. After conducting nearly two hundred in-depth interviews with avid readers, Ross found that readers are driven to read narrative fiction and nonfiction not only for entertainment but also for the information, or insight, that reading could offer their lives. These readers, in discussing significant books or books that changed their lives, revealed seven main reasons they read, including to find: (1) new perspectives, (2) models for identity, (3) reassurance, comfort, confirmation of self-worth, or strength, (4) connection with others, (5) courage to make a change, (6) acceptance, and/or (7) a disinterested understanding of the world.[12]

While Ross's research focused on adult readers, it is our assumption that if lifelong booklovers read for the reasons Ross identifies, then we

CHAPTER 2 | Reader Appeals and Book Appeals

should probably be tapping into these motives when suggesting books for children and teens. Again, our goal is not only to match children with books they find pleasurable and entertaining but also to spark a deeper connection with, and appreciation for, reading. We want children to discover the pleasures of reading so that they can also develop into lifelong, avid readers who, again, can enjoy all the associated benefits that come with reading literacy.[13]

More recent scholarship into reading behavior has also found that among reader-driven appeal elements, "the most crucial one is curiosity, followed by readers' personal situations, needs, and mood at the moment."[14] While themes (explained in the next section) can be used to identify books that will satisfy a reader's curiosity about a particular topic, "personal situations, needs, and mood" — that is, motivation for reading — is addressed in the "For those coping with (challenges)" field.

These "challenges" may mirror potential aspects of the reader's own situation or mood. For example, if a child is dealing with the death of a parent and looking for, in Ross's language, "comfort" or "connection with others," the challenges index uses the labels "death of a parent," "death of a loved one," or "grief." In this case, one may identify and offer Patrick Ness's *A Monster Calls* to a teen reader, as the story's protagonist is facing the same challenge and his story may help them feel less alone in their loss.

Again, using this field takes for granted an understanding of the child's or teen's reading context: their personality, social environment, and/or present living situation. For another reader, Emily X. R. Pan's *The Astonishing Color of After*, or Libba Bray's *A Great and Terrible Beauty* may be a better fit. It is also possible that *none* of these titles is appropriate — just because a child or teen is bereaved does not automatically mean they want, at that moment, a book that mirrors their experience. Rather, this field is helpful only in those cases when a reader is seeking ways of coping with a particular challenge.

For Those Drawn to (Book-Driven Appeals)

While we are advocating for a more reader-centered approach to readers' advisory, the fact remains that genre, setting, pace, and other book-related appeals also matter to readers. While each chapter begins with a summary of the genre's conventions, genre alone does not account for all the book-related appeals in a specific title. For example, a reader might be drawn to "romance," a "witty tone," or "strong female characters" — none of which is specific to a particular genre. Thus, this field is meant to identify outstanding book-appeal elements specific to each individual title.

In this way, you might begin to see the potential of genre blends to extend the range of categories from which you select your reading as well as how genre blends may appeal to broader audiences. For example, a reader who alludes to the fact she hates Fantasy or "made-up worlds" may be better matched with Realistic Fiction, Biographical Novels, or Memoir. But by using this index, they can also find a genre blend that has these book-related appeals as well. In other words, readers may discover new genres they have never considered reading before—a Verse Novel, for example, or Graphic Novel—as many of these titles also feature Memoir and other types of Narrative Nonfiction.

While most of the headings in this index are self-explanatory, one requires further explanation: culturally responsive literature. Recognizing the desire among many educators to raise critical consciousness about systems of inequality, and also recognizing the role children's literature can play in raising this awareness, we created this heading to help teachers and librarians quickly identify titles that speak to these issues. For example, Jerry Craft's Graphic Novel *New Kid* and Ann E. Burg's Verse Novel *Serafina's Promise* are both tagged with this heading because of the way they describe present and past examples of systemic racism in schools. Similarly, Melanie Crowder's Verse Novel *Audacity* is also given this heading because it examines historical examples of gender-based discrimination in the workplace. In short, we assigned this heading to novels we think can best inform and generate discussion in the classroom about equity issues.

It is also important to keep in mind that book-related appeals extend beyond this field as well. For example, a book's author, the themes/informational value, and whether or not it is part of a series are also appeals to consider. Some readers will simply want to read anything written by their favorite author. The same is also true for series (which is why we indicate titles that are part of a series with the symbol 📕) and themes/subjects.

Themes/Subjects

This field includes themes and subjects that describe what a particular title is *about*—the story's content. "Themes and subjects" can be thought of as either book-related appeals or reader-driven appeals, depending on the context. For example, sometimes readers find themselves on a particular kick, wanting to read anything about aliens, or zombies, or witches. In this case, the Subjects/Themes/Appeals Index can be used to find titles that address the reader's curiosity, which, again, is a crucial reader-driven appeal. On the other hand, it is also easy to imagine librarians or teachers wanting to create a book display or curriculum centered on a particular theme (labeled "medieval settings," "the Great Depression") or issue ("bullies," "immigration"), in which case the index can be regarded as a tool to identify titles based on book-related appeal.

NOTES

1. Neal Wyatt, "Readers' Advisory: We Owe Our Work to Theirs," *Reference & User Services Quarterly 54*, no. 2 (2014): 25.
2. Joyce Saricks, *Readers' Advisory Service in the Public Library* (Chicago: American Library Association, 2005), 44, 50, 55, 58.
3. Ibid., 66
4. Ibid., 40.
5. See Keren Dali, "Hearing Stories, Not Keywords: Teaching Contextual Readers' Advisory," *Reference Services Review 41*, no. 3 (2013): 474–502.
6. David Beard and Kate Vo Thi-Beard, "Rethinking the Book: New Theories for Readers' Advisory," *Reference & User Services Quarterly 47*, no. 4 (2008): 332.
7. Kathryn E. Kelley and Lee B. Kneipp, "Reading for Pleasure and Creativity among College Students," *College Student Journal 43*, no. 3 (2009): 1137–44.
8. Jude D. Gallik, "Do They Read for Pleasure? Recreational Reading Habits of College Students," *Journal of Adolescent & Adult Literacy 42*, no. 6 (1999): 480–88.
9. See Raymond A. Mar, Keith Oatley, and Jordan B. Peterson, "Exploring the Link Between Reading Fiction and Empathy: Ruling Out Individual Differences and Examining Outcomes," *Communications: The European Journal of Communications Research 34*, no. 2 (2009): 407–28; and David Comer Kidd and Emanuel Castano, "Reading Literary Fiction Improves Theory of Mind," *Science 342* (2013): 377–80.
10. See Gay Ivey and Karen Broaddus, "'Just Plain Reading': A Survey of What Makes Students Want to Read in Middle School Classrooms," *Reading Research Quarterly 36*, no. 4 (2001): 350–77; Yaacov Petscher, "A Meta-analysis of the Relationship between Student Attitudes towards Reading and Achievement in Reading," *Journal of Research in Reading 33*, no. 4 (2010): 335–55; and Lunetta Williams and Karen Hall. "Exploring Students' Reading Attitudes," *Journal of Reading Education 35*, no. 2 (2010): 35–41.
11. Stephen D. Krashen, *The Power of Reading* (Westport, CT: Libraries Unlimited, 2004), x.
12. Catherine Sheldrick Ross, "Finding Without Seeking: The Information Encounter in the Context of Reading for Pleasure," *Information Processing & Management 35*, no. 6 (1999): 783–99.
13. See Catherine Sheldrick Ross, Lynne McKechnie, and Paulette M. Rothbauer, *Reading Matters: What the Research Reveals about Reading, Libraries, and Community* (Westport, Conn: Libraries Unlimited), 2006.
14. Keren Dali, "From Book Appeal to Reading Appeal: Redefining the Concept of Appeal in Readers' Advisory," *Library Quarterly 84*, no. 1 (2014): 36.

Part II

Annotations

3

Graphic Novels for Children and Young Adults

Introduction to the Genre

At first glance, Graphic Novels can easily be confused for comic books. Both use words and pictures to tell a story. Both divide pages into panels and frames. Graphic-novel art also sometimes looks like comic-book art.[1] The difference, however, lies in their narrative approach.

Like traditional prose novels, Graphic Novels tell a complete story with a beginning, middle, and end. They are longer than comic books, which are, by design, short and episodic, serialized so that the narrative stretches over many issues. That said, it is possible for a series to be compiled into a single work so that it becomes a Graphic Novel; Allen Moore and Dave Gibbons's seminal work from 1987, *Watchmen*, is such an example. The novel was originally published as twelve separate issues. Most Graphic Novels, however, are conceived and produced like traditional novels—as standalone works complete unto themselves.

Graphic Novels also differ from comic books in terms of the way writers use verbal and graphic content to tell the story. Illustrations in Graphic Novels do not merely repeat or reinforce the text, but add new information that helps drive the narrative. In other words, verbal content is more than a caption, and graphic content is more than a description of the text. The reader must interpret visual elements—panels and frames, space (including empty space, or "gutters"), font styles, speech bubbles and thought bubbles—in addition to the text in order to fully comprehend the story.

Technically, Graphic Novels are a blended *format*, not a blended genre. They combine two mediums, comics and novels, which does not necessarily result in a genre blend. And yet, the visual aspect of this format—particularly, the way it conveys the role of media representations such as television, film, and social media in everyday life—lends itself to new modes of expression that nonetheless often result in genre blends. For example, Cece Bell's *El Deafo* is a Memoir, but as it is told in the visual form of anthropomorphized rabbits, it is also an Animal Fantasy. Similarly, Chanani Nidhi's *Pashmina* is a Graphic Novel that depicts magical realist scenes. In other words, hybridity, either in terms of format or genre, is almost inevitable in the creation of a Graphic Memoir.

With regard to hybrid formats, it is worth noting that a good number of Graphic Novels are Memoirs. This is not surprising given the Graphic Novel's earliest origins. Will Eisner's *A Contract with God* (1978), considered to be the first Graphic Novel, draws on the author's experiences growing up in a Bronx tenement; Art Spiegelman's *Maus* (1980), probably the most widely recognized Graphic Novel, is also a Memoir, one that describes the author's troubled relationship with his father, a Holocaust survivor. More recent examples of Graphic Novel Memoirs include Marjane Satrapi's *Persepolis* and Alison Bechdel's *Fun Home*. Though originally targeted to adult audiences, Satrapi's and Bechdel's works have gained popularity with young adults as well.

Not all Graphic Novels in this chapter are Graphic Memoirs. And, again, not all Graphic Novels are blended genres, but this chapter focuses on those that are.

Matching Readers and Graphic Novels: Appeal Factors as Bridges

Like Verse Novels, Graphic Novels focus primarily on subjectivity. They are almost exclusively first-person narratives, written in the present tense, and so intimate that at times the protagonist may break through the fourth wall to address the reader personally. However, because of the visual component, Graphic Novels capture not only the protagonists' interior world, but also their outward dramas so that the experience of reading is much like watching a film. Characters are literally seen in action, in dialogue, and in a distinct setting.

The visual power of the Graphic Novel cannot be underestimated. Unlike traditional prose, Graphic Novels are able to literally give visibility to those who have historically been shadowed out or made invisible by mainstream media. Thus, the format tends to attract those who want to expose such dominant narratives/representations and call their authority into question. LGBTQIA narratives, immigration narratives, and disability narratives are frequently found in Graphic Novels. For example, Cece Bell's *El Deafo*, which describes her experience of hearing loss after contracting meningitis at a very young age, uses graphic art to capture frustrated encounters with hearing-abled classmates and adults. Bell includes depictions of teachers who lecture while facing the chalkboard and friends who shout loudly, or speak extremely slowly, in a mistaken effort to help her understand their speech. Bell's cartoons put readers in her place; a traditional Memoir, told only in words, could not translate this subjective experience nearly as well.

It is also important to keep in mind that artists and writers are likely drawn to the graphic-novel format because illustrations (as opposed to real-life representations) allow them to portray difficult topics at a safe remove. This quality makes these topics more digestible for children and young adult readers, too. For example, in *Hey, Kiddo*, Jarrett Krosoczka describes his mother's heroin addiction by interspersing frames of typical childhood experiences—Jarrett playing with toys, Jarrett posing in a Halloween costume—with others that depict strangers coming in and out of his house using drugs. These illustrations immediately reveal the horror of the young child's vulnerability and his lack of understanding of the danger while creating psychic distance so that the horror of the subject matter does not become overwhelming. The reader still wants to turn the page.

Given these features, Graphic Novels tend to appeal to readers who are looking for comfort and reassurance—who want, in other words, to feel less alone. Depending on the reader, Graphic Novels can also serve as a doorway to other worlds, helping readers gain insight into experiences different from their own and expanding their sense of empathy. Breezy, straightforward dialogue also makes the Graphic Novel accessible to and suitable for English Language Learners or reluctant readers.

Key Novels/Sure Bets

Gene Luen Yang is one of the leading authors of Graphic Novels for young adults, and his *American Born Chinese* has become a modern-day classic. For younger readers, the works of Cece Bell, Jerry Craft, and Raina Telgemeier have also become widely recognized for providing outstanding examples of counternarratives that promote awareness and sensitivity to otherness.

PART II | Annotations

Bell, Cece. *El Deafo*. **Grades 3–7.**

Cece Bell is only four years old when she contracts meningitis and loses most of her hearing. While her "Phonic Ear" helps her understand her teacher and classmates so she can attend school like other children, it is an awkward, bulky contraption that draws a lot of unwanted attention. Both children and adults mistakenly assume they need to shout at her, or speak *extremely slowly*, in order for her to understand them — or they turn their backs so that she can't read their lips, and she is excluded from the conversation completely. Cece feels left out a lot, and her self-esteem takes a hit. But when Cece discovers some of the advantages of her Phonic Ear — like how she can use it to spy on her teacher's private conversations in the teacher's lounge — she begins to recognize her self-worth and assert herself.

In this Memoir, told as an animal story, characters are depicted as anthropomorphized bunny rabbits, whose large ears emphasize the central conflict in the story while keeping the mood light. Told with warmth and humor, this story is also touching in its subtlety. While readers with disabilities may be able to identify with Cece's struggles and the assumptions able-bodied people make about her, this story will make any reader laugh, and it has great potential to expand empathetic imaginations.

For those coping with: being different, concern with what others think, disability, domineering friend, unassertiveness/timidity

For those drawn to: animal stories, character-driven novels, culturally responsive literature, humor, likeable/relatable characters, Memoir, suburban settings, witty tone

Themes/subjects: disability (deafness), education/learning, friendship, resilience, self-esteem

Read-alikes: Shannon Hale's Graphic Memoir *Real Friends* takes up similar themes and has the same feel-good tone. Brian Selznick's *Wonderstruck* also features a deaf protagonist.

Craft, Jerry. *New Kid*. 📖. **Grades 4–7.**

Jordan Banks isn't exactly thrilled to be starting middle school. His heart had been set on going to the arts school, but his parents insist that Riverdale Academy, a prestigious New York City prep school, will offer more opportunities. The problem, though, is that Riverdale isn't very diverse. Most of the students come from white families that are so rich, some of the school's buildings are named after them. Jordan, middle class and African American, obviously stands out. Although his teachers and classmates are friendly enough, their

🎧 available as an audiobook   📖 part of a larger series

CHAPTER 3 | Graphic Novels for Children and Young Adults 27

comments often betray their mistaken assumptions about him and the people who look like him. One obnoxious loudmouth named Andy isn't making things any easier. Jordan longs for his own neighborhood; but if he wants to go to art school, he has to prove to his parents he has given Riverdale a chance. However, once he begins to befriend his Riverdale classmates, he discovers that he isn't the only one who feels like the "new kid," and he isn't alone.

Told with irony and humor, this Newbery Award–winning novel provides a nuanced illustration of intersectionality, particularly how race, class, and gender identities overlap to create varied experiences of discrimination and privilege. Its attention to systemic inequalities within schools makes it an ideal fit for reflexive classroom discussions, and teachers might also want to use it to introduce the concept of microaggressions and explain why they are harmful. Extremely relatable—anyone who has felt like an outsider will feel less alone reading this book.

For those coping with: anxiety/fear, bullying, feeling entitled, moving to a new school, racism, recognizing privilege in oneself

For those drawn to: character-driven novels, culturally responsive literature, humor, likeable/relatable characters, Realistic Fiction, witty tone

Themes/subjects: African Americans, art as coping strategy, Asian Americans, boy artists, bullies, class/socioeconomic differences, comics (love of), education/learning, friendship, gentrification, Latino/a Americans, media influence on identity, middle school life, New York City (twenty-first century), racism, sports, video games/gaming

Read-alikes: A similar plot but from an African American female perspective plays out in Karen English's novel *It All Comes Down to This*. The protagonist in Jason Reynolds's novel *Ghost* also attends an elite middle school where he faces similar challenges.

Telgemeier, Raina. *Smile.* 🔖. Grades 5+.

Raina thought getting braces was bad enough, but then she accidently falls and knocks out her front teeth. Now she endures retainers, braces, headgear, and the other accoutrements of orthodontia while beginning middle school. All of a sudden, her childhood friends become snide and sarcastic, and because of her "vampire" gear, Raina becomes the constant butt of their jokes. At the same time, she is getting pimples and her straight hair is becoming curly, and her crush doesn't seem to know she exists. For all these reasons, Raina is finding it hard to smile.

Telgemeier's Graphic Memoir captures the essence of 1990s suburban Central California, but her observations of middle school relationships remain timeless. In fact, the distant setting and memoiristic style help build her authority. Every reader could use the encouraging reminder that middle school is just a stage in everyone's development and that they are not totally powerless against bullying. They can choose their friends and how they treat others, and they can seek their own self-worth instead of relying solely on outward validation.

For those coping with: body image, broken friendships/growing apart, bullying, concern with what others think, infatuation, lack of confidence, unassertiveness/timidity

For those drawn to: character-driven novels, humor, likeable/relatable characters, Memoir, suburban settings, witty tone

Themes/subjects: bullies, California, cliques, crushes, dental work, earthquakes, friendship, middle school life, self-esteem

Read-alikes: Fans of *Smile* should not only finish the series (*Sisters* and *Guts*) but also check out Telgemeier's fiction (*Drama* and *Ghosts*). A similar middle school story about friendship plays out in *Roller Girl* by Victoria Jamieson.

Yang, Gene Luen. *American Born Chinese*. Grades 7+.

Jin Wang was born in San Francisco and has been living in the suburbs of California most of his life, but the only thing his classmates seem to see is that he's Asian. They tease him about everything: the way he looks, the foods he eats, the mere fact that his parents are Chinese. It goes on this way for most of elementary school, and Jin is basically friendless until Wei-Chen, a Chinese immigrant, joins their classroom. Although Jin initially tries to distance himself from other Asian students, he has to admit that he and Wei-Chen have a lot in common. They become best friends and are pretty much inseparable until middle school. But then things change. Jin falls hard for a girl, a white girl, and when their date doesn't turn out the way he planned, he blames Wei-Chen—and everything Chinese.

Two additional storylines—a legend about a monkey king and a mock television sitcom featuring the character Chin-Kee (a composite of popular Asian and Asian American stereotypes)—interconnect with Jin's narrative to explore issues about self-image, transformation, and cultural identity. Yang's comic-strip style adds depth to these issues; he uses the form to comment on and subvert racist depictions of Asians and Asian Americans in all media, but especially comic books. (This novel would complement an assignment that asks students to identify and analyze stereotypes in current media and/

CHAPTER 3 | Graphic Novels for Children and Young Adults   **29**

or propaganda.) Anyone struggling with self-acceptance will find a kindred spirit in Jin.

For those coping with: being different, bullying, concern with what others think, feeling entitled, (the) immigrant experience, infatuation, overly critical view of self, racism, rejection, sense of inferiority

For those drawn to: Asian-inspired novels, character-driven novels, coming-of-age stories, culturally responsive literature, multiple intertwined storylines

Themes/subjects: Asian Americans, bullies, cliques, crushes, cultural differences, friendship, influence of popular culture, myths/legends, self-esteem

Read-alikes: Robin Ha's *Almost American Girl* addresses similar themes but from a female perspective. The protagonist in Rick Detorie's *The Accidental Genius of Weasel High* shares Jin's teenage-male angst.

More Excellent Graphic Novels

Anderson, Laurie Halse, and Emily Carroll. *Speak: The Graphic Novel.* **Grades 7+.**

The summer before high school, Melinda Sordino attends a house party with her best friend. Even though she is younger than everyone else and doesn't feel like she fits in, Melinda tries to mingle. She wanders outside, where an older classmate, a handsome senior, starts to flirt with her. Flattered, she accepts his invitation to dance. Music drifts from the house, and she enjoys their embrace—that is, until she feels his grip is tightening around her. When Melinda tries to pull away, he holds her harder. When she struggles, he pins her to the ground, then rapes her. Afterward, shaking from fright, Melinda runs home without telling anyone what happened—not the police, not her parents, not even her best friend. Melinda can't say anything and can't stand up for herself because Melinda has lost the words, and the courage, to speak.

While this story does tend to perpetuate the dominant rape narrative of the stranger-perpetrator, obscuring the fact that most female victims of sexual assault report being raped by an intimate partner or acquaintance, *Speak* remains one of the few well-written narratives available on the topic. This graphic adaptation adds to the original by evoking the feelings Melinda cannot articulate as well as capturing the realities of cyberbullying. Strongly recommended for young men and women, this book is a great way for teachers to introduce and discuss consent.

For those coping with: being a victim of gossip/slander, being misunderstood by parents, bullying, cruelty toward oneself, depression, domineering friend, family conflict, loneliness, physical violence, sexual assault

For those drawn to: character-driven novels, poetic language, psychological focus, postmodern stories

Themes/subjects: art as coping strategy, artists, assertiveness, bullies, courage, depression, dysfunctional families, friendship, high school life, secrets, sexual violence

Read-alikes: Girl psychology is a major theme in Tillie Walden's *Spinning*. Finding a voice in the midst of family dysfunction is a central theme in Alison Bechdel's Graphic Memoir *Fun Home*.

Colfer, Eoin, and Andrew Donkin. *Illegal*. Illustrated by Giovanni Rigano. Grades 6+.

Ebo is twelve years old when he leaves his desert village in Ghana, alone, to search for his older brother, Kwame, who has set out for Europe to find their older sister. As orphans living in extreme poverty, leaving their village is the only way they can survive. But the journey poses incredible obstacles. Ebo has no idea where Kwame is and no way of calling or getting word to him. He must also figure out money and transportation. Fortunately, he is a talented singer, and he is able to busk his way toward Europe. Still, he must cross the Sahara and communicate in languages other than his own, and he must do all of this while avoiding capture, as young Ebo is still considered an illegal immigrant.

Realistic color drawings enhance this narrative by capturing concretely what many Western readers may otherwise struggle to comprehend: extreme poverty; the scorching heat of the Sahara; and the multiple dangers that Ebo and other refugees face, such as illness, violence, and death. At the same time, the story promotes a message of community building—of loving and caring for one another in small ways. It is almost impossible to read this book and not expand one's capacity for empathy.

For those coping with: (the) immigrant experience, injustice/unfairness, loneliness, poverty, powerlessness

For those drawn to: dangerous adventures, dual intertwined storylines, streetwise characters, survival stories

CHAPTER 3 | Graphic Novels for Children and Young Adults   **31**

Themes/subjects: Africa (Ghana), art as coping strategy, community, deserts, escapes, family, gun violence, illness, immigration, music, oceans, poverty, refugees, rescues, self-reliance, self-sacrifice, smugglers, thieves/robbery

Read-alikes: Pair this novel with Victoria Jamieson and Omar Mohamed's Graphic Memoir *When Stars Are Scattered*, about life in a Kenyan refugee camp. Sibling relationships and survival are central themes in Padma Venkatraman's novel *The Bridge Home*.

Holm, Jennifer L., and Matthew Holm. *Swing It, Sunny.* 🗎. Grades 4–6.

A lot changes for twelve-year-old Sunny Lewin in 1976. Her older brother, Dale, whom she adores, falls into a bad crowd, flunks out of the twelfth grade, and winds up in boarding school. At the same time, she starts junior high, discovers she's allergic to mold, and becomes addicted to almost everything on television. She misses Dale deeply; but when he returns for a visit, she is saddened and confused by his hostility—they used to have so much fun together—and feels rejected. When he goes back to school, she is almost relieved.

Cheerful color illustrations complement this story about resilience in the face of familial heartbreak. While Sunny cannot comprehend her brother's behavior, she learns to add up the little pieces of joy in her life to find comfort. The novel is also Historical Fiction, and its illustrations of classic television help convey and call into question how media influences identity. Teachers could use these examples to deepen discussions about the use of media (especially social media).

For those coping with: adjusting to change, worry/anxiety about a loved one

For those drawn to: character-driven novels, Historical Fiction, humor, suburban settings

Themes/subjects: addiction (drugs/alcohol), brother-sister relationships, friendship, grandfathers, media influence on identity

Read-alike: Jerry Spinelli's novel *Jake and Lily* is also about a brother and sister growing apart.

Jamieson, Victoria. *Roller Girl.* Grades 4–8. 🎧.

Astrid usually dreads her mother's "Evenings of Cultural Enrichment," which usually involve dragging her to dull museum visits or art films. But the Rose City Roller Derby is just the opposite. With their punked-up makeup, powerful athleticism, and unapologetic aggression, these women turn the rink into a riveting, action-packed theater. Astrid is instantly hooked and begs her mom to enroll her in the junior roller derby camp during the summer break. But roller skating is harder than it looks, and Astrid spends more time on the ground than on her wheels. Meanwhile, Nicole, her best friend since first grade, would rather hang out with her ballet friends than with her. Astrid wants to give up, but with some encouraging words from her favorite Rose City Roller, Astrid finds the courage to keep trying, despite all the bruises—literal and figurative.

This novel stands out in its complex presentation of female gender roles. For instance, Astrid's mother is a nurturing single parent who also works as an academic librarian. Rather than fall into false binaries (for example, ballet is girly and therefore bad), this novel encourages readers to be true to themselves and embrace their own curiosity. Teachers can use this novel to generate classroom discussion of gender roles by assigning students to identify contemporary examples of men and women who both perpetuate and defy social expectations.

For those coping with: adjusting to change, anxiety/fear, being an outsider/misfit, broken friendships/growing apart, concern with what others think, lack of confidence, needing to prove oneself

For those drawn to: likeable/relatable characters, strong female characters, witty tone

Themes/subjects: ambitions, competitions/testing, friendship, gender roles (twenty-first century), heroes/mentors, jealousy, lying, media influence on identity, middle school life, mother-daughter relationships, Oregon, single-parent families, sports

Read-alikes: The heroine in Celia Perez's novel *The First Rule of Punk* is another middle school girl with unconventional interests, and female friendship is a major theme in Cathy G. Johnson's Graphic Novel *The Breakaways*.

Krosoczka, Jarrett. *Hey, Kiddo*. Grades 7+.

At first, Jarrett doesn't understand why he has to move in with his grandparents, or why he can't live at home anymore. It's not that he doesn't love his grandparents, or his grandma's meatball sandwiches; it's just that life isn't the same without his mom around. While she sends him letters from time to time (greeting him, "Hey, Kiddo"), and they occasionally visit each other, she also misses his birthday parties and school events. She misses everything. Jarrett doesn't understand why it has to be like this. He never knew his dad in the first place, but his mom's absence is felt. When she first disappears, Jarrett is too young to understand the reason: she is a drug addict. Finding solace

CHAPTER 3 | Graphic Novels for Children and Young Adults

in art, Jarrett also finds compassion and learns to value his family's love, however imperfect. At the same time, he discovers he can use his talents to make a better future for himself.

A finalist for the National Book Award, this Memoir/Artist's Novel blends lyricism, drawing, and artifacts from the writer's actual childhood—letters, childhood drawings, newspaper clippings—to create a truly original work of art. Tender and often witty, Krosoczka navigates this difficult subject matter with grace. He also inspires hope while acknowledging painful realities. Any reader who has experienced a difficult childhood will feel less alone reading this work.

For those coping with: abandonment/desertion, absent parent, family conflict, feeling ashamed of family, parental neglect

For those drawn to: character-driven novels, coming-of-age stories, Memoir, postmodern stories, psychological focus

Themes/subjects: abandoned children, addiction (drugs/alcohol), ambitions, art as coping strategy, boy artists, comics (love of), dreams/nightmares, family (extended), friendship, grandfathers, resilience

Read-alikes: The protagonists in both *The Dark Matter of Mona Starr*, a Graphic Novel by Laura Lee Gulledge, and *The Absolutely True Diary of a Part-Time Indian*, by Sherman Alexie, use art to stave off despair.

Lemire, Jeff. *The Collected Essex County*. Grades 10+.

This trilogy of Graphic Novels tells a multigenerational story about rural life in Ontario's Essex County. *Tales from the Farm*, which takes place circa 2006, tells the story of Lester, a young boy who has just lost his mother to cancer. Orphaned, he moves to Essex to live on his uncle's farm. At first, Lester is so consumed with grief he can barely speak, but he takes comfort in reading comics as well as writing and illustrating his own. His comics draw the attention of the gas station attendant, a former hockey star, who becomes an unexpected friend. Then, in *Ghost Stories*, an elderly, Alzheimer's-afflicted Lou Lebeuf reflects on growing up in Essex County with his younger brother and best friend, Vince, in the 1940s, both talented hockey players. Lou and Vince are eventually drafted by Toronto's professional hockey team, the Grizzlies. But, while the two of them take their team to the play-offs, their love for the same woman threatens to drive them apart. The story concludes with *The Country Nurse*, which follows Lou's nurse, Anne. As she drives throughout the county checking on patients, Anne reveals key details that tie all three stories together.

Stark black-and-white illustrations beautifully depict these characters' grief and isolation and guide the reader as the story shifts quickly between space and time. This extremely moving story is a meditation on love, memory, and the importance of family, especially extended family. This is a story to read to feel less alone.

For those coping with: absent parent, death of a loved one, death of a parent, emotional detachment or avoidance, family conflict, loneliness

For those drawn to: character-driven novels, poetic language, psychological focus, postmodern stories

Themes/subjects: art as coping strategy, boy artists, brothers, Canada (twentieth century), comics (love of), country versus city, crushes, death, family, forgiveness, friendship, grief/loss, guilt, illness (terminal), jealousy, sports

Read-alikes: A similar graphic style and themes of loneliness and unrequited love are found in Craig Thompson's *Blankets*. Per Petterson's *Out Stealing Horses* is another adult novel that appeals to young adults and also deals with grief.

Nidhi, Chanani. *Pashmina*. Grades 4–8.

Like most high school students, Priyanka Das is just trying to survive. But with a name like Priyanka, she doesn't exactly fit in with her Laguna Beach classmates—she is a minority among the wealthy and white, and no one appreciates her thrift-store style. Fortunately, "Pri" can grumble to her best friend, Eddie, who shares her passion for drawing and making comics, and to her uncle Jatin, whom she treats more like her father. Pri's family is small—she lives alone with her mother—so when Uncle Jatin decides to start his own family, Pri can't help but feel jealous. Uncle Jatin's announcement also stirs up questions about her own parents: Why did her mother leave India before she was born, and why does she refuse to return? Why won't her mother tell her about her father? What happened to him? Having no explanations, Pri begins to search for answers on her own and discovers among her mother's possessions a magic pashmina whose supernatural powers finally lead her to some clarity.

More than an immigration story, *Pashmina* will surprise readers with its nuance and critique. It not only captures the challenges first-generation American teenagers experience but also reveals these challenges from a feminist point of view, expanding readers' understanding of why immigration is often not a choice so much as a necessity.

CHAPTER 3 | Graphic Novels for Children and Young Adults **35**

For those coping with: absent parent, being different, class/socioeconomic differences, family conflict, guilt, (the) immigrant experience, worry/anxiety about a loved one

For those drawn to: ghost stories, strong female characters, unexpected plot twists

Themes/subjects: artists, cultural differences, comics (love of), factories/factory workers, family secrets, gender roles (twentieth century), ghosts, India, mother-daughter relationships, single-parent families

Read-alikes: An Asian American protagonist also learns about her heritage in a magical-realism setting in Tae Keller's novel *When You Trap a Tiger*. Similar themes and artwork are found in Vera Brosgol's *Anya's Ghost*.

Selznick, Brian. *Wonderstruck*. Grades 4–8.

Ever since his mother died, Ben has been haunted by the same nightmare: a pack of wolves chase him through the dark forest. Although wolves can be found near Gunflint Lake, where Ben lives with his aunt and uncle in Minnesota, they are much more threatening in his dream than in real life. Still, Ben can't shake the feeling that the wolves are trying to tell him something, urging him toward some discovery, which is why he decides to search his mother's bedroom in their old house. He discovers some things he did not know she had: a heart-shaped locket and a book about the Museum of Natural History. At first, Ben thinks that the book was intended for him because his mom knew how much he loves museums and anything to do with collecting. But an inscription leads him to believe that they might be gifts from his father, whom Ben has never met. Driven by this mystery, Ben decides to run away to New York, where he suspects his father is living. But the quest is not easy. He has to learn how to navigate an unfamiliar landscape, New York in the 1970s, and he must do so in total silence, as Ben is deaf.

Dual storylines—one about Ben and one about Ben's grandmother, who is also deaf—converge to reveal the identity of Ben's father. Notably, the grandmother's story is told completely in pictures, which helps readers who are not hearing impaired appreciate the deaf person's experience. While providing this insight, the central narrative remains on survival, particularly surviving loss. Anyone who has ever struggled to find a sense of place and belonging will take comfort in Ben's story.

For those coping with: being different, death of a parent, desire to find birth parent, disability

For those drawn to: arresting/original settings, dual intertwined storylines, Historical Fiction, mystery/suspense, richly detailed descriptions, secret codes/clues

Themes/subjects: art as coping strategy, collectors/collections, disability (deafness), dreams/nightmares, family secrets, film/film history, friendship, journeys/quests, museums, New York (post–World War II), orphans, runaways, wolves

Read-alikes: Those drawn to the novel's intertwined plot should check out Pam Muñoz Ryan's *Echo*, in which characters are connected by the same harmonica, and Emily Rodda's intricately plotted *His Name Was Walter*.

Smy, Pam. *Thornhill*. Grades 5–9.

As Ella unpacks and settles into her new bedroom at her dad's, she discovers an eerie sight outside her window: a house, boarded up and overgrown with vegetation. Once, it had been an orphanage, the Thornhill Institute for Children, where young girls waited and hoped to be adopted by loving families. When Ella notices a figure on the orphanage's grounds, she is compelled to trespass. She discovers the diary of a former resident, a mute girl named Mary who was badly bullied by the other girls. When summer comes, Ella starts to jump across the fence and sneak into to the orphanage to gather other clues about Mary. She finds a puppet, and another puppet, and a key. With each object, Ella gets a little closer to understanding who Mary was and the terrible thing that happened to her. Consumed with chasing Mary's ghost, Ella does not realize her own life is in danger, too.

Two stories, one in words and one in pictures, intersect to tell a haunting tale of child abuse. Both girls are alone and neglected. As Mary deals with her bully, she has no helping adults, and, as she is mute, she cannot speak up for herself. She keeps to herself and pours herself into art: she sculpts her own puppets, sews them clothes, and pretends they are her family. Ella's parents are also never around (it is unclear what has happened to her mother), and although it is a different danger she faces—trespassing on unsafe grounds—the cause is also neglect. Smy makes several allusions to Frances Hodgson Burnett's *The Secret Garden*, another story of child neglect, but her own work departs greatly from the classic's happy ending—perhaps to greater effect, as this book's ending surprises in such a way that it makes it hard to forget.

CHAPTER 3 | Graphic Novels for Children and Young Adults

For those coping with: bullying, false accusations, favoritism, lack of friends, loneliness, parental neglect, preoccupied/busy parents, self-doubt, sense of inferiority

For those drawn to: arresting/original settings, boarding school stories, classics-inspired fiction, dual intertwined storylines, ghost stories, Gothic settings/atmosphere, mystery/suspense, richly detailed descriptions

Themes/subjects: abandoned children, appearance versus reality, art as coping strategy, bullies, cliques, depression, disability (mutism), gardens, ghosts, haunted houses, orphans, revenge, suicide, toys (dolls and puppets)

Read-alikes: Pair this novel with Frances Hodgson Burnett's *The Secret Garden*, a must–companion read. Parallel narratives separated by time are also found in *Wonderstruck* by Brian Selznick.

TenNapel, Doug. *Ghostopolis*. Grades 7+.

Garth has just learned he may have an incurable disease when a skeleton-horse ghost flies through his bedroom and accidentally drags him into the afterlife. There he meets family members he didn't expect to meet and discovers superpowers he didn't know he had. But when Garth's mother discovers her only son is missing, she is devastated. He was the only family she had left. Fortunately, the Supernatural Immigration Task Force was established to solve such problems, and Special Agent Frank Gallows makes it his personal mission to return Garth to his home. For backup, Frank looks to his ex-girlfriend Claire, a ghost posing among the living; together they use her Plasmapod to travel to the underworld city of Ghostopolis. Once they arrive, though, they discover the city is ruled by a terrorist named Vaugner, who, threatened by Garth's powers, tries to hunt him down before Frank and Claire can save him.

Part myth, part Science Fiction, part Fantasy, *Ghostopolis* is fast paced, highly imaginative, and deeply philosophical. The constant presence of death naturally yields to characters reflecting on life choices and questions about the relationship between free will and moral responsibility. Garth's deceased/estranged grandfather tells him after meeting him for the first time: "You don't have to repeat our mistakes . . . Being an idiot isn't cast in stone." Readers are left with the encouraging reminder that they, too, have agency in their lives—they can be a part of their families but still distinct from them. Like Garth, they can change who they become.

For those coping with: being underestimated by others, being unloved by a parent, death's finality, forgiving others

For those drawn to: chase stories, classics-inspired fiction, eccentric characters, ghost stories, humor, multiple intertwined storylines, romance, supernatural stories

Themes/subjects: abandoned children, afterlife, demons, detectives (adult), escapes, free will, ghosts, goblins, illness (terminal), jealousy, journeys/quests, political oppression, self-sacrifice, skeletons, traitors, wars/battles (imaginary)

Read-alike: The graphic adaptation of Neil Gaiman's *The Graveyard Book* offers another ghost-world setting and probes into complex familial relationships.

Thrash, Maggie. *Honor Girl.* Grades 9+.

Every summer since Maggie could remember, she has visited Camp Bellflower, an all-girls camp located in the remote forests of Kentucky. Far away from her home in Atlanta, she stages lip-synching performances to the Backstreet Boys and learns how to build campfires and shoot a rifle. But the summer of 2000, when Maggie turns fifteen, is different. She falls in love with a young female camp counselor. Her name is Erin, and though she returns Maggie's affections, neither one is ready or free to come out. Homosexuality is not welcome at Bellflower, where campers aspire to become "Honor Girl"—that is, the "perfect" lady.

While this is a poignant description of Thrash's first sexual awakening, the characters in the story actually never even kiss. They don't need to. In Bellflower culture, just the thought of loving a woman is deviant enough, and this is one of the reasons Thrash's Memoir stands out. Her story is placed within a larger narrative about the pressure on young women—especially in conservative environments—to conform. Her observations of her campmates' depression, for example, draw attention to the rise in teenage suicide in the United States since the mid-2000s. Thrash's willingness to point out hypocrisy and be different makes her a model of courage not just for LGBTQIA readers but all readers.

For those coping with: ambivalence about romantic feelings, being an outsider/misfit, being different, bullying, concern with what others think

For those drawn to: character-driven novels, culturally responsive literature, humor, Memoir, romance, strong female characters, witty tone

Themes/subjects: camping, cliques, competitions/testing, courage, crushes, friendship, gender roles (twentieth century), homosexuality, jealousy, media influence on identity, self-esteem, wealthy girls

Read-alikes: A changing friendship is also the subject of Mariko Tamaki's *This One Summer* and Tillie Walden's *Are You Listening?*

Tolstikova, Dasha. *A Year without Mom.* **Grades 5+.**

The Soviet Union is dissolving, and twelve-year-old Dasha is all alone. Her mother has gone to study at an American university for the year and has left her in Moscow with her grandparents. Although Dasha loves her grandparents and has her friends and her art to keep her company (she is an excellent illustrator), she misses her mother. So much happens while she is gone: Dasha falls in love with an older boy she meets over summer vacation. She skips a grade in math. She studies and applies for admission to a prestigious secondary school all on her own. And because this is the era before smartphones or e-mail, her mother misses it all.

The combination of text and illustration in this Memoir mimics the look and feel of a twelve-year-old's journal so that each page is a pleasure to behold. The monochromatic gray drawings are occasionally punctuated with bursts of pink, blue, or red—emphasizing the joy to be found in the quotidian. While readers gain an appreciation of the relationship between Russia and the West, this book appeals more broadly, as Dasha models resiliency in the face of environmental factors she cannot control and exercises her own agency. Teachers should pair this with a social studies unit and/or use this book to introduce journaling (especially as a coping mechanism).

For those coping with: absent parent, being different, change, loneliness, moving/relocating

For those drawn to: likeable/relatable characters, Memoir, richly detailed descriptions, urban settings

Themes/subjects: art as coping strategy, artists, cliques, crushes, cultural differences, divorce, family, friendship, immigration, jealousy, middle school life, mother-daughter relationships, resilience, Russia (twentieth century)

Read-alike: Artistic endeavors are the subject of Julie Billet's Graphic Historical Novel about Nazi-occupied France, *Catherine's War.*

Vernon, Ursula. *Hamster Princess: Harriet the Invincible.* 📕. Grades 3–5.

Harriet is a princess who has a problem with the word *princess*. Her mother seems to think it means standing with perfect posture, looking "ethereal," and "sighing a lot," but Harriet is happiest and most confident when she is going on adventures—jumping off cliffs or sword fighting with ogres. Her courage, though, isn't quite her own. When she was born, an evil fairy cast a spell to make her invincible... but only until her twelfth birthday. Then she will prick herself on a hamster wheel, and the curse will take full effect: she will fall under a sleeping spell until a prince rescues her with his kiss. Harriet, though, is determined to save herself. She devises a plan to outsmart the evil fairy, but the plan backfires. Everyone in the kingdom *but* Harriet falls into a trance, including the evil fairy, so that only Harriet is left to break the curse.

This new adaptation of "Sleeping Beauty" is full of wit and snarky one-liners as it gently turns gender stereotypes on their head. Harriet is bold, confident, sometimes arrogant, but completely self-possessed. She offers an alternative model of female identity and a new meaning for "princess." On the other hand, the prince, who becomes Harriet's friend instead of her husband, is far less athletic but the stronger of the two in terms of empathy and emotional intelligence. This modern-day allegory has something to teach everyone while also being fast paced and fun to read—boys and girls have much to learn from it.

For those coping with: being underestimated by others, gender identity, gender inequality

For those drawn to: Animal Fantasies, comic adventures, Fairy Tale–inspired stories, humor, strong female characters, witty tone

Themes/subjects: curses/hexes, gender roles (twenty-first century), journeys/quests, mice/rodents (talking), princesses, rescues

Read-alikes: Another Fairy Tale–inspired story that challenges gender stereotypes is Rebecca Solnit's *Cinderella Liberator*. Lincoln Peirce's *Max and the Midknights* is another amusing Graphic Novel series that is aimed more toward male readers.

Walden, Tillie. *Spinning*. Grades 8+.

Tillie has been a competitive figure and synchronized skater for twelve years. At first, skating was an escape—from bullies, from her parents, from fear of her own sexuality. But now, at seventeen, Tillie is tired of 5 a.m. practices, pancake makeup, and tiny outfits. She is tired of the pressure to perform. Most of all, she is tired of pretending. She would rather read, or play the cello, or draw. But the urge to conform and please others runs deep. It's hard to let go. Before she can find the courage to leave, Tillie must first disentangle her own needs from others' expectations.

Each chapter of this artfully drawn novel is more like a sketch from the writers' adolescent past. Although skating is the recurring theme, this novel is really a coming-of-age story that reveals the many gendered expectations and situations that young American girls continue to encounter today. But in showing the physical demands and discipline needed to skate, Walden elevates the perception that it's just a ladies' sport. Those who are struggling to find the courage to make a big life decision will take comfort in reading this work.

For those coping with: anxiety/fear, being an outsider/misfit, homophobia, parental neglect, self-blame, self-doubt, sexual assault, sexual identity

For those drawn to: coming-of-age stories, Memoir, psychological focus, strong female characters

Themes/subjects: bullies, cliques, competitions/testing, courage, crushes, gender roles (twenty-first century), heroes/mentors, homosexuality, ice-skating, purpose in life, sexual violence

Read-alikes: In contrast to this novel, *Tomboy: A Graphic Memoir*, by Liz Prince, is a humorous Graphic Novel about resisting feminine stereotypes. For those looking for something focused more on sexual identity, see Maggie Thrash's *Honor Girl*.

NOTE

1. Emma Carlson-Berne, *What Are Graphic Novels?* (Minneapolis: Lerner, 2014), 8.

4

Historical Fantasies for Children and Young Adults

Introduction to the Genre

Historical Fantasies yoke together two genres that conflict with each other: Reality-Based Histories and Reality-Defying Fantasies. Although they appear antithetical, they are, on closer examination, complementary: The historical settings help readers accept the fantasy world, increasing its plausibility and credibility. Conversely, the Fantasy elements intensify the emotional impact of the historical issues, highlighting them in fresh and unusual ways. Dark fantasy elements also heighten the air of treachery and depravity that accompanied low points in history.

Historical Fantasies for children and teens began in the twentieth century with Arthurian legends (Rosemary Sutcliff's King Arthur Trilogy, Kevin Crossley-Holland's Arthur Trilogy, Jane Yolen's *The Dragon's Boy*) and stories of Supernatural Adventures (Elizabeth Marie Pope's *The Perilous Gard*, Philip Pullman's *Count Karlstein*, William Pène du Bois's *The Twenty-One Balloons*).

In the twenty-first century, the scope of the genre has expanded significantly. Novelists combine Historical Novels with Fairy Tales (*Stepsister, West of the Moon*), ghost stories (*The Poisoned House, The Haunting of Falcon House*), folk magic and superstitions (*Midnight Magic, Grayling's Song*), eerie Gothic elements (*A Great and Terrible Beauty, The Charmed Children of Rookskill Castle*), talking animals (*Secrets at Sea, Whittington*), spiritual beliefs such as miracles (*The Passion of Dolssa, The Inquisitor's Tale*), Horror stories (*Dread Nation, The Night Gardener*), or characters with psychical powers (*The Diviners, Yesternight*). The boundary line between the real and the unreal is often blurred; this lack of clear demarcation makes readers question traditional ideas about reality.

Historical Fantasies are set in a variety of countries, but the majority take place in Britain and America. The Victorian era is depicted more often than other historical periods. Authentic to the era are the settings, social conditions, major historical events, and period detail, but less often the actual personages.

Although action is plentiful in Historical Fantasies, detailed descriptions slow their pace. Atmosphere is the feature that really distinguishes these novels. Eerie, gloomy, desolate, and haunting stories are especially prominent. Some Historical Fantasies are humorous or witty, but most are serious in tone.

Even though many protagonists are white, they experience prejudice of various kinds (gender, ethnicity, religion, class, or socioeconomic). Although such marginalization still occurs today, the entrenched attitudes that facilitate it were especially prominent in past centuries.

Many adults who play significant roles in the lives of protagonists fail them. Historical Fantasies depict parents who are distant, domineering, preoccupied, disapproving, or cruel. The novels also present teachers, clergy, employers, and officials who are corrupt, manipulative, and exploitative. Kind and supportive adults exist, but more often than not, children and teens must face problems on their own, without the support of the adults in their lives.

Some of the biggest names and most prolific authors in the genre are Libba Bray, Frances Hardinge, and Robin LaFevers. Fans of series novels will also be interested in the novels of Edward Carey, Justina Ireland, and Jennifer A. Nielsen.

Matching Readers and Historical Fantasies: Appeal Factors as Bridges

Set in both a fantasy world and a past era, Historical Fantasies are doubly removed from the here and now. These novels will appeal to readers who are looking for an escape from the present, be it the broader turbulent world they inhabit or inescapable personal problems. The genre will also appeal to those who simply love immersing themselves in a world that is markedly different from their own. Listen for clues that readers enjoy novelists who excel at world building.

Young people who love stories about girls and young women will be attracted to the plethora of narratives about them. Readers who have experienced gender inequality will find inspiration in the many protagonists who have coped with the issue.

Children and teens who enjoy Historical Mysteries may also like Historical Fantasies. The element of suspense characterizes both these history-based genres. *Jackaby*, *Newt's Emerald*, and *The Wizard of Dark Street* are examples of Historical Fantasies that are also Historical Mysteries. And if atmosphere is important to readers, they will relish such novels.

Those who are interested in the inexplicable, the inscrutable, and the mystical in life will gravitate to Historical Fantasies. Readers who appreciate stories with ambiguity and those who enjoy the suspense of not knowing what to believe in a novel will be a natural audience for these books.

Key Novels/Sure Bets

Auxier, Jonathan. *Sweep: The Story of a Girl and Her Monster*. Grades 5–8. 🎧

> Six-year-old orphan Nan Sparrow wakes up one morning to find her beloved guardian gone. Alone without her chimney sweep, she possesses only one object: a lump of coal. Five years later, as an indentured chimney sweep to the evil Mr. Crudd, Nan leads a dismal life. One day, when she gets stuck in a chimney, a hostile fellow sweep drops a lit match down the flue. After Nan awakens, she realizes she has somehow survived the chimney fire. Moreover, her lump of coal has come to life. Afraid that Mr. Crudd will find her, she hides in an empty house with the newly awakened coal. Nan names it Charlie, looking after the coal as she would a young child. As Charlie grows, he looks more and more unusual; observers who do not know him think he is a monster.
>
> Although Auxier does not gloss over the horrors of a chimney sweep's life, he creates a magical, uplifting story that is poignant, whimsical, and wondrous. The immensely likeable Nan, lovable Charlie, and streetwise Sweep view life in a highly unconventional and inspiring way. Teachers looking for an engrossing curricular tie-in for lessons on Victorian London or child labor will find in this book a much-loved tale that will that fire their students' imaginations. The story will resonate especially with readers who have been neglected or exploited by the adults in their lives.
>
> **For those coping with**: entrapment in a way of life, evil/manipulative adults, exploitation of one's poverty, homelessness, lack of parental guidance, orphanhood, poverty

🎧 available as an audiobook   📖 part of a larger series

For those drawn to: humor, likeable/relatable characters, nineteenth-century settings, streetwise characters

Themes/subjects: child labor, chimney sweeps, London (Victorian era), monsters

Read-alikes: Like Nan, twelve-year-old Serafina in Robert Beatty's *Serafina and the Black Cloak* lives in an old estate and foils a villain who is ensnaring children. Eleven-year-old Annabelle learns to cope with bullying and manipulation in Lauren Wolk's Historical Novel, *Wolf Hollow*.

Bray, Libba. *A Great and Terrible Beauty.* 📖. Grades 9+. 🎧.

In 1895, a sixteen-year-old named Gemma Doyle witnesses the inexplicable suicide of her mother in the streets of Bombay. Authorities cover up the suicide, and Gemma's father sends her to a prestigious boarding school in London. The school feels prisonlike to the lonely, grieving girl. Her roommate is sullen, and the other girls are cruel to Gemma, especially the popular Felicity and Pippa. Even more concerning is the fact that Gemma starts seeing visions of the future. A mysterious boy from Bombay who has followed her to London threatens her if she does not somehow put an end to these visions.

Bray combines the daily life of boarding school with an arresting otherworld and a haunting Gothic atmosphere. She also skillfully depicts the interpersonal dynamics between Gemma and her fellow students. When Gemma first meets Felicity and Pippa, she is appalled by their deviousness and cruelty. But as she is drawn into their clique, she becomes more like them. The vulnerability and powerlessness of the girls make them easy prey for manipulation in the otherworld they visit. This *New York Times* best seller and Goodreads First Choice for Historical Teen Novels will appeal to readers who have been bullied or left out of social circles.

For those coping with: bullying, cliques, cruelty, death of a parent, gender inequality, unpopularity

For those drawn to: boarding school stories, nineteenth-century settings

Themes/subjects: boarding schools, friendship, mother-daughter relationships, secret societies

Read-alikes: In Laura E. Weymouth's *The Light Between Worlds*, another vulnerable sixteen-year-old stumbles upon a blissful magical world that makes her forget her problems. Something magical also helps a teen who has lost her former happy life in Jaclyn Dolamore's *Magic under Glass*.

CHAPTER 4 | Historical Fantasies for Children and Young Adults **47**

Carey, Edward. *Heap House.* 🗐. **Grades 7–9.** 🎧.

Fifteen-year-old Clod Iremonger lives with his eccentric extended family in Heap House, a sprawling mansion in Victorian London. The mansion itself lies in the midst of trash heaps, the leftover junk of Londoners. Also odd are the offbeat characters. Every Iremonger is associated with a birth object, a common household items that helps define his or her character. Clod's birth object is a universal bath plug, which he wears like a watch fob. The other Iremongers think something is wrong with Clod because he can hear birth objects calling out their names. When Clod and a teenage servant named Lucy defy Iremonger conventions, they place themselves in grave danger.

This highly original, deliciously peculiar story will appeal to fans of Roald Dahl and Stefan Bachmann. Illustrations by the author are an added appeal, expertly capturing the oddity of the characters and settings. The Victorian obsession with possessions is turned on its head as objects get their revenge on humans.

Clod is timid and unsure of himself, a character who is easily victimized and afraid of challenging the status quo. *Heap House* is the perfect book for those who are intimidated by domineering figures, or readers who feel like their world is out of control.

For those coping with: being different, bullying, domineering relatives, lack of control over events, parent/guardian controlling one's destiny, unassertiveness/timidity

For those drawn to: arresting/original settings, eccentric characters, nineteenth-century settings, offbeat stories, witty tone

Themes/subjects: garbage/junk, London (Victorian era), mansions, materialism, servants, snobbery/elitism

Read-alikes: Readers who enjoy witty, offbeat stories that challenge the status quo will also like Stefan Bachmann's Steampunk novel *The Peculiar* and Terri Pratchett's Fantasy novel *Truckers*.

Hardinge, Frances. *The Lie Tree.* **Grades 7+.** 🎧.

When her family decides to suddenly leave their English home to live on the remote island of Vane, fourteen-year-old Faith suspects her parents of hiding secrets from her. But hearing rumors of a scientific scandal involving her clergyman father, Faith refuses to believe it. Soon after moving to the island, her father is found dead, allegedly having committed suicide. Faith, however, believes he has been murdered. When she finds his diary, she discovers his strange passion for a magical tree. After Faith locates the tree, she becomes entangled in an inextricable web of lies and secrets.

Those who wonder what it would have been like to experience gender inequality in the Victorian era will feel the cumulative, crushing weight of misogynist opinions. The novel also skillfully depicts the profound impact that Darwin's *On the Origin of Species* had on the deeply held religious beliefs of the time. The story will inspire debate between creationists and evolutionists.

Although Faith appears meek and docile, she hides an inner life of stormy emotions and intense curiosity. "Nobody good could feel what I feel," she thinks. "I am wicked and deceitful and full of rage." Faith's story will resonate with those who are harsh critics of themselves. Readers who have been emotionally abused or unfairly treated will also see themselves in Faith. *The Lie Tree* is a masterful coming-of-age story that provides great hope for readers who feel they do not deserve it. Depicted in stunningly evocative prose, this claustrophobic Victorian world is palpable in its intensity.

For those coping with: abuse (emotional), being misunderstood by a parent, distant/uncommunicative parent, flirtatious mothers, gender inequality, overly critical view of self, revenge (desire for), scandal, sense of inferiority

For those drawn to: coming-of-age story, lyrical prose, mystery/ suspense, psychological focus, richly detailed descriptions, Victorian settings, sinister atmosphere

Themes/subjects: archaeologists/archaeology, creationism versus evolution, England (Victorian era), father-daughter relationships, gender roles (nineteenth century), islands, lying, magical trees, mother-daughter relationships, murder, science versus faith, secrets

Read-alikes: Maryrose Wood's *The Poison Diaries* contains the same intense psychological focus, magical vegetation, and strained father-daughter relationship. When Ileni moves to an unwelcoming community in Leah Cypess's *Death Sworn*, she also becomes enmeshed in secrets and deceit.

LaFevers, Robin. *Grave Mercy*. 📖. Grades 9+. 🎧.

Growing up in fifteenth-century Brittany, seventeen-year-old Ismae believes in the power of the old pagan gods. Sired by the god of death, beaten by a cruel father figure, and abused by her husband, she is unexpectedly sent on an enigmatic journey to an isolated, austere convent. An abbess who poisons her as a test of her abilities tells Ismae that the convent will train her to be a covert assassin. Three years later, the abbess sends her to the Court of Brittany as an undercover agent.

CHAPTER 4 | Historical Fantasies for Children and Young Adults   **49**

A thrilling story of spies, treason, double agents, and court intrigue, *Grave Mercy* is also a compelling love story set at the end of the Middle Ages—a time of dark superstitions and Old World beliefs. The Fantasy elements seamlessly integrate with the meticulously researched historical setting. Contending with a series of repressive situations and environments, Ismae must figure out how to cope, who to trust, and what to believe. A story of survival in a dark world and personal hell, the novel is powerful, moving, and haunting. Anyone who feels pulled in two directions in life will not feel so alone after reading Ismae's struggles. Her story will also resonate with those who must live with domineering, abusive, or overly strict parents.

For those coping with: abuse (physical), being unloved by a parent, death's finality, moral dilemmas, questioning one's faith

For those drawn to: court/palace settings, medieval settings, political intrigue, romance

Themes/subjects: assassins, brainwashing/indoctrination, Brittany (fifteenth century), convents, courts/courtiers, death, nuns, poisoning/poisons

Read-alikes: A teen struggles with her deadly magical ability in Kristin Cashores's *Graceling*, another spellbinding book of court intrigue. Another teenage girl is removed from a nightmarish life and trained to be an assassin in Sarah J. Maas's *Throne of Glass*.

Peck, Richard. *Secrets at Sea*. Grades 3–5. 🎧.

When the "upstairs" Cranstons decide to travel by ship to England in order to find a husband for the eldest daughter, the "downstairs" Cranston mice resolve to sneak aboard in the luggage. The eldest mouse, Helena, does not make the decision lightly, as two of her siblings died by water. Once aboard, the Cranston mice meet their English-society counterparts in this witty sea adventure. Sitting on spools of thread at yardstick tables and drinking out of thimbles, Helena not only maneuvers the intricacies of high society, but also contends with the dangers of the high seas and looks after her headstrong, often foolhardy siblings.

Peck's novel is clever, imaginative, and heartwarming, following in the footsteps of Beatrix Potter's Peter Rabbit stories. It is an especially appealing book for younger readers and an excellent choice to read aloud—what Helena calls "a rodent's view of society." The reader sees the Victorian era from such unusual vantage points as inside jacket pockets and on top of hats. The charming, whimsical illustrations are an additional appeal. Chosen as a best book of the year by both the *New York Times* and *Kirkus*, this novel is a perfect choice for children who must overcome fears and anxieties.

For those coping with: anxiety/fear, sibling issues/rivalry, snobbery/elitism

For those drawn to: Animal Fantasies, humor, likeable/relatable characters, sea adventures

Themes/subjects: aristocracy/upper classes, class/socioeconomic differences, mice, Queen Victoria's Diamond Jubilee, sea voyages, ships, Victorian social life and customs

Read-alikes: A mouse must overcome his fears in Kate DiCamillo's *The Tale of Despereaux*. William Steig's witty Fantasy novel, *Abel's Island*, recounts the adventures of an endearing mouse.

More Excellent Historical Fantasies

Berry, Julie. *The Passion of Dolssa*. Grades 7+. 🎧.

After surviving a harsh childhood by stealing whatever Botille and her two sisters could, the trio takes over a derelict tavern in thirteenth-century Provensa. In the meantime, friars question a devout adolescent girl named Dolssa and condemn her to death for heresy. Forced to watch her mother burn at the stake, Dolssa escapes the same fate by running away. The story of how these four characters cross paths and affect one another's lives is a profoundly moving one.

The story builds momentum as Dolssa's whereabouts are tracked by a relentless friar. The characters themselves are unlikely heroic figures, very human in their weaknesses yet stirring in their actions. Readers who have ever wondered about the possibility of religious miracles will find this story deeply absorbing. Berry brings to life a period in history that might seem dull by infusing it with emotional intensity. This Printz Honor book is a must-read for anyone studying the Inquisition or medieval France. The story will resonate with readers who have experienced any form of injustice.

For those coping with: injustice/unfairness, orphanhood, questioning one's faith, religious prejudice

For those drawn to: likeable/relatable characters, medieval settings, multiple intertwined storylines, multiple perspectives, survival stories

Themes/subjects: France (medieval period), friars, inns/taverns, Inquisition, miracles, religious faith

Read-alikes: Also set in medieval Europe, Mary Hoffman's *The Falconer's Knot: A Story of Friars, Flirtation and Foul Play* features

CHAPTER 4 | Historical Fantasies for Children and Young Adults

friars and religious life. Alice Hoffman's *Incantation*, set three centuries later, is another powerful tale of religious persecution and the Inquisition.

Bray, Libba. *The Diviners.* 📗. Grades 9+. 🎧.

After upsetting her parents by exposing an acquaintance's secret, seventeen-year-old Evie is sent to live with her uncle in New York. Uncle Will, the proprietor of the Museum of American Folklore, Superstition, and the Occult, reluctantly allows Evie to accompany him when he investigates a strange death. Using her psychic ability to read objects, Evie provides clues that her uncle and the police rely on to capture a serial killer. Set during the "roaring twenties," the novel depicts a bizarre series of events that terrorize New Yorkers. This exciting plot, with its paranormal events and multiple murders, will appeal to readers who love high drama and suspense. Bray introduces a large cast of characters who initially appear unrelated to one another; readers will become increasingly rivetted as the separate stories converge.

Evie is a larger-than-life character—high-spirited, feisty, and rebellious. Her quick wit and unflagging zest for life are strong appeals in the novel. Teens living in the shadow of a preferred sibling and those who are coping with the disapproval of a parent or teacher will find in Evie a kindred spirit. Teachers looking for a novel that conveys the exuberance of America in the 1920s will find an excellent candidate in *The Diviners*.

For those coping with: being unconventional, death of a sibling, disapproval, favoritism, parental disapproval

For those drawn to: early twentieth-century settings, gradually unfolding stories, multiple intertwined storylines, richly detailed descriptions, strong female characters

Themes/subjects: cults (religious), flappers, New York (early twentieth-century), psychic ability, serial killers

Read-alikes: Destiny Soria's *Iron Cast* is a Historical Fantasy about a sassy teenage girl who hunts down a murderer in the 1920s. Although set earlier in Victorian England, Matthew J. Kirby's *A Taste for Monsters* is another Historical Fantasy about a highly feared serial killer.

Carey, Janet Lee. *Dragon's Keep.* 📗. Grades 6–10. 🎧.

After King Uther banishes his daughter from England, she makes her home on remote Wilde Island. Merlin prophesizes that her descendant, the twenty-first queen of the isle, will "end war with the wave of her hand." Six hundred years later, in the twelfth century, Princess Rosalind is born with a dragon's claw in place of her ring finger; the golden gloves that this twenty-first queen-to-be wears hide her secret. As she draws closer to marriageable age, all the remedies to remove the claw fail, and she becomes increasingly anxious. Then, one day, a dragon kidnaps her, forcing her into a life of misery and servitude. The princess loses all connections with her former life and the people in it.

Few readers will forget this incredibly moving story. Rosalind, who feels "like a monster" because of her claw, also endures a deep sense of guilt over the criminal actions her mother takes to keep the claw secret. Rosalind's nuanced, complicated relationship with both her mother and the dragons is skillfully depicted. The psychological richness is as impressive as the storyline itself. The quiet wisdom and bittersweet tone of the narrative will appeal to fans of Ursula K. Le Guin's novels. Readers who feel trapped between two cultures or ways of life will view their circumstances in a different light after reading Rosalind's story.

For those coping with: being an outsider/misfit, corrupt or criminal parent, death of a loved one, guilt, poor body image, shame

For those drawn to: character-driven novels, epic/grand-scale stories, medieval settings

Themes/subjects: dragons, friendship, heroism, islands, mother-daughter relationships, princesses, prophecies/omens, secrets

Read-alikes: Tenar is taken away from her family, too, and forced into a harsh new life that changes her in Ursula K. Le Guin's memorable novel *The Tombs of Atuan*. Like Rosalind, Seraphina is ashamed of the dragon part of herself in Rachel Hartman's Fantasy novel, *Seraphina*.

Chokshi, Roshani. *The Gilded Wolves.* Grades 9+. 🎧.

Interweaving late nineteenth-century Parisian history with a richly imagined fantasy world, Chokshi creates a magical, decadent realm that reflects the electrifying Belle Époque. In order to restore hotelier Séverin to his rightful place as patriarch of the Order of Babel, he and his assembled crew of gifted misfits must find and steal an ancient artifact. The fate of civilization depends on the actions of these characters. The story is told from multiple perspectives as members of Séverin's crew variously relate the events. Chokshi is especially talented at depicting each character's thoughts, emotions, and motivations.

CHAPTER 4 | Historical Fantasies for Children and Young Adults   **53**

An exciting heist story with several surprising plot twists, *The Gilded Wolves* will also appeal to those who love Historical Fiction. After finishing the novel, readers will want to know more about the Belle Époque as well as the 1889 Exposition Universelle. An exotic world that combines eastern and western mythological elements, the novel will not disappoint those who love spellbinding fantasies. Readers who have experienced injustice or those who have endured an unhappy childhood will be drawn to Séverin's tale.

For those coping with: being an outsider/misfit, being wronged, biracialism, foster families, orphanhood

For those drawn to: heist stories, multiple perspectives, nineteenth-century settings, political intrigue, romance, richly detailed descriptions

Themes/subjects: Belle Époque, brothers, colonialism, Exposition Universelle (Paris, 1889), France (nineteenth century)

Read-alikes: Another group of talented outcasts works together to pull off a heist in Leigh Bardugo's *Six of Crows*. Set four centuries earlier, Robin LaFevers's masterful *Courting Darkness* is the story of two operatives working separately in Paris on a deadly mission.

Ford, Michael. *The Poisoned House*. Grades 6–10. 🎧.

Fourteen-year-old Abigail tries unsuccessfully to run away after the cruel housekeeper of Greave Hall abuses her physically and emotionally. A scullery maid whose mother died from cholera a year earlier, Abigail works grueling hours and endures constant bullying in a countryside Victorian household. After she sees a ghost at the window, she begins to suspect that the house is haunted by her mother's spirit.

The story is told through Abigail's eyes, and we are never sure if we can trust her perceptions. Is the house truly haunted? Is there a murderer in her midst? Readers are left guessing until the end and will find this novel hard to put down. As they become immersed in the life of a Victorian teenage servant, they realize what it must have been like to be young, vulnerable, and destitute in the nineteenth century. Ford creates a plausible and convincing ghost story by grounding the eerie events and suspenseful atmosphere in the harsh realities of the household's daily routines.

Abigail is a very engaging character who is enmeshed in a series of inexplicable incidents. Readers who feel powerless in their current situation and those who have been abused or wronged will relate to Abigail's story.

For those coping with: abuse (emotional), abuse (physical), being wronged, evil/manipulative adults, orphanhood

For those drawn to: ghost stories, Gothic settings/atmosphere, nineteenth-century settings, psychological suspense

Themes/subjects: ghosts, haunted houses, séances, secrets, servants, war veterans

Read-alikes: Although the focus is more psychological, Frances Hardinge's *The Lie Tree* depicts the haunting events that another fourteen-year-old experiences in nineteenth-century England. Also set in the nineteenth century, Katherine Paterson's highly readable *Lyddie* is the story of a fourteen-year-old who must work full time in grueling conditions.

Fox, Janet. *The Charmed Children of Rookskill Castle.* **Grades 6+.** 🎧

During the London bombing of World War II, twelve-year-old Kat and her younger siblings are sent to live in a Scottish castle, the home of a distant relative. Converted into a boarding school, this isolated structure provides an eerie backdrop to the story. The boarders are locked in their rooms at night and wonder if they are being drugged. They also hear mysterious sounds that come from secret rooms. Corridors in the castle seem to disappear and later reappear. Then, one by one, children begin to vanish. Kat suspects that the castle harbors a war spy who is somehow involved in the mysterious incidents. Interspersed in this story are chapters describing the life of a previous inhabitant of the castle, a woman who practices black magic.

Readers who enjoy haunting ghost stories with a menacing atmosphere will find themselves addicted to this novel. The dark-fantasy elements heighten the general air of suspicion and treachery that existed at an oppressive time in history. Unaided by adults, Kat must face life-threatening problems on her own. Overwhelmed at times, she keeps recalling her father's advice to simply "carry on." Her story will inspire readers who face serious issues and must do so without the support of the adults in their lives.

For those coping with: evil/manipulative adults, lack of parental guidance

For those drawn to: dual intertwined storylines, Gothic settings/atmosphere, ghost stories, homefront stories, sinister atmosphere

Themes/subjects: Blitz, boarding schools, castles, codes/ciphers, ghosts, mechanical or clockwork creatures, missing persons, spies/spying, witches, World War II (homefront life)

CHAPTER 4 | Historical Fantasies for Children and Young Adults

Read-alikes: The events of World War II affect the life of another twelve-year-old in Frances Hardinge's strange and haunting *Cuckoo Song*. Nina Bawden's *Carrie's War* is about a girl and her brother who are sent to a stranger's home during the Blitz.

Gidwitz, Adam. *The Inquisitor's Tale, or, The Three Magical Children and Their Holy Dog.* **Grades 5–10. 🎧.**

Guests at a French medieval tavern tell one another what they know about three infamous children who have become enemies of the king of France. Each of the guests knows part of the story of how these children became embroiled in dangerous events. Adopting the narrative technique of *The Canterbury Tales*, Gidwitz uses multiple narrators to tell interconnected stories about a peasant girl, a Jewish boy, and a biracial African oblate. Some characters believe the children and their greyhound dog are actual saints because of their magical abilities. Earthiness combines with saintliness in a way that skillfully evokes life in thirteenth-century Europe. Readers unfamiliar with the period will discover that religion played a large and influential role in children's lives.

A Newbery Honor book that is filled with suspense, danger, poignancy, and humor, *The Inquisitor's Tale* will appeal to both boys and girls. Readers who feel isolated because they are different from others and those who have suffered from prejudice of any kind will identify with the children in the story.

For those coping with: being an outsider/misfit, being different, religious intolerance or persecution

For those drawn to: medieval settings, multiple perspectives

Themes/subjects: France (medieval), friendship, inns/taverns, Inquisition, Jews, miracles, peasants, religious faith, saints, stories, visions

Read-alikes: Catherine Gilbert Murdock's *The Book of Boy* recounts a boy's adventures as he travels across medieval Europe. Circumstances also bring three children together in Matthew J. Kirby's more-modern, adventure-filled Steampunk novel, *The Clockwork Three*.

Hardinge, Frances. *Cuckoo Song.* **Grades 5+. 🎧.**

Eleven-year-old Triss wakes up one day confused and disoriented, unable to remember falling into a pond the previous day. Her parents whisper behind her back—an action that increases her anxiety.

Her younger sister, who has always despised Triss, is now consumed by hatred of her. Then strange, unexplained events begin to occur, and Triss is afraid she is losing her sanity. Straddling the boundary between reality and fantasy, the initial chapters lure readers into the enigmatic narrative, making them wonder if the unexplained events are caused by a vindictive sister, an unbalanced protagonist, a mysterious stranger known to her father, or a supernatural force. The unsettling events are well suited to a world in which the old certainties have been undermined by an unprecedented world war.

Family dynamics are shaped by the tragic loss of Triss's brother in the war. A mesmerizing tale of psychological suspense, *Cuckoo Song* probes the deep recesses of characters' minds. A strange, haunting tale, it will appeal to those who love Neil Gaiman's *Coraline*. Readers dealing with a poisonous sibling relationship, grieving parents, or overprotective ones will be drawn to this story.

For those coping with: death of a sibling, grieving parents, overprotective parents, secretive adults, sibling animosity or hatred

For those drawn to: psychological focus, psychological suspense, richly detailed descriptions, sinister atmosphere

Themes/subjects: England (post–World War I), postwar life

Read-alikes: The sinister, menacing atmosphere of Neil Gaiman's *Coraline* will appeal to readers who love *Cuckoo Song*. Holly Black's *Doll Bones* is another eerie story about preteens channeling their emotions into dolls.

Ireland, Justina. *Dread Nation.* 🔖. Grades 9+. 🎧.

In the uneasy years following the American Civil War, government officials forcibly remove African American teen Jane McKeene from her home and enroll her in Miss Preston's School for Combat. In this alternative history, dead soldiers have risen from graves and turned into zombies. The government takes advantage of African Americans and Indigenous peoples by forcing them to combat and destroy the horrific zombies. Jane trains for this role; but when she stumbles upon a secret government plot, she is caught and exiled to a western outpost. Once she arrives at Summerland, she realizes that officials are hiding sinister, deadly secrets.

The witty tone and self-deprecating humor offset the horrors of this *New York Times* best seller. Jane's favorite novel is *Tom Sawyer*, and it becomes apparent that she is the female counterpart of the likeable "bad boy."

CHAPTER 4 | Historical Fantasies for Children and Young Adults

Although slavery had been officially outlawed in the era described, a racist mentality still dominated large pockets of post–Civil War America. No one depicts the discriminatory stereotypes, and so-called "scientific theories" of the time, better than Ireland. Readers who must cope with their own monsters will draw strength from Jane's indomitable determination.

For those coping with: abuse (emotional), biracialism, racism

For those drawn to: nineteenth-century settings, strong female characters, witty tone, zombie stories

Themes/subjects: African Americans, friendship, post–Civil War era (American), slavery/slaves, zombies

Read-alikes: Set in the present, Sierra also fights back against zombies in Daniel José Older's *Shadowshaper*. Seventeen-year-old Zelie battles tyranny and oppression in Tomi Adeyemi's Afrofuturistic Fantasy, *Children of Blood and Bone.*

Jones, Kelly. *Murder, Magic, and What We Wore.* **Grades 9+.**

Sixteen-year-old Annis lives with her aunt in Regency-era London. After she learns that her father has died overseas, she also discovers that his money has vanished and his death may have been a murder. Annis, suspecting that he worked as a spy, decides to follow in his footsteps and investigate his death. But when her aunt reveals that they are destitute and must become governesses, Annis must convince her that her burgeoning talent for magical dressmaking can support them. Annis becomes a part-time spy and full-time dressmaker.

Combining Regency life, high fashion, and spy craft, this delightfully inventive story is lighthearted and witty. Readers know more than the intrepid but naïve Annis—a situation that lures them into the suspenseful plot. The creation of "glamours," or enhanced appearances, through the art of dressmaking is a particularly original aspect of the story, one that blends seamlessly with a spy's need for disguises. Annis's witty observations on characters' clothes as an indication of their character are a clever addition to this fashion-themed novel. Readers whose family fortunes have diminished and those whose parents doubt their abilities will be energized by Annis's plucky perseverance.

For those coping with: financial loss of parents, gender inequality, needing to prove oneself

For those drawn to: likeable/relatable characters, nineteenth-century settings, Regency novels, witty tone

Themes/subjects: deception and disguises, dressmaking, England (Regency period), fashion/dress, murder investigation, spies/spying

Read-alikes: Readers who enjoy fantasy-tinged Regency novels with intrepid teenage heroines will delight in Garth Nix's *Newt's Emerald* and Alison Goodman's *The Dark Days Club*.

Moriarty, Chris. *The Inquisitor's Apprentice.* 📖. Grades 4–7. 🎧.

In Moriarty's alternate history, early twentieth-century New York is riddled with magical crime. When thirteen-year-old Sacha discovers that he can see witches, he joins the New York police force as an inquisitor's apprentice. Since Sacha and his extended family share a crowded two-room apartment with another family, the money he earns is sorely needed. Ashamed of his poverty, he lies about his family to Inquisitor Wolf, an action that entangles him in further lies. Teamed up with a girl from a wealthy New York family, Sacha resents her privilege and self-confidence. After he begins working with the inquisitor, he is followed by a shadowy figure, a situation that increases his anxiety.

A highly relatable character, Sacha loves his family but is embarrassed by their humble roots. Readers become immersed in what it must have been like to live in crowded tenements a century ago. Those who have felt discriminated against will relate to the prejudice that the Jewish boy experiences.

Turn-of-the-twentieth-century New York is reimagined as a larger-than-life magical city. Moriarty presents famous historical figures such as Teddy Roosevelt and Thomas Edison in a vividly imagined way, making their stories memorable for readers unfamiliar with their lives and accomplishments.

For those coping with: entanglement in lies, feeling ashamed of family, feeling unprepared for roles/responsibilities, poverty, prejudice

For those drawn to: dangerous adventures, early twentieth-century settings, mystery/suspense

Themes/subjects: apprentice magicians, apprentices, Edison (Thomas), inventions/inventors, Jewish boys, New York (early twentieth century)

Read-alikes: A boy in early twentieth-century America faces danger when trying to solve a mystery in Cynthia Voigt's *The Book of Lost Things*. Also set in late nineteenth-century New York, Avi's *City of*

CHAPTER 4 | Historical Fantasies for Children and Young Adults 59

Orphans recounts the dangerous adventures of a poverty-stricken thirteen-year-old who lives in a crowded tenement.

Nielsen, Jennifer A. *Mark of the Thief.* 📖. Grades 6–9. 🎧.

Nic, a young slave miner in ancient Rome, unwillingly obeys the commands of his tyrannical master. When forced to retrieve an amulet from the depths of a dangerous mine, Nic is attacked by a griffin and trapped in a cavern after a tunnel collapses. Unbeknownst to him, the amulet possesses magical properties, a relic that supposedly provided Caesar with great power. High-level political figures who know about the amulet's magic stalk the boy.

The precarious situation immediately lures readers into the story. Hunted by evil officials, double-crossed by those he trusts, and unsure who to believe, Nic flees for his life. He must outwit powerful enemies and learn how to use his newly acquired magical power. As readers are drawn into his pulse-pounding adventures, they also learn what life was like for young people in the ancient Roman world. This fast-paced story is an excellent choice for reluctant readers.

Children who feel overwhelmed by events they cannot control and those who are unsupported by the adults in their lives will gain renewed confidence in their ability to cope after reading the novel.

For those coping with: absent parent, being underestimated by others, evil/manipulative adults, lack of control over events

For those drawn to: ancient world settings, likeable/relatable characters, political intrigue, survival stories

Themes/subjects: amulets, ancient Rome, brother-sister relationships, slavery/slaves

Read-alikes: In Megan Whalen Turner's Historical Fantasy, *The Thief*, Gen's fate is also intertwined with a gemstone he must steal. Another story of magic and political intrigue, Jonathan Stroud's fast-paced *The Amulet of Samarkand* is about a twelve-year-old boy who steals an amulet.

Ruby, Laura. *Thirteen Doorways, Wolves behind Them All.* Grades 9+. 🎧.

This World War II homefront story follows the lives of two girls over the course of their teenage years. Left at an orphanage by her poverty-stricken father, Frankie endures harsh conditions and cruel treatment by abusive nuns. When her father remarries, he takes her brother out of the orphanage to live with this new blended family. Leaving Frankie and her sister behind in the Chicago orphanage, the rest of the family moves across the country. Frankie's story alternates with Pearl's, a ghost who endured similar injustice when she was alive.

As the title suggests, all options are equally dismal for Frankie and Pearl. They feel powerless and unsupported by those who should protect them. Their poignant stories will resonate with readers who have faced multiple cruel blows in life. This coming-of-age novel will provide hope and comfort to anyone who has faced inhumane treatment by adults, crippling injustice, or the death of a loved one. A National Book Award finalist, *Thirteen Doorways* also provides readers with an immersive, engrossing experience of what it was like to be a disadvantaged teen during World War II.

For those coping with: abandonment/desertion, abuse (emotional), being unloved by a parent, blended families, death of a loved one, deception, lack of control over events, stepparents

For those drawn to: coming-of-age stories, dual intertwined storylines, homefront stories, likeable/relatable characters

Themes/subjects: Chicago (mid-twentieth century), ghosts, orphans, orphanages

Read-alikes: Judy Blundell's *What I Saw and How I Lied* is another homefront story about a girl who is cruelly deceived and let down by a parent. Although more psychologically intense, Nova Ren Suma's *A Room away from the Wolves* is a story containing ghostly characters and a teen forsaken by a parent.

Schlitz, Laura Amy. *Splendors and Glooms*. Grades 4–8. 🎧.

As the sole surviving child in her family, Clara is spoiled by her parents. Seven years have passed since her four siblings died of cholera, but her grieving parents still dote on their memories. On Clara's twelfth birthday, she persuades her reluctant parents to invite a puppeteer named Grisini to perform in their home. After the party, Clara goes missing and her wealthy father receives a ransom note. When the police start looking for Grisini, the two children who work for him realize they are in grave danger: Unbeknownst to thirteen-year-old Lizzie Rose and eleven-year-old Parsefall, the evil puppeteer is also a powerful magician. The clever interconnections between various strands of the suspenseful plot is a strong appeal in this Newbery Honor book.

Schlitz evokes a darkly Gothic Victorian world in which children must rely on their own resources to extricate themselves from dangerous, neglectful, and manipulative adults. *Splendors and Glooms* is populated with an array of unforgettable characters from maudlin parents and creepy magicians to entitled children and streetwise urchins. The story will appeal to readers who feel like puppets in their own worlds and believe they have little control over their own lives.

For those coping with: death of a sibling, evil/manipulative adults, favoritism, feeling entitled, grieving parent, poverty, powerlessness

For those drawn to: Gothic settings/atmosphere, multiple intertwined storylines, streetwise characters

Themes/subjects: kidnapping, London (Victorian era), magicians, missing persons, puppets/puppeteers, witches

Read-alikes: Jonathan Auxier's *Sweep: The Story of a Girl and Her Monster* is a Victorian Fantasy about a girl who must outsmart evil-intentioned adults. Janet Fox's *The Charmed Children of Rookskill Castle* features dark magic, manipulative adults, and the disappearance of children.

Read On: Matching Readers and Historical Fantasies

Children

Author	Title	For those coping with
Auxier, Jonathan	*The Night Gardener*	authoritarian figures, death of a parent, disability, hostility, poverty, strict/controlling adults
Cushman, Karen	*Grayling's Song*	feeling unprepared for roles/responsibilities, self-doubt, unassertiveness/timidity
LaFevers, Robin	*Theodosia & the Serpents of Chaos*	being gifted, being underestimated by others, gender inequality, preoccupied/busy parents
O'Dell, Kathleen	*The Aviary*	death of a loved one, evil/manipulative adults, loneliness, overprotective parent, unassertiveness/timidity
Odyssey, Shawn Thomas	*The Wizard of Dark Street*	death of a parent, finding a career path, self-blame
Peck, Richard	*The Mouse with the Question Mark Tail*	being different, being underestimated by others, identity formation

| Weyr, Garret | *The Language of Spells* | being an outsider/misfit, lack of control over events, lack of friends |
| Yelchin, Eugene | *The Haunting of Falcon House* | death of a parent, idolized or famous relatives, recognizing privilege in oneself, snobbery/elitism |

Teens

Author	Title	For those coping with
Donnelly, Jennifer	*Stepsister*	being an outsider/misfit, jealousy, lack of beauty, lack of confidence, parental disapproval
George, Jessica Day	*Silver in the Blood*	domineering relatives, evil/manipulative adults, parent/guardian controlling one's destiny, secretive adults
Goodman, Alison	*The Dark Days Club*	ambivalence about romantic feelings, domineering relatives, hereditary traits, parent/guardian controlling one's destiny
Hardinge, Frances	*A Skinful of Shadows*	gender inequality, guilt, powerlessness, secretive adults, traumatic memories
Kirby, Matthew J.	*A Taste for Monsters*	being overweight, disfigurement, lack of beauty, lack of confidence, past wrongdoing, poverty
LaFevers, Robin	*Courting Darkness*	ambivalence about romantic feelings, distrust of others, fear of inheriting parental depravity, finding a purpose/direction in life, moral dilemmas, overly critical view of self, questioning one's faith, sense of inferiority

CHAPTER 4 | Historical Fantasies for Children and Young Adults

Lu, Marie	*The Kingdom of Back*	being a child prodigy, desire for parental approval, favoritism, gender inequality, jealousy, sibling issues/rivalry
Nix, Garth	*Newt's Emerald*	being underestimated by others, gender inequality, powerlessness
Ritter, William	*Jackaby*	being an outsider/misfit, concern with what others think, finding a career path, gender inequality, separating from parents/leaving home
Soria, Destiny	*Iron Cast*	being a black sheep, being an outsider/misfit, betrayal, disapproval, prejudice,
Thorley, Addie	*An Affair of Poisons*	corrupt or criminal parent, guilt, parental disapproval, parent/ guardian controlling one's destiny
Weymouth, Laura E.	*The Light Between Worlds*	grief, guilt, responsibility for younger siblings, self-harm
Winters, Cat	*In the Shadow of Blackbirds*	being an outsider/misfit, death of a loved one, epidemic/ pandemic threat, gender inequality, post-traumatic stress disorder

5

Historical Mysteries for Children and Young Adults

Introduction to the Genre

Unlike their counterparts for adults, Historical Mysteries for young people contain few real detectives. More often, highly curious children and teens investigate a mystery that crosses their path or is personally connected with them. Although some Historical Mysteries are set long ago, far more take place in the nineteenth and twentieth centuries. Victorian-era mysteries largely dominate the genre for children and teens. The pioneering novels of Avi, Leon Garfield, and Philip Pullman are still popular today.

Some Historical Mysteries examine shameful and horrific practices, such as widespread discrimination against Jewish people or the practice of exiling citizens to leper colonies. Even more Historical Mysteries focus on a personal rather than public past. Novels such as *Glow, Dreamland Burning*, and *Draw the Dark* explore dark secrets in a familial past.

Because people can never experience the historical past firsthand, it is a perfect setting for books of mystery, secrecy, and obscurity. The mystery element in these novels takes various forms. Gothic Mysteries such as *Elizabeth and Zenobia*, or *The Hidden Gallery* are set in shadowy, haunted landscapes and evoke a sinister atmosphere. Puzzle Mysteries such as *The Blackthorn Key* or the Mister Max books involve cracking codes, ciphers, or other clues. Less often, Historical Mysteries feature protagonists who view themselves as detectives-in-training (*The Girl Is Murder*, the Murder Most Unladylike series, the Sally Lockhart series).

65

While working to uncover secrets from a recent or distant past, young people discover clues to their own identity. They frequently investigate dark secrets that are hidden in their ancestral past. Secrets exist about characters' identity, parents, grandparents, friends, and even strangers. Solving such a mystery provides characters with clues to their roots and identity. Uncovering these clues helps them move forward in life with a sense of direction and purpose. In some novels, the mystery is shrouded in adulthood, in situations children don't understand. Solving such mysteries involves a loss of innocence but a gain in maturity.

Many Historical Mysteries provide readers with a sense of perspective on the present. Readers gain a sense of perspective on their own world as well as their own problems. Historical Mysteries such as *Glow, Dreamland Burning,* and *Draw the Dark* alternate between the past and present, drawing parallels between them and highlighting their interdependence.

Mysteries set in the past often explore issues such as gender inequality or racial prejudice. As protagonists uncover secrets, they also unearth systematic, institutionalized discrimination. Katherine Paterson reminds us that "the characters in history or fiction that we remember are those who kicked against the walls of their societies."[1] Their acts of rebellion and defiance help them mature and define their identities.

Matching Readers and Historical Mysteries: Appeal Factors as Bridges

Readers who are deeply interested in secrets and enigmas are perfect candidates for Historical Mysteries. Curiosity about the unknown drives readers of both Historical Novels and Mysteries.

Fans of Historical Fiction are good contenders for Historical Mysteries. Mystery fans who believe that history is dry may be willing to try a Historical Mystery. Readers will find themselves swept along by the mystery and suspense, surprised that the historical part is equally interesting. Teachers looking for curriculum tie-ins for history lessons will find a winning combination of historical narrative and suspense. Historical Mysteries include an incredibly wide range of choices. Asking readers if they have a favorite historical period will help narrow the selection.

Listen for clues that suggest a child or teen is exploring his or her own identity, background, and roots; he or she may want to read about a character who is doing the same. The stories may especially resonate with children who are adopted or have become interested in their heritage.

Readers of Fantasy who enjoy escaping to a totally different realm may find the historical setting so different from their own that they become completely immersed in it. Those looking for reassurance or comfort will be drawn to a genre in which loose ends are tied up, the mystery is solved, and unity is reestablished. The unchangeable past provides readers with a temporary respite from the unpredictable here and now.

Books set during wartime or other traumatic periods in history will appeal to readers who enjoy survival novels. Readers will gain a renewed appreciation of ordinary life after reading about horrific events. As Margaret Atwood has written, "The *Titanic* may be sinking, but we're not on it."[2]

Although the genre includes several male characters, females dominate the central roles. Gender inequality in particular seems to have captured novelists' imaginations. Female readers—and especially those coping with injustice or not conforming to the norm—are good candidates for Historical Mysteries.

Readers who are attracted to series should consider those written by Kevin Sands, Phillip Pullman, Maryrose Wood, Nancy Springer, and Robin Stevens.

Key Novels/Sure Bets

Blundell, Judy. *What I Saw and How I Lied.* **Grades 9+.** 🎧.

Winner of the National Book Award, the story is told through the eyes of fifteen-year-old Evie. The year is 1947, and Evie's veteran stepfather takes his wife and daughter on vacation to Palm Beach. Evie falls in love with a private who served under her stepfather's command in World War II. Although the mystery in the novel is not immediately apparent, small clues make readers aware that something is not right. The reader only gradually realizes that Evie is an unreliable narrator, unaware of the treachery surrounding her.

Blundell depicts the adults in the novel as products of the historical forces of the 1940s. While war helped shape a generation of men who served, stereotypical ideas of women affected and restricted the choices of females.

Blundell depicts the process of growing up with great psychological astuteness. Her lucidly written coming-of-age story captures the hopes, illusions, and anxieties of a girl who desperately wants to become a woman like her stunningly beautiful mother. Evie's startling lie at the height of the novel sets her apart from others and marks her entry into adulthood. Her story will resonate with readers faced with a heartbreaking loss, those betrayed by people they trust, or anyone living in the shadow of an idolized parent.

🎧 available as an audiobook   📖 part of a larger series

For those coping with: betrayal, corrupt or criminal parent, death of a loved one, idolized or famous relatives

For those drawn to: mid-twentieth-century settings, psychological focus, romance, well-developed characters

Themes/subjects: anti-Semitism, gender roles (twentieth century), hotel life, media influence on identity, mother-daughter relationships, secrets, war veterans, World War II (aftermath)

Read-alikes: Kathryn Miller Haines's Historical Mystery, *The Girl Is Murder*, is about another teenage girl whose life is deeply affected by World War II. Josie must also cope with a mother who fails her in Ruta Sepetys's poignant novel *Out of the Easy*.

Donnelly, Jennifer. *A Northern Light*. Grades 8+. 🎧.

After her mother dies in 1906, sixteen-year-old Mattie takes over the role as farmwoman and mother to her three younger sisters. She earns a scholarship to college and is desperate to leave her Adirondack village but has neither the money nor paternal approval to do so. As a talented writer, Mattie feels trapped in a life to which she is unsuited. She also makes promises to people who died, promises that imprison and oppress her. When Mattie's father allows her to work at the Glenmore Hotel, she is delighted with the independence such a life brings. But after a guest drowns and another one goes missing, she is drawn into the mystery of Grace Brown's life. Grace's true-life story weaves in and out of Mattie's tale, acting as a counterpoint.

Readers hear Mattie's tale from her own perspective—from a candid, probing voice that inexorably draws them into her story. Anyone who wishes they were understood by those closest to them, those who are not suited to the life expected of them, readers who struggle with a distant or uncommunicative parent, and anyone who suffers from poverty or prejudice will find in this Michael L. Printz Honor book a stirring, insightful, and deeply resonant story.

For those coping with: being an outsider/misfit, death of a parent, distant/uncommunicative parent, gender inequality, lack of beauty, moral dilemmas, poverty, racial prejudice

For those drawn to: early twentieth-century settings, romance, strong female characters

Themes/subjects: ambition, books (love of), farm life, hotel life, single-parent families, teachers as mentors, village/small-town life, words (power of), writers (aspiring)

Read-alikes: Teenage girls also become working women and must battle hardships and injustice in two novels set in early

CHAPTER 5 | Historical Mysteries for Children and Young Adults   **69**

twentieth-century America: Kirby Larson's *Hattie Big Sky* and Laura Amy Schlitz's *The Hired Girl*.

Sands, Kevin. *The Blackthorn Key.* ▓. Grades 5–8. 🎧.

The debut novel in a compelling Historical Mystery series, Sands's *The Blackthorn Key* opens with a warning about the dangerous recipes and remedies concocted by the seventeenth-century pharmacists in the tale. As an orphan apprentice to a London apothecary, fourteen-year-old Christopher leads a harsh life, but one that is softened by a kind master. When he finds his master dead—most likely murdered—he is devastated and terrified. After finding a coded message from his master, he leaves home to escape from the deadly cult he suspects of the murder.

Sands's use of ciphers is inventive and engaging, making readers co-detectives with Christopher. As the murders increase and get closer to home, readers are inexorably drawn into this adrenaline-charged story. Sands is also skilled at depicting the everyday life of London in the 1760s—particularly the sights, smells, appalling conditions, and utter precariousness of existence without a safety net. Christopher's story will resonate with readers who have little control over the conditions of their lives. His success in adjusting to the death of the only person who mattered to him will provide consolation to those who have faced the death of a loved one.

For those coping with: death of a loved one, lack of control over events, orphanhood, poverty

For those drawn to: dangerous adventures, killer stalking a character, seventeenth-century settings, solve-the-puzzle stories, survival stories, unexpected plot twists

Themes/subjects: alchemists/alchemy, avenging death, codes/ciphers, cults (religious), England (seventeenth century), friendship, inheritance and wills, murder, orphans, pharmacists/apothecaries, secret societies

Read-alikes: Although set in the present, Laura Ruby's *York: The Shadow Cipher* is another story with puzzles and ciphers that the main characters need to decode. Milo follows a series of clues to solve the mysteries of a smuggler's inn in Kate Milford's *Greenglass House*.

Sepetys, Ruta. *Out of the Easy.* Grades 9+. 🎧.

This *New York Times* best seller is the moving story of seventeen-year-old Josie, the neglected daughter of a manipulative prostitute.

Working in a New Orleans bookstore and living by herself above the shop, Josie also cleans rooms in her mother's brothel. When a well-read man enters the shop, Josie is drawn to his wise words but later shocked when she hears of his murder.

Enmeshed in a 1950s world of what she terms "gutter trash," Josie dreams of leaving the Big Easy for Smith, the elite Massachusetts college. But even if she can figure out how to pay the tuition, she lacks the necessary social connections to get in. And with no successful role model to guide her, she faces an insurmountable psychological barrier.

Although the murder investigation is riveting, it is the characters whom readers will never forget. What really sets this compelling story apart from others is the depiction of the relationship between mother and daughter. Despite the fact that Josie deeply resents her, "wishing that she could be like other mothers," she knows she must somehow come to terms with her. Readers who have been neglected, abused, or ill-treated will find in Josie's example a way to cope with and accept the situation. The wisdom Josie receives is from unlikely sources, from characters who find a permanent place in readers' hearts.

For those coping with: corrupt or criminal parent, entrapment in a way of life, exploitation of one's poverty, moral dilemmas, parental neglect, troubled mother-daughter relationships

For those drawn to: character-driven novels, mid-twentieth-century settings, mystery/suspense, streetwise characters

Themes/subjects: children of prostitutes, New Orleans (mid-twentieth century), mother-daughter relationships, murder investigation, prostitution

Read-alikes: Megan E. Bryant's *Glow* is another Historical Mystery about a seventeen-year-old who must postpone her educational dreams because of her mother. A clever girl in the American South is caught in circumstances that entrap her in Stacey Lee's masterful Historical Novel, *The Downstairs Girl*.

Wolk, Lauren. *Beyond the Bright Sea*. Grades 5–8. 🎧.

Raised by a kindly man who found her washed ashore on one of Maine's Elizabeth Islands, twelve-year-old Crow wonders why the other islanders are aloof toward her. Although her guardian cannot read, Osh is a man of deep wisdom and simple good-heartedness. The self-sufficiency and pared-down lifestyle of island existence have always made Crow happy. But once she starts investigating her past, her contentment with this simplicity is threatened. One secret leads to another in this highly suspenseful novel.

CHAPTER 5 | Historical Mysteries for Children and Young Adults

Crow's character is thoughtful and reflective—strongly influenced by the man who has raised her. Although she looks for answers, she does not find what she expects. Her story will help others look differently at their own problems, enabling them to live with uncertainty and ambiguity. Readers who wish to know more about their past or discover their birth parents will find in this novel wisdom and insight. Crow's story will also resonate with those who have experienced any form of rejection. Winner of the Scott O'Dell Award for Historical Fiction and shortlisted for the Carnegie Medal, *Beyond the Bright Sea* is a poignant and gratifying tale that will appeal to those who love Scott O'Dell's *Island of the Blue Dolphins*.

For those coping with: abandonment/desertion, desire to find birth parent, ostracism/rejection

For those drawn to: early twentieth-century settings, island settings, likeable/relatable characters, poetic language, simplified lifestyles

Themes/subjects: buried/hidden treasure, leprosy, nature versus civilization, secrets

Read-alikes: Karana is also left on an island and unsure what happened to her parent in Scott O'Dell's *Island of the Blue Dolphins*. Eva Ibbotson's *The Star of Kazan* is another Historical Mystery about the mysterious parentage of a twelve-year-old girl.

More Excellent Historical Mysteries

Avi. *Midnight Magic.* 📖. Grades 5–8. 🎧.

One stormy midnight in 1491, twelve-year-old Fabrizio hears a sudden knocking at the door. Courtiers summon Fabrizio's master, Mangus the Magician, to appear before the king. Mangus brings Fabrizio with him to the ominous Castello Pergamontio. The king asks Mangus to investigate his ten-year-old daughter's claim to have seen a ghost. The young Princess Teresina gets Fabrizio aside to tell him that her brother is missing. Moreover, the evil Count Scarazoni wants to marry her. Shortly afterward, Teresina's tutor is found dead.

Those who would not read a Historical Novel about the Renaissance will find *Midnight Magic* a compelling story of secrets, intrigue, plot twists, and missing persons. Most of the novel takes place in an ominous Italian castle, one complete with secret passageways, dark dungeons, trap doors, and ghostly sightings. Intriguing historical details such as the fact that ten-year-olds can and do marry; printed books are considered a novelty; and people believe that the world is flat are interspersed throughout the novel. In an audio interview, Avi said he was intrigued by the fact that the Renaissance "marks a point between old ways of thinking and new," a dichotomy represented by Fabrizio and his master.

To escape the gallows, Fabrizio must be brave and resourceful. Readers who feel trapped in difficult situations or who must cope with manipulative adults will be reassured by his story.

For those coping with: being underestimated by others, evil/ manipulative adults

For those drawn to: ghost stories, Gothic settings/atmosphere, mystery/suspense, unexpected plot twists

Themes/subjects: conspiracies, ghosts, heirs/heiresses, Italy (fifteenth century), magicians, missing persons, nobility, Renaissance, servants

Read-alikes: Readers who love suspenseful novels about magicians will enjoy Sid Fleischman's *The Midnight Horse* and Kate DiCamillo's *The Magician's Elephant*.

Donnelly, Jennifer. *These Shallow Graves*. Grades 9+. 🎧.

When seventeen-year-old Josephine Montford is summoned to the school office, the headmistress tells her that her father died while cleaning his gun. But when Jo subsequently learns that his death was a suicide, not an accident, she suspects foul play. Teaming up with a young reporter, Jo investigates her father's death, even though a young lady of her class would not do so in 1890. The twists and turns of the plot lead to several unexpected revelations.

These Shallow Graves is no dry history. Readers become immersed in the world of the 1890s, learning about the growing field of forensic pathology, the treatment of the mentally ill, and the lives of nineteenth-century prostitutes and pickpockets. The epigraph to the novel by William Faulkner—"The past is never dead. It's not even past"— highlights the inextricability of the past and the present in this story. Unearthing the past shakes the very foundations of Jo's existence. But by investigating her familial history, she learns about herself and her identity. Readers who need courage to make changes in their lives will find Jo's story inspirational.

For those coping with: being an outsider/misfit, death of a parent, finding a purpose/direction in life, gender inequality, murder of a loved one, overprotective parent

For those drawn to: detective novels, Gilded Age settings, nineteenth-century settings, romance, strong female characters, unexpected plot twists

CHAPTER 5 | Historical Mysteries for Children and Young Adults

Themes/subjects: aristocracy/upper classes, murder investigation, newspaper industry/reporters, New York (Gilded Age), police corruption, prostitution, psychiatric institutions

Read-alikes: Readers who enjoy Mysteries set in the late nineteenth century and featuring smart, resourceful teenage girls will also like Lucinda Gray's *The Gilded Cage*. Although Libba Bray's *The Diviners* involves the supernatural, it also is about a seventeen-year-old girl who investigates murder.

Haines, Kathryn Miller. *The Girl Is Murder.* 🖥. Grades 7–10. 🎧.
Fifteen-year-old Iris recently moved from the affluent Upper East Side New York to the Lower East Side. Her father, a veteran amputee of Pearl Harbor, resumes work as a private detective after his wife commits suicide and their inheritance runs out. Still grieving for her mother, Iris wishes that her father would not be so preoccupied with his work. She also feels out of place in her new public school, an establishment far different than the posh private school she used to attend. Although her father forbids her to do detective work, Iris secretly undertakes her own investigation when a classmate goes missing.

Readers unfamiliar with postwar America will be interested in the way World War II affected people's everyday lives on the homefront. To Iris, "the war ruined everything." Her resourcefulness in coping with its aftermath will motivate readers who are dealing with the harmful effects of social and political forces.

Iris must face a host of problems: the death of her mother, the inexplicability of her suicide, the disability of her father, his lack of attention to her, the change in the family fortune, and the move away from her friends. However, she does not recognize the enormity of these challenges. Both she and her father are grieving for their many losses, but neither knows how to express their feelings. This Edgar Award nominee will appeal to readers who are coping with loss of any kind.

For those coping with: death of a parent, disabled loved ones, distant/uncommunicative parent, financial loss of parents, loneliness, moving/relocating, snobbery/elitism, suicide of a loved one

For those drawn to: detective novels, homefront stories, mid-twentieth-century settings

Themes/subjects: detectives (child/teen), father-daughter relationships, high school life, Jewish descent, missing persons, New York (post–World War II), single-parent families

74 PART II | Annotations

Read-alikes: Another World War II homefront novel, Laura Ruby's *Thirteen Doorways, Wolves behind Them All*, is about a teen who experiences a multitude of cruel blows in life. Set during WWII, Katherine Paterson's *Jacob Have I Loved* is a moving story of a girl who learns to cope with being unfairly deprived.

Ibbotson, Eva. *The Star of Kazan*. Grades 7–10. 🎧.

After cook Ellie and maid Sigrid find a baby girl in a church in early twentieth-century Vienna, they raise her in the home of the three professors that they work for. Despite her humble life, Annika is grateful for a home that is rich in love and simple pleasures. When Annika is twelve years old, a beautiful, stately aristocrat visits the house, announcing that she is Annika's long-lost mother. Annika is overjoyed, but she is also apprehensive of the new life she will lead at Spittal, her mother's vast estate in northern Germany. After she arrives in this desolate environment, she discovers a number of mysterious events and puzzling situations. The novel's disquieting Gothic atmosphere, suspenseful plot, and psychological manipulation of characters will keep readers riveted.

Annika must leave home to discover the worth of what she left behind. Community and family are strong values in the novel, outweighing those of wealth and class. Readers who have been manipulated by cunning adults and those who have been deceived or abused by loved ones will relate to Annika's story.

For those coping with: abandonment/desertion, absent parent, corrupt or criminal parent, deception, desire to find birth parent, evil/manipulative adults, moral dilemmas

For those drawn to: early twentieth-century settings, idealized village settings, likeable/relatable characters

Themes/subjects: abandoned children, aristocracy/upper classes, class/socioeconomic differences, community, horses, inheritance and wills, lying, mother-daughter relationships, poverty, servants, stealing

Read-alikes: Gloria Whelan's *Listening for Lions* is about another orphan girl who is ensnared by manipulative adults who plot an impersonation scheme. Jeanne Birdsall's *The Penderwicks* is a reassuring, character-driven novel about girls growing up in a charmingly old-fashioned world.

Johnson, Varian. *The Parker Inheritance*. Grades 5–7. 🎧.

Twelve-year-old Candice and her mother move into her late grandmother's home while their own is being renovated. Not happy about

CHAPTER 5 | Historical Mysteries for Children and Young Adults 75

her parent's divorce and upset at having to leave her friends behind, Candice is delighted when she finds a mysterious letter addressed to her deceased grandmother. A secret treasure is promised to the person who solves the clues in the letter. The present-day story alternates with flashbacks to the letter writer's life in the Civil Rights era.

A Coretta Scott King Honor book, *The Parker Inheritance* depicts life during the time of racial segregation. Johnson uses alternating narratives to show how the past intertwines with the present and is still part of it. By learning about her grandmother and her heritage, Candice gains knowledge about her roots and identity. Those who must cope with divorced parents, racial prejudice, homophobia, bullying, or a gay parent will find a source of comfort and strength in the novel. Combining social injustice, romance, history, and riddles, *The Parker Inheritance* will appeal to a wide range of readers.

For those coping with: biracialism, bullying, divorced/separated parents, gay parent, homophobia, moving/relocating, racism

For those drawn to: dual intertwined narratives, romance, solve-the-puzzle stories

Themes/subjects: African Americans, buried/hidden treasure, grandmothers, racial segregation, secret identities, secrets

Read-alikes: Ellen Raskin's *The Westing Game*, which is referred to in the novel, is a classic Puzzle Mystery. Chris Grabenstein's *Escape from Mr. Lemoncello's Library* is another highly readable Puzzle Mystery.

Latham, Jennifer. *Dreamland Burning*. Grades 8+. 🎧.

When laborers find a skeleton on the Chase property, seventeen-year-old Rowan Chase is both intrigued and unsettled. After learning that the skeleton was buried there a hundred years ago, she becomes absorbed in the mystery of the person's death. The story of Will Tillman, a seventeen-year-old who grew up in Tulsa, Oklahoma, in 1921, alternates with Rowan's tale. When Will witnesses an African American man sitting beside a white girl, he confronts him—a situation that leads to the man's beating and death. After the Ku Klux Klan infiltrates Tulsa, Will begins to question his long-held beliefs.

Exploring such topics as Jim Crow laws, prohibition, the Ku Klux Klan, and the 1921 Tulsa Race Riot, the novel brings history to life in a highly engaging way. Racist attitudes are depicted in obvious as well as subtle ways. The story will resonate with readers who have experienced racism or other forms of discrimination. The novel provides words of wisdom for those looking for meaning in life and anyone hoping to make a difference in the lives of others.

For those coping with: being wealthy or privileged, biracialism, finding a career path, finding a purpose/direction in life, racism

For those drawn to: dual intertwined storylines, early twentieth-century settings, likeable/relatable stories

Themes/subjects: African Americans, class/socioeconomic differences, Ku Klux Klan, racial segregation, skeletons, Tulsa Race Riot (1921)

Read-alikes: Cat Winters's *The Steep and Thorny Way* also explores biracialism, the Ku Klux Klan, and racial prejudice in the 1920s. Although set entirely in the present, Kekla Magoon's *Light It Up* is another powerful story of racial violence and injustice.

Miller, Jessica. *Elizabeth and Zenobia*. Grades 4–7. 🎧📱.

Elizabeth's mother has run off with another man, so father and daughter move into Witheringe House, a haunted Edwardian mansion. A lonely child who is ignored by a preoccupied father, Elizabeth turns to Zenobia for companionship. Although very real to Elizabeth, Zenobia is not visible to anyone else. With Zenobia's prompting, Elizabeth explores the forbidden parts of the house and discovers secrets from the past.

Those who love scary stories about ghosts, séances, and haunted mansions will enjoy the ominous atmosphere and mysterious events. Using traditional Gothic-story features, Miller adds original touches, such as a mysterious gardener who performs eerie plant grafts.

Miller makes brilliant use of the doppelganger or evil-twin motif as well. Is Zenobia the dark and daring side of timid Elizabeth; is she an imaginary friend; or is she real? Yelena Bryksenkova's illustrations are haunting, suggestive, and psychologically penetrating. Children who are timid, those who are anxious and fearful, and others who have parents who are uncommunicative or preoccupied with their own problems will not feel so alone after reading Elizabeth's story.

For those coping with: absent parent, distant/uncommunicative parent, moving/relocating, shyness, unassertiveness/timidity

For those drawn to: Gothic settings/atmosphere, richly detailed descriptions, sinister atmosphere

Themes/subjects: ghosts, governesses, haunted houses, imaginary friends, missing persons, séances, secrets, single-parent families

Read-alikes: Lucy Strange's *The Secret of Nightingale Wood* is another eerie Gothic novel about a girl experiencing the loss of a loved one. Kathleen O'Dell's *The Aviary* is a Historical Mystery about a lonely, isolated young girl who lives in a crumbling mansion.

CHAPTER 5 | Historical Mysteries for Children and Young Adults

Pullman, Philip. *The Ruby in the Smoke.* 📕. Grades 7+. 🎧.

In 1872, a young woman named Sally receives a mysterious message: "Beware of the Seven Blessings. Marchbanks will help." Once Sally investigates, she learns that her inheritance has disappeared, her fate is somehow intertwined with that of a priceless ruby, and her father's death aboard the *Lavinia* may have been murder. Living with a cruel, calculating aunt who continually undermines her, Sally decides to leave. Alone and homeless, she learns to survive on her own. Sally disregards the limited options available to females of her time and pursues a job in business and finance. Although she wants to ignore the mysterious circumstances of her father's death, she tells herself that she is the only one who can set it right.

The Ruby in the Smoke is a rousing yarn complete with shipwrecks, murders, kidnappings, double-crossings, blackmail, and a legendary cursed gemstone. Pullman evokes a darkly brooding, Dickensian atmosphere in this underworld of London slums, shady criminals, and opium dens.

Sally's plucky resilience in the face of opposition and grave danger is a strong appeal in the novel. Readers who feel odd or unusual because they do not conform to conventional expectations will see their differences as strengths after reading this novel.

For those coping with: being different, death of a parent, evil/ manipulative adults, orphanhood

For those drawn to: detective novels, killer stalking a character, mystery/suspense, nineteenth-century settings, richly detailed descriptions, strong female characters

Themes/subjects: addiction (drugs/alcohol), assertiveness, buried/ hidden treasure, cursed gemstones, detectives (child/teen), females in unconventional jobs, London (Victorian era), opium trade, photography (nineteenth century), secrets, slums

Read-alikes: Orphan Mary uses skills that are untraditional in nineteenth-century England to make a career for herself in Y. S. Lee's *A Spy in the House*. Suspecting that her parents' deaths were murders, sixteen-year-old Meg investigates in Kristin Bailey's Victorian Steampunk novel, *Legacy of the Clockwork Key*.

Springer, Nancy. *The Case of the Missing Marquess.* Grades 4–8. 🎧.

On her fourteenth birthday, Enola, the much younger sister of Sherlock Holmes is puzzled when her mother does not return home to their countryside estate outside London. An unconventional Victorian woman, Enola's mother greatly resents the fact that her eldest son inherited the family estate after her husband died. When it becomes obvious that her mother is not returning home, Enola writes to her two older brothers. After Sherlock and Mycroft arrive, they discover that the money Mycroft had been sending for upkeep of the estate was never used to do so. When Mycroft tells Enola that she must go to boarding school, she disguises herself as a widow, sneaks out of the house, and travels to London in search of her mother.

An exciting tale of mysterious events that are set in the shadowy, gaslit world of Holmesian London, the novel ranks near the top of the Goodreads Historical Mystery Book List for teens and middle schoolers. What particularly distinguishes the novel is the way females outsmart their male counterparts by using the very instruments that oppress them. A naïve narrator, Enola initially views the world through very innocent eyes. But her adventures in London introduce her to a world of injustice—an experience that stimulates an untapped resourcefulness that will inspire readers who have been underestimated by others.

For those coping with: abandonment/desertion, absent parent, being underestimated by others, gender inequality, idolized or famous relatives, loneliness

For those drawn to: detective novels, mystery/suspense, nineteenth-century settings

Themes/subjects: brother-sister relationships, codes/ciphers, deception and disguise, detective (child/teen), kidnapping, missing persons, mother-daughter relationships

Read-alikes: Female teenage detectives investigate the death of a parent in Kathryn Miller Haines's *The Girl Is Trouble* and Philip Pullman's *The Ruby in the Smoke*.

Stevens, Robin. *Murder Is Bad Manners.* 📗. Grades 5–8. 🎧.

Even though Hazel Wong and Daisy Wells form a detective society, they find only trivial incidents to investigate. But then Hazel accidently discovers the body of Miss Bell, the science teacher at their English boarding school. When she returns with Daisy, the body is gone. As the girls investigate, they conclude that Miss Bell was murdered by one of their teachers.

The Murder Most Unladylike series is modeled on the Golden Age detective story, making use of features such as red herrings, an intricate puzzle plot, a British interwar-years setting, well-to-do characters, a closed circle of suspects, and the use of observation and rational deduction to solve the mystery.

CHAPTER 5 | Historical Mysteries for Children and Young Adults **79**

Even though thirteen-year-old Hazel views herself as the plodding Watson to the brilliant Holmes-like Daisy, the facts do not bear this out. Hazel is the one who makes many of the most intelligent deductions in the case. The fascinating interpersonal dynamics between the girls raises the novel from a plot-driven work to a more complex plot- and character-driven story, one that includes Hazel's adjustment as an immigrant from Hong Kong. Readers who are adapting to a new school or even a new country will find Hazel's story a rich source of inspiration.

For those coping with: being an outsider/misfit, domineering friend, (the) immigrant experience, moving to a new school

For those drawn to: boarding school stories, dangerous adventures, detective novels, mystery/suspense, strong female characters

Themes/subjects: boarding schools, deceptiveness of appearances, friendship, murder investigation

Read-alikes: Girls investigate a murder at their school in Julie Berry's humorous *The Scandalous Sisterhood of Prickwillow Place*. A plucky female detective stars in Elizabeth C. Bunce's witty Historical Mystery, *Premeditated Myrtle*.

Voigt, Cynthia. *The Book of Lost Things*. 📕. Grades 5–8. 🎧.
It is the early 1900s and the Maharajah asks Max's actor parents to set up a theater company in Kashmir. But when Max meets his parents at the dock to leave for Kashmir, they are not there and neither is the ship. He is given a cryptic unsigned letter that neither he nor Grammie can figure out. Although Max can't immediately solve the mystery of his parent's whereabouts, he turns detective to make a living.

At the age of twelve, Max is ambivalent about being independent. Although Grammie's house adjoins his parent's home, he is initially unsure of which place to live. He also has a number of questions with no immediate answers: Was he deliberately left behind? Was foul play involved? What did his parents know of the plan? Describing Max's thought processes in detail, Voigt provides readers with a number of coping strategies for dealing with seemingly impossible problems. Chief among them is focusing on the solvable when the unsolvable presents itself. Max also uses his knowledge of drama, playing roles that make him feel more courageous and resolute. Readers who are plagued by doubts and those whose parents have abandoned them will find Max's example a valuable support.

Set during the early years of the twentieth century, the novel's historical background is charmingly conveyed through Iacopo Bruno's whimsical illustrations.

For those coping with: abandonment/desertion, absent parent, finding employment, self-doubt, worry/anxiety about a loved one

For those drawn to: character-driven novels, early twentieth-century settings

Themes/subjects: abandoned children, actors/acting, children of actors/actresses, class/socioeconomic differences, detectives (child/teen), disguises, grandmothers, grandmothers as guardians, missing persons, problem-solving, self-reliance

Read-alikes: Also living in the early twentieth century, thirteen-year-old Sacha works at solving mysteries in Chris Moriarty's *The Inquisitor's Apprentice*. Brian Selznick's *The Invention of Hugo Cabret* is about another twelve-year-old boy who learns to live on his own after his father dies.

Winters, Cat. *The Steep and Thorny Way*. Grades 8+.

When Hanalee learns that Joe, the teenager who ran over and killed her father, is out of jail, she confronts him with a loaded gun. Just as she is about to fire, the teenager says it was Hanalee's stepfather who killed him. Sowing seeds of doubt in Hanalee's mind, Joe tries to convince her to poison her stepfather. Although Hanalee does not know who to believe, she argues with her stepfather and leaves home. One mystery leads to another as Hanalee probes the secrets that her family, friends, and townspeople are hiding. As the story progresses, the reader becomes suspicious of nearly all the characters in the novel.

Living during a time of deep racial prejudice, Hanalee is accustomed to signs like the one on her local nickelodeon that reads, "NO NEGROES, JEWS, CATHOLICS, CHINESE, OR JAPANESE." The 1920s Oregon photographs interspersed throughout are a perfect accompaniment to the tale, providing readers with an immersive experience of the past.

Children and teens who have experienced prejudice of any kind, those who have had to adjust to a new family, and anyone who has felt the desire for revenge will be drawn to this story. "If the pages of this book," Winters writes, "bring hope and inspiration to even one person who's found himself or herself on a steep and thorny path in life, then I'll feel I have done my job as its writer."

For those coping with: biracialism, death of a parent, homophobia, ostracism/rejection, racism, revenge (desire for), stepparents

For those drawn to: early twentieth-century settings, mystery/suspense

Themes/subjects: eugenics, ghosts, Ku Klux Klan, murder, secrets

Read-alikes: Biracialism is also explored in Richard Peck's *The River Between Us*, a Historical Novel about a spirited teenage girl. Angie Thomas's powerful present-day novel, *The Hate U Give*, depicts a senseless death caused by racism against African Americans.

Wood, Maryrose. *The Mysterious Howling.* 📕. Grades 5–7. 🎧.

A proud graduate of the Swanburne Academy for Poor Bright Females, fifteen-year-old Penelope anxiously awaits her interview for governess. Although alone in a strange place, she reminds herself that she is "a Swanburne girl, through and through." The interview itself, although somewhat strange, is overshadowed by the bizarre howling from outside. When Penelope tracks down the source of commotion, she discovers Lord Ashton's three wards, children who have been raised by wolves and are now huddled together in the stables.

Civilizing and educating the three Incorrigibles is Penelope's mission. But it soon becomes apparent that the wealthy Ashtons and their friends are the barbarians, not the feral children. The mystery of the children's parentage reminds Penelope of her own mother and father, a couple who, for some unknown reason, left her at age five in the care of the Academy.

The children and their governess are incredibly likeable and endearing characters. The humorous asides, witty observations, and chatty armchair-style narration are strong attractions in the novel. The discrepancy between the children's animal-like tendencies and the erudite academic texts they learn is delightfully funny and inspiring. Readers who feel discouraged by insurmountable difficulties will look at them in a new light after reading this novel. Jon Klassen's whimsical illustrations evoke a bygone world of Victorian charm.

For those coping with: absent parent, evil/manipulative adults

For those drawn to: Gothic settings/atmosphere, humor, likeable/relatable characters, mystery/suspense, nineteenth-century settings

Themes/subjects: aristocracy/upper classes, governesses, hunting/hunters, orphans, wild/feral children

Read-alikes: Lemony Snicket's *The Bad Beginning* and Lois Lowry's *The Willoughbys* are also witty, tongue-in-cheek novels about neglected siblings and their adventures.

Yelchin, Eugene. *Spy Runner*. Grades 5–7. 🎧.

It is 1953, the height of the Cold War—a time of paranoia, suspicion, and propaganda in the United States. Twelve-year-old Jake dreams of finding his father, an Air Force pilot, MIA from World War II. After his mother rents their attic to a Russian-born boarder, Jake suspects him of being a Communist spy. After his best friend spreads the story of this boarder, Jake is ostracized by his classmates. When Jake decides to spy on the man, he is stalked by strangers, interviewed by FBI agents, and almost killed by unknown assailants.

A riveting Noir Mystery featuring multiple deceptions, a menacing atmosphere, and intriguing plot twists, *Spy Runner* will appeal to hard-boiled Mystery fans. In true noir fashion, Jake hurtles headlong into the path of destruction. People in authority and even parents are not what they seem; in fact, none of the adults can be relied upon for support or guidance. Jake's story will resonate with readers facing rejection, betrayal, or an absent parent.

Spy photography is central to the plot and highlighted in the clever illustrations. As Yelchin has observed, these illustrations "cast doubt on everything the protagonist holds as true while contributing to the vertiginous sense of a nightmare he finds himself in."[3] Readers wondering what it was like to live during the Cold War must read *Spy Runner*.

For those coping with: absent parent, being a victim of gossip/slander, ostracism/rejection, secretive adults

For those drawn to: Cold War settings, dangerous adventures, mid-twentieth-century settings, Noir novels

Themes/subjects: Cold War, Communism, deception and disguise, influence of popular culture, McCarthyism, propaganda, secret identities, spies/spying

Read-alikes: Readers who enjoy books about boys as amateur spies will love Rebecca Stead's *Liar & Spy* and Deborah Hopkinson's *How I Became a Spy*, the first a present-day novel, the second a World War II book.

Read On: Matching Readers and Historical Mysteries

Children

Author	Title	For those coping with
Avi	*Murder at Midnight*	being underestimated by others, being unloved by a parent, false accusations, needing to prove oneself, sense of inferiority
Berry, Julie	*Scandalous Sisterhood of Prickwillow Place*	being underestimated by others critical/faultfinding parent, entanglement in lies
Bunce, Elizabeth C.	*Premeditated Myrtle*	being gifted, being unconventional, gender inequality, unpopularity
Golding, Julia	*The Diamond of Drury Lane*	orphanhood, poverty, racism
Haines, Kathryn Miller	*The Girl Is Trouble*	anti-Semitism, death of a parent, distant/uncommunicative parent, overprotective parent, racism, single-parent dating
Hopkinson, Deborah	*How I Became a Spy*	guilt, lack of confidence, past wrongdoing, self-blame
Lawson, Jessica	*Nooks & Crannies*	abandonment, adoption, being unloved by a parent, cruelty, lack of friends, parental neglect
Sands, Kevin	*Mark of the Plague*	epidemic/pandemic threat, evil/manipulative adults, lack of parental guidance
Stevens, Robin	*First Class Murder*	anti-Semitism, being underestimated by others, racism, strained relationship with a father
Stevens, Robin	*Poison Is Not Polite*	false accusations, parental affair, worry/anxiety about a loved one
Strange, Lucy	*The Secret of Nightingale Wood*	absent parent, death of a sibling, guilt, moving/relocating, parent with post-traumatic stress disorder, powerlessness

Teens

Author	Title	For those coping with
Baldwin, Kathleen	*A School for Unusual Girls*	being a misfit/outsider, being unloved by a parent, death of a sibling, gender inequality
Bick, Ilsa J.	*Draw the Dark*	abandonment/desertion, absent parent, anti-Semitism, being an outsider/misfit, bullying, self-blame
Bryant, Megan E.	*Glow*	gender inequality, jealousy, moral dilemmas, obsessions, poverty, sexual harassment in the workplace
Cameron, Sharon	*The Dark Unwinding*	abuse (emotional), autistic loved ones, being different, powerlessness, poverty
Gray, Lucinda	*The Gilded Cage*	death of a sibling, evil/manipulative adults, moving/relocating, orphanhood, powerlessness
Hoffman, Mary	*The Falconer's Knot*	being an outsider/misfit, being wronged, betrayal by a friend, gender inequality, parent/guardian controlling one's destiny
Landman, Tanya	*Hell & High Water*	absent parent, being wronged, evil/manipulative adults, racism
Lee, Y. S.	*A Spy in the House*	biracialism, feeling unprepared for roles/responsibilities, gender inequality
Wein, Elizabeth	*The Pearl Thief*	being wealthy or privileged, financial loss of parents, racism, sexual identity
Zettel, Sarah	*Palace of Spies*	abandonment/desertion, gender inequality, unloved by guardian

NOTES

1. Katherine Paterson, "Connecting Past and Present to Ourselves," *Signal* 23, no. 2 (1999): 13.

2. Margaret Atwood, "In Search of *Alias Grace*: On Writing Canadian Historical Fiction," *American Historical Review* 103, no. 5 (1998): 1511.

3. Eugene Yelchin, interview by Elizabeth Bird, "Review of the Day: *Spy Runner* by Eugene Yelchin," *School Library Journal*, March 21, 2019, http://blogs.slj.com/afuse8production/2019/03/21/review-of-the-day-spy-runner-by-eugene-yelchin-bonus-interview-included/.

6

Magical Realism for Children and Young Adults

Introduction to the Genre

As paradoxical as it sounds, Magical Realism is exactly what the name implies, a blend of both extraordinary occurrences—anything that defies scientific explanation—and elements that are true to life, present or historical. While borrowing many of Fantasy's motifs (time displacement and time distortion; animal, toy, and mythical characters), Magical Realism stories differ in that they take place on the same plane of reality as our own. In other words, unlike L. Frank Baum's *The Wizard of Oz* or C. S. Lewis's Narnia novels, there are no secondary or alternative worlds, only this one. Furthermore, the magical things must be accepted as part of material reality, whether visible or invisible, and not simply the imaginings of one's mind.

Critics, authors, and theorists have been debating the origins of Magical Realism since the last century. Franz Roh first applied the term to visual art in his 1925 essay, "Magic Realism: Post-expressionism," but it was the Latin American critic Angel Flores who first applied it to literature—specifically, Latin American literature.[1] The concept developed in the early twentieth century as a response to the changing modern world and an increasingly disordered reality. As the postcolonial scholar Brenda Cooper explains, "Magical realism arises out of particular societ[ies]—postcolonial, unevenly developed places where old and new, modern and ancient, the scientific and the magical views of the world co-exist."[2]

Given this explanation, it is no wonder that so many of us associate Magical Realism with the Latin American Boom and post-Boom writers such as Gabriel García Márquez and Isabel Allende. In rejecting Western, postindustrial notions of the division between reality and fantasy, Magical Realism becomes a resource—a method for subverting colonial influence and challenging assumptions of Western history and science. As our world becomes more globalized, and the list of existential threats (artificial intelligence, climate change, global pandemics) continues to grow, writers everywhere—especially women writers and writers of color—have turned to this mode as well. In other words, Magical Realism is no longer a uniquely Latin American phenomenon.

Consequently, what constitutes reality and magic will depend on the author's and the reader's cultural context. Nonetheless, the key characteristic of this genre is that magical events are deliberately treated as ordinary occurrences. As Wendy B. Faris notes, "The narrative voice reports extraordinary—magical—events, which would not normally be verifiable by sensory perception, in the same way in which other, ordinary events are recounted."[3] In this way, magical realist writers challenge Western science and logic and the modern tendency to reduce everything to the knowable. Through metaphor, Magical Realism makes visible, the nonvisible, nonempirical forces that also move and shape the world; in Allende's words: "dreams, legends, myths, emotion, passion, history."[4] In fusing dream and reality, the conscious and the unconscious, Magical Realism is able to mirror the natural world and, at the same time, change the way we see it.

In the face of a reality that is becoming progressively more disordered, it is not surprising that Magical Realism has expanded its presence into children's literature. By providing a fictive order to the universe and human existence, Magical Realism affirms life in the face of oppressive realities. It makes space for hope—which is, after all, the aim of all children's literature.

Matching Readers and Magical Realism: Appeal Factors as Bridges

Again, the *magic* in *Magical Realism* does not refer to magicians or a rabbit being pulled out of a hat but rather to magical occurrences. Characters have wings or travel through dreams; trees or animals can talk; ghosts haunt. Other examples include disappearances, extraordinary talents, and strange atmospheres.[5] The protagonist accepts these real and magical happenings with the same matter-of-fact manner as they would in a realistic setting.

For example, in Anna-Marie McLemore's *When the Moon Was Ours*, no one in the story questions the strange arrival of the protagonist, Miel, the fact that she washes out of a tipped-over water tower, or that roses grow out of her wrist. No rational explanations are offered (as in Science Fiction); rather, it is assumed that something extraordinary actually has happened, and it is treated as a given, even ordinary.

The scholar Maggie Ann Bowers describes Magical Realism as a mode of writing suited to exploring and transgressing boundaries. It is subversive in that "it alternates between the real and the magical using the same narrative voice"; and it is transgressive in that it "crosses the borders between the magic and the real to create a further category—the magical real."[6] As a result, the reader is led to question not just the nature of reality, but "all assumptions of truth."[7]

The protagonists of magical realist stories tend to live on the fringes, as outsiders. In the US, the word *outsider* usually refers to anyone outside the privileged class of males who are white, heterosexual, cisgender, middle to upper class, and able bodied. This, of course, is because Magical Realism is rooted in a desire to challenge and offer alternative approaches to reality other than that offered by Western philosophy. As such, many Magical Realism stories may provide "mirrors" for readers who do not usually see themselves reflected in literature and "windows" for others.[8]

Metaphors like Miel's roses offer an indirect means of addressing difficult, complex, or unexplained aspects of reality: rejection and abandonment; anxiety and depression; death and dying; violence, including sexual violence; and even, as in Amy Sarig King's *Me and Marvin Gardens*, the Anthropocene.

Given their subject matter and abstraction, Magical Realism stories are suited for more mature, sophisticated audiences. With a few exceptions, most of the novels included in this chapter are written for middle-aged readers or older. Readers who like ambiguity, and who are more interested in posing questions than finding definitive answers, will find much to love about Magical Realism.

Key Novels/Sure Bets

McGhee, Alison. *Pablo and Birdy*. Grades 4–6. 🎧.

> Pablo knows he's about to turn ten—he's just not exactly sure when. He doesn't know anything about his birth, only that when he was an infant, he washed up on the shores of Isla after a great storm, and his only company was a parrot, now his pet, named Birdy. Luckily, Pablo and Birdy were found and adopted by Immanuel, a shop owner in

🎧 available as an audiobook   📖 part of a larger series

Isla, and together they make a family out of their small community. Still, Pablo longs to know where he comes from. When Birdy suddenly begins to speak—after ten years of complete silence—Pablo begins to suspect that she may be the rare, rumored-to-be-true but never-seen-before seafaring parrot. Seafarers are supposed to remember everything, which means Birdy may remember Pablo's parents and, therefore, the truth behind their separation.

Deeply affecting, and full of wit and memorable characters, this story is hard to put down. As Pablo uncovers the truth behind his missing parents, and as he begins to openly discuss his grief, his community of loved ones reveal to readers that families are not just inherited, they are also made. Teachers may use this novel to complement a science unit on animal classification (particularly birds) or climate change. Although the novel is set in a fictional seaside town, McGhee references Latino/Caribbean culture, particularly in the context of immigration.

For those coping with: adoption, death's finality, desire to find birth parent, (the) immigrant experience, moral dilemmas

For those drawn to: alternating perspectives, Animal Fantasies, chase stories, dual intertwined storylines, eccentric characters, humor, idealized village settings

Themes/subjects: anger, birds, birthdays, (the) Caribbean, community, courage, dogs, dreams/nightmares, grief/loss, heritage/ancestry, immigration, nontraditional families, seaside towns, village/small-town life

Read-alikes: Crow, the protagonist in Lauren Wolk's *Beyond the Bright Sea*, is also set adrift as an infant and makes a family out of her island community. Magical Realism, coming-of-age themes, and charming characters feature in Christina Uss's *The Adventures of a Girl Called Bicycle* as well.

Ness, Patrick. *A Monster Calls*. Grades 7+. 🎧.

Connor has been waking from the same nightmare for weeks—a nightmare so awful he can't bring himself to repeat it out loud. But this particular night, he also wakes to the sound of someone calling out his name. Looking outside, he recognizes the yew tree that grows in the cemetery behind his house. Only now the tree has mean eyes and a sneer, and it stands—literally stands—in his backyard. Connor might have felt afraid if his waking life wasn't so much scarier: his mum has cancer, and since his dad has remarried and gone off to America, it is up to Connor to take care of them both. He has never felt so alone, and now this monster won't stop bothering him. Every

CHAPTER 6 | Magical Realism for Children and Young Adults 89

night, at 12:07 a.m., the monster brings his strange tales and won't stop, he says, until Connor tells him *his* story, *his* truth. But the truth is something Connor cannot admit to himself, much less anyone else.

Inspired by the late children's writer Siobhan Dowd, Ness has expanded her ideas and characters into a gorgeous fable about the grieving process and healing after terrible loss. This novel will appeal to anyone, any age, who has suffered the loss of a close loved one. As Connor must accept death's finality, his story also highlights the power of love and the promise of hope, of life, even after death.

For those coping with: anxiety/fear, death of a parent, death's finality, emotional detachment or avoidance, guilt, loneliness, powerlessness, strained relationship with a father

For those drawn to: mystery/suspense, ominous atmosphere, poetic language, psychological focus, supernatural stories

Themes/subjects: anger, bullies, cancer, death, dreams/nightmares, England (twenty-first century), father-son relationships, forgiveness, grandmothers, grief/loss, guilt, illness (terminal), magical trees, monsters, stories, supernatural beings

Read-alikes: Helena Fox's *How It Feels to Float* is about a teenage girl managing her grief after the death of her father. Parental illness, rather than death, is the main focus of Jordan Sonnenblick's *Falling Over Sideways*.

Ruby, Laura. *Bone Gap*. Grades 9+. 🎧.

Most of the people of Bone Gap don't remember how Roza came to their town or how she wound up living with poor Sean and Finn O'Sullivan. But everyone in Bone Gap loves Roza, and they all feel her absence now that she has disappeared.

Only Finn, the younger of the O'Sullivan boys, knows the truth: Roza was kidnapped. Finn knows because he was with her when it happened. He saw the man grab Roza's arm. He saw him push her into an SUV. But no one in Bone Gap, not even his brother, Sean, Roza's *boyfriend*, believes him. For some reason that not even Finn can explain, he can't remember or describe the face of the man who took her. Now, two months later, with no other leads, everyone begins to conclude that Roza must have chosen to leave, just like Sean and Finn's mother did. Finn, however, refuses to give up the search.

An adaptation of the Orpheus and Eurydice myth, this novel primarily focuses on two mysteries: Finn and Roza. Roza's imprisonment is described in dreamy fragments set in different time periods and locales—a house, a medieval castle, her childhood home in

Poland—in order to tell a larger, more universal narrative about the female experience and the history of violence toward women. Finn's story also hooks into magical elements—whispering cornstalks, a horse he travels on through dreams—all of which help him tap into his own instincts, leading him not only to Roza but also to his first romantic love. Spare and beautiful, this novel is ultimately about how we see ourselves and how we see others, and why looking deeper, beyond appearances, is essential not only to human connection but also survival.

For those coping with: abandonment/desertion, absent parent, bullying, concern with what others think, poor body image, sexual assault, traumatic memories, trusting instincts, unpopularity, village/small-town life, worry/anxiety about a loved one

For those drawn to: alternating perspectives, classics-inspired fiction, eccentric characters, Gothic settings/atmosphere, mystery/suspense, poetic language, psychological focus, Realistic Fiction, romance, secret codes/clues, survival stories

Themes/subjects: abandoned children, appearance versus reality, beauty, bees, body image, bullies, class/socioeconomic differences, courage, crushes, cultural differences, disability (cognitive), dreams/nightmares, farm life, gender roles (twenty-first century), imprisonment/entrapment, kidnapping, literary allusions, (the) Midwest (United States), sexual violence, survival, village/small-town life

Read-alikes: While more realistic, John Corey Whaley's *Where Things Come Back* is also a multilayered story about small-town guys missing loved ones. Ruby's lyricism and beautiful imagery call to mind Anna-Marie McLemore's *When the Moon Was Ours*, which examines love and identity in a small town.

Zoboi, Ibi. *American Street*. Grades 9+. 🎧.

In Haiti, Fabiola remembers only struggle: poverty and crime, the ruins of earthquakes, the legacy of dictators. She and her mom flee to the United States hoping for a better life. But the moment they leave, a new struggle begins. Fabiola's mother is not a US citizen and gets detained along the way, leaving Fabiola to continue on her own to Detroit, where her three cousins and her Matant Jo wait.

CHAPTER 6 | Magical Realism for Children and Young Adults 91

But once Fabiola settles into their home on American Street, she discovers she is still surrounded by poverty, drugs, and violence—just a different kind. While Fabiola goes to school and tries to adjust to American ways, she aches for her mother, and her home in Haiti, where families at least cooked and ate their meals together instead of alone, out of paper wrappers. Every night, she prays for their reunion, appealing to her beloved saints and "Iwas" for courage, and it seems like her prayers are answered when a detective surprises her with an offer to release her mother in exchange for some information about her cousin's boyfriend, Dray. Dray is a known womanizer and abuser, so Fabiola would be glad to be rid of him. She agrees, but as she uncovers information about Dray, Fabiola also uncovers some unsettling details about her own family and must choose between loyalties.

A metaphor for intersectionality, *American Street* exposes how race, gender, class, and other identities work to create different modes of privilege and discrimination in contemporary America—that is, why the American Dream is achievable for some but not for others. Zoboi's crisp, effortless prose and efficient use of detail also make this novel a total pleasure to read.

For those coping with: being an outsider/misfit, bullying, cliques, desire to find absent parent, family conflict, homesickness, (the) immigrant experience, loneliness, moving/relocating, poverty, racial segregation, recognizing privilege in oneself, secretive adults

For those drawn to: ghost stories, gradually unfolding stories, multiple intertwined storylines, mystery/suspense, ominous atmosphere, secret codes/clues, supernatural stories

Themes/subjects: accents (language), addiction (drugs/alcohol), African Americans, ambitions, anger, body image, bullies, capitalism, class/socioeconomic differences, cliques, courage, crushes, cultural differences, failings of the legal system, family, gender roles (twenty-first century), gun violence, high school life, mother-daughter relationships, poverty, religious faith, secrets, sex, supernatural beings, survival, twins, violence/abuse

Read-alikes: Echo Brown's *Black Girl Unlimited* blends Magical Realism and Autobiography to explore intersectionality. Romina Garber's *Lobizona* is also a magical realist story about a teenage immigrant (from Argentina) who is separated from her mother while she is in the US.

More Excellent Magical Realism

Applegate, Katherine. *Crenshaw*. Grades 3–6. 🎧.

A believer in science and facts, Jackson is "not an imaginary friend kind of guy." And yet, he once had an imaginary friend. He hates to admit it, but the friend's name was Crenshaw, and he was an enormous cat, except that he also had fingers instead of paws, and he could talk, and he loved to take bubble baths. Jackson met him just after the first grade, when his dad was diagnosed with multiple sclerosis and his mother lost her job. Times became so hard that Jackson's family had to live in their minivan because they could no longer afford their rent. But eventually, they found jobs and their life went back to normal. Jackson started a new school, and once he made a real best friend, Marisol, he no longer needed an imaginary one. So why, after so many years, is Crenshaw back?

Written in crisp, straightforward prose, *Crenshaw* is a quick, laugh-out-loud read. It is also a poignant poem about food insecurity, homelessness, and the working poor. Anyone who has experienced these challenges, young or old, will feel seen in this book, while others may become more conscious of their privilege after reading. This is a story that expands hearts and teaches the importance of empathy.

For those coping with: anxiety/fear, being wealthy or privileged, change, family conflict, financial loss of parents, homelessness, lack of control over events, lack of friends, loved ones with a physical disability, poverty, worry/anxiety about a loved one

For those drawn to: Animal Fantasies, eccentric characters, humor, likeable/relatable characters, Realistic Fiction, witty tone

Themes/subjects: brother-sister relationships, cats (talking), class/socioeconomic differences, community, education/learning, family, friendship, homelessness, hunger/food insecurity, imaginary friends, literary allusions, lying, pets, poverty, San Francisco, saving and investment, science versus magic, stealing, work

Read-alikes: In Wendy Mass and Rebecca Stead's award-winning *Bob*, the protagonist also rekindles a relationship with an imaginary friend as she works through her anxiety. Michelle Cuevas's *Confessions of an Imaginary Friend*, written as an autobiography, is more offbeat, as funny as it is wise.

CHAPTER 6 | Magical Realism for Children and Young Adults **93**

Funke, Cornelia. *The Thief Lord*. Grades 6–8. 🎧.

After their mother dies, Prosper and Bo run away to Venice in order to evade their aunt, who threatens to split them apart by sending Prosper to boarding school. They go to Venice, the "City of Canals," because of all the wonderful stories their mother used to tell them about it. The reality, however, is much grittier. Venice is an expensive tourist town, and Prosper and Bo have no money. They must figure out how to survive on their own. This is how they meet a gang of young pickpockets and their leader, the "Thief Lord," and wind up living in an abandoned movie theater called the Star Palace. When a rich count hires the gang to steal a cherished object from a famous photographer's house, their money woes may finally be over—that is, until they discover that Prosper and Bo are being followed by a private detective.

The Magical Realism in this story is suspended until the end. The cherished object, a wooden wing, turns out to be the missing part of an enchanted carousel with the power to make one grow older or younger. Adults who are terrible to children become child-size again, and poetic justice is served. On the other hand, the Thief Lord, who is actually the neglected child of an aristocrat, is able to use the carousel to transform into a liberated young adult—an inverse Peter Pan. In this way, the novel raises questions about the social construction of childhood and what constitutes "childish" behavior. The characters, and the conclusion, are extremely satisfying.

For those coping with: abandonment/desertion, being underestimated by others, being wealthy/privileged, critical/faultfinding parent, evil/manipulative adults, homelessness, parental neglect, recognizing privilege in oneself

For those drawn to: arresting/original settings, chase stories, gradually unfolding stories, heist stories, humor, multiple perspectives, streetwise characters, survival stories, unexpected plot twists

Themes/subjects: abandoned children, authoritarian figures, buried/hidden treasure, class/socioeconomic differences, community, deception and disguise, detectives (adult), foster children, gangs, homelessness, hunger/food insecurity, imposters/charlatans/frauds, orphans, runaways, thieves/robbery, Venice, Italy (twentieth century)

Read-alikes: Katherine Rundell's *Rooftoppers* is also about an unconventional family of orphans and misfits who are on the run, but in Paris. Jonathan Auxier's Fantasy novel, *Peter Nimble*

and His Fantastic Eyes, is about a ten-year-old blind orphan, also living in the streets, who goes on a quest to rescue a lost kingdom.

King, Amy Sarig. *Me and Marvin Gardens*. Grades 3–7. 🎧.

A hundred years ago, Obe's great-grandpa owned and farmed all the land that surrounds Delvin Creek. Unfortunately, a hundred years ago, his great-grandpa also had a drinking problem and "drank it all away." Still, Obe thinks of the creek as *his*, and therefore *his* responsibility. Now that developers have bulldozed all the cornfields and orchards to make room for new housing, construction workers are constantly leaving behind litter. Plastic bags, lids, and bottles line the creek. While his best friend, Tommy, used to help him, Tommy has since become obsessed with name-brand sneakers and bullying around with his new friends. It's like Obe doesn't exist anymore. So the day he discovers the strange animal rooting along the creek's bank, he is all alone. Immediately, Obe knows he has made a discovery. The animal, who he names Marvin Gardens, not only looks strange—maybe part aardvark, part dog, and part slime—but also acts strange. Marvin Gardens eats plastic, *only* plastic, which also produces the worst-smelling scat Obe has ever encountered. But this may mean he has found a possible solution to the pollution problem. Before he can find out, though, Obe must keep Marvin Gardens safe from the developers—and from Tommy.

Tender and highly original, this novel recognizes children's power to be agents of change. King deftly introduces the tensions between environmental sustainability and capitalism without being alarmist. On the contrary, this novel inspires hope. In emphasizing how individual decisions have global effects, King reveals our connection to the planet and to one another—now and throughout history—and, therefore, our obligation to environmental justice.

For those coping with: being misunderstood by parents, broken friendships/growing apart, bullying, climate change, injustice/unfairness, powerlessness, strained relationship with a father

For those drawn to: Animal Fantasies, character-driven novels, culturally responsive literature, humor, Realistic Fiction, suburban settings

Themes/subjects: brother-sister relationships, bullies, capitalism, class/socioeconomic differences, climate change, courage, ecosystems, environmental justice, friendship, garbage/junk, Indigenous peoples (United States), pollution, teachers as mentors

CHAPTER 6 | Magical Realism for Children and Young Adults

Read-alikes: Nicole Lea Helget's *The End of the Wild* also examines environmental issues (fracking) from a working-class perspective. Carl Hiaasen's classic *Hoot* is also Eco-Fiction, and the protagonist is also a boy who struggles with bullies.

Leno, Katrina. *Summer of Salt*. Grades 8+.

Georgina Fernweh and her twin sister, Mary, have never been anywhere but By-the-Sea, the tiny island town where they were born. But this summer, they will celebrate their eighteenth birthdays and soon be off to college. Until then, they help their mother run their family's small inn, which fills every summer with tourists in search of the rare flicker that roosts on the island. Georgina, though, is feeling apprehensive. It's not just the anticipation of moving away, or the crush she develops on one of the inn's guests, or the fact that the bird has yet to appear. It's her upcoming birthday. Almost every Fernweh woman in her family's history has possessed magical powers. Mary has always known hers—she was born with the ability to walk on air—and their mother can brew potions and cast spells. Georgina, however, seems to possess no powers at all. But when a terrible tragedy strikes, Georgina begins to understand that magic comes in many forms.

Between the mystery and the crisp, fluent prose, this novel is hard to put down. While sibling relationships are a significant theme, the novel turns on the discovery of Mary's sexual assault by a family friend. Rather than graphic depictions, Leno uses the missing bird, and the violence that befalls it, as a metaphor for the violence Mary also suffers: she transforms from a confident, exuberant young woman into a small, hollow bird. The allusions to Edgar Allan Poe's poem "Annabel Lee" add resonance. While the subject matter is difficult, Georgina's wit sparkles, bringing both light and hope.

For those coping with: ambivalence about romantic feelings, change, sense of inferiority, sexual assault, shame, sibling issues/rivalry, village/small-town life

For those drawn to: likeable/relatable characters, mystery/suspense, psychological focus, romance, supernatural stories, unexpected plot twists

Themes/subjects: birds, birthdays, crushes, friendship, heritage/ancestry, LGBTQIA, literary allusions, secrets, self-esteem, sexual violence, sisters, trauma (emotional or physical), twins, words (power of), wrongfully accused

Read-alikes: Caroline O'Donoghue's *All Our Hidden Gifts*, set in Ireland, blends the normal and paranormal, and the protagonist also uncovers a tragic mystery in the midst of a queer romance. Sister relationships are also the subject of Anna-Marie McLemore's *Blanca & Roja*, and an animal (bird) transformation is also a major plot point.

McLemore, Anna-Marie. *When the Moon Was Ours.* **Grades 9+.** 🎧📖

Miel and Sam, also known as Honey and Moon, have been friends ever since the day Miel spilled out of the town's water tower. As outsiders in their town—Sam because he is a Pakistani immigrant, Miel because of the roses that mysteriously grow out of her wrist's pulse—a bond has developed naturally between the two of them. But now, older, they find that they are more than classmates, more than neighbors, and more than friends: they are in love. But the Bonner Girls, four sisters known both for their beauty and for always getting what they want—and also rumored to be witches—threaten to destroy their reputations. They know that Sam was really born Samira, and they also know about Miel's secret past. The sisters demand Miel's roses, which they believe possess magic, or else they will expose both Miel and Sam.

Painted paper moons that hang from trees, a field of pumpkins that turn to glass, a stained-glass coffin, the fragrance of rose and lemon: these are just some of the ways that McLemore's gorgeous prose engages the senses. By riffing on Fairy-Tale tropes, McLemore challenges gender roles and explores questions about gender identity. Notably as the Bonner girls threaten to out Sam just as he is beginning to understand and realize his own gender identity, the novel impresses upon readers the indignity of labeling and/or outing others. At the same time, the metaphorical depiction of Miel's traumatic childhood as a deep-rooted phobia of pumpkins gently probes at how one's own psychology develops. Readers who enjoy such contemplation will feel seen in this work.

For those coping with: abuse (emotional), abuse (physical), being a victim of gossip/slander, being an outsider/misfit, bullying, concern with what others think, gender identity, identity formation, lack of confidence, ostracism/rejection, racism, sexual identity, village/small-town life

For those drawn to: alternating perspectives, arresting/original settings, character-driven novels, culturally responsive literature, Fairy Tale–inspired stories, gradually unfolding stories, mystery/suspense, ominous atmosphere, psychological focus, richly detailed descriptions, romance

CHAPTER 6 | Magical Realism for Children and Young Adults

Themes/subjects: body image, bullies, courage, curses/hexes, family secrets, farm life, forgiveness, friendship, gender identity, gender roles (twenty-first century), healing/healers, LGBTQIA, kidnapping, literary allusions, sex, sisters, stealing, trauma (emotional or physical), village/small-town life, violence/abuse, witches

Read-alikes: Francesca Lia Block's *Love in the Time of Global Warming* has elements of Magical Realism and portrays relationships between characters with different LGBTQIA identities. Those drawn to this story's imagery and love potions should read Alice Hoffman's classic *Practical Magic*.

Murdock, Catherine Gilbert. *The Book of Boy*. Grades 4–6. 🎧📖.

The year is 1350, and the Plague, or "Black Death," has reached France and devastated most of the country. The manor on which Boy lives—that's his name—is no exception. Only his lord and a few other servants have survived. But Boy is not lonely because he can talk, literally *talk*, to any animal—on the manor, or elsewhere. Boy is perched in a tree, chatting with the goats when a stranger—a pilgrim, he soon learns—notices him. The pilgrim, Secundus, observes that although Boy is hunchbacked, he is an excellent climber, and this skill may prove useful to Secundus on his pilgrimage to Rome. Despite some reservations, Boy is pulled into Secundus's journey and hopes that once they reach their destination, the tomb of St. Peter, he may also be granted a miracle: to be made into a "normal" boy. But, as Boy begins to discover on their journey, there may be more power in his body than he had initially realized.

By the end of their journey, Boy learns Secundus's true motivations: the Plague has cost him both his wife and son, and he is desperate for God's forgiveness so that he might meet them again in Heaven. At the same time, Boy also learns the truth about himself: he is not a hunchback but a fully winged angel. Blending Magical Realism with Historical Fiction, this heartwarming story describes the struggle for, and the power of, self-acceptance. Its setting during a global pandemic also offers opportunities for teachers and students to compare aspects of the Plague to COVID-19.

For those coping with: being an outsider/misfit, being different, epidemic/pandemic threat, guilt, identity formation, lack of confidence, ostracism/rejection, poor body image, self-doubt

For those drawn to: Animal Fantasies, comic adventures, gradually unfolding stories, Historical Fiction, humor, mystery/suspense, supernatural stories, witty tone

Themes/subjects: angels, biblical allusions, body image, Catholicism, corruption, deceptiveness of appearances, dreams/ nightmares, escapes, exploration of unknown lands/places, feudalism, forgiveness, France (medieval period), grief/loss, guilt, journeys/quests, literacy/illiteracy, Middle Ages, miracles, the Plague, robbery/thieves, saints, serfdom

Read-alikes: For those more interested in Historical Fiction, Avi's *Crispin* offers an intense quest story set in the Middle Ages. Adam Gidwitz's *The Inquisitor's Tale* is set in a similar time period and is also a quest story about three magical misfit children (and a holy dog).

Ness, Patrick. *Release*. Grades 9+ 🎧.

It's summer break, just a few weeks before Adam Thorn begins his senior year, and tonight is the going-away party for Enzo, his ex-boyfriend and first love. Adam will be there, but as far as his church-leading parents know, it's just a small get-together with him and his best friend Angela. Adam exaggerates his plans not only to throw off their suspicions—his parents would never accept him if they found out he is gay and had a boyfriend—but also because a classmate was recently murdered in the same lakeside area where the party is to be held. Until then, Adam has an uneventful Saturday planned: a run, work, and a tryst with his new boyfriend, Linus. But each scheduled event is interrupted by one shocking discovery after another. It begins to feel like the worst day of his life. Meanwhile, the ghost of Katie haunts the small town, seeking vengeance against her murderer, making her a threat to anyone who crosses her path.

Set over the course of a single day, this story is an engrossing page-turner. More than another coming-out story, this novel touches on universal themes of love, intimacy, and acceptance. While those struggling to feel seen will relate especially to Adam's character, his friends (particularly the precocious Angela, a Korean adoptee) are excellent foils, providing more alternative points of view.

For those coping with: being unloved by a parent, evil/manipulative adults, homophobia, needing to prove oneself, parental disapproval, parent/guardian controlling one's destiny, questioning one's faith, sexual harassment in the workplace

For those drawn to: alternating perspectives, culturally responsive literature, ghost stories, likeable/relatable characters, ominous atmosphere, psychological focus, romance

CHAPTER 6 | Magical Realism for Children and Young Adults

Themes/subjects: addiction (drugs/alcohol), anger, authoritarian figures, class/socioeconomic differences, courage, crushes, forgiveness, friendship, ghosts, guilt, LGBTQIA, murder, religious faith, secrets, sex, supernatural beings, violence/abuse

Read-alikes: Adam Silvera's *They Both Die at the End* is Speculative Fiction but also a twenty-four-hour story about an LGBTQIA romance, as is Bill Konigsberg's realistic *The Music of What Happens*. Both also feature culturally diverse protagonists.

Oppel, Kenneth. *The Nest.* Grades 5–8. 🎧.

The dreams begin soon after Steven's brother is born, after his parents discover that the baby needs surgeries and might not recover. Steven has always been an anxious person, but watching his parents worry makes him feel even worse. So, in the first dream, when a pretty voice comes to him promising to help save his brother, Steven wants to believe it. Only later, when he realizes the speaker's true identity, does he begin to sense a threat. This dream visitor knows too much — things only he and his family should know. Steven would like to confess his concerns to his parents, but how could they ever believe him? These are only dreams, after all, and dreams should have no power over him. And yet, they do. But by the time Steven realizes just how real the danger is, he has no choice but to face it alone. His and his brother's lives will depend on it.

In revealing the ways that dreams shape our reality and vice versa, *The Nest* is Magical Realism at its best. Steven's nightmares are dominated by a demanding wasp, an insect that Steven is also allergic to, and therefore deeply afraid of, in real life. While Steven is ashamed of his anxiety (he has been diagnosed with an anxiety disorder), it is ultimately his profound sensitivity — his intuition — that allows him to sense real-life danger and save his little brother and himself. Readers who struggle with perfectionism or feelings of inadequacy will find a sympathetic spirit in Steven, who struggles for self-acceptance.

For those coping with: anxiety/fear, being an outsider/misfit, being different, disability, disabled loved ones, panic attacks, preoccupied/busy parents, sense of inferiority, shame, trusting instincts, worry/anxiety about a loved one

For those drawn to: character-driven novels, gradually unfolding stories, Horror elements, mystery/suspense, ominous atmosphere, poetic language, postmodern stories, psychological focus

Themes/subjects: appearance versus reality, bees, courage, dreams/ nightmares, family, illness, self-esteem

Read-alikes: This novel resembles David Almond's classic *Skellig*, which is also about a boy worried about his sick infant sibling. Patrick Ness's *A Monster Calls* shares the same dark atmosphere but is more about the grieving process than managing anxiety.

Pan, Emily X. R. *The Astonishing Color of After.* **Grades 9+. 🎧.**

While Leigh was kissing her best friend, Axel, her mother was back home—committing suicide. Now Leigh can't shake the guilt. If only she hadn't gone to her friend's after school, her mother might still be alive. Leigh has no idea what led her to this awful decision. Her mother left no note, no explanation. But the night before the funeral, Leigh hears her mother's voice calling out her name. She follows the sound and finds her mother outside her window, transformed into a large, scarlet-feathered bird. Leigh follows her—all the way to Taipai. In Taiwan, Leigh finally meets her mother's parents and discovers her missing heritage and begins to piece together her mother's painful past.

Lushly written, this novel is a synesthetic experience of both grief and healing. Other strands of the story pick up on the power of love (Leigh and Axel's friendship turned relationship), art (Leigh is also a gifted painter), and courage (Leigh pursues her art despite her father's dismissiveness). For those who have experienced loss like Leigh's, Pan's language offers comfort and a means to acceptance. As a biracial character, Leigh also gives fresh insight into understanding cultural differences and ethnocentrism.

For those coping with: biracialism, critical/faultfinding parent, death of a parent, death's finality, family conflict, grieving parent, jealousy, mentally ill family member, self-blame, suicide of a loved one

For those drawn to: arresting/original settings, character-driven novels, culturally responsive literature, ghost stories, multiple intertwined storylines, poetic language, postmodern stories, psychological focus, romance

Themes/subjects: appearance versus reality, art as coping strategy, artists, Asian Americans, biracialism, boy artists, China (twenty- first century), courage, crushes, cultural differences, death, deceptiveness of appearances, depression, dreams/nightmares, Emily Dickinson, family, father-daughter relationships, friendship, ghosts, gifted children or teens, grief/loss, guilt,

CHAPTER 6 | Magical Realism for Children and Young Adults

heritage/ancestry, high school life, learning a new language, literary allusions, mother-daughter relationships, poetry, reconciliation, secrets, suicide

Read-alikes: A Chinese American teen artist deals with grief over a friend, romantic feelings, and family secrets in Kelly Loy Gilbert's *Picture Us in the Light*. Those drawn to Chinese culture and Fantasy should check out Amy Tan's classic *The Hundred Secret Senses*.

Pyron, Bobbie. *Lucky Strike*. Grades 4–6.

When Nate Harlow wakes up in a hospital room on his eleventh birthday after being struck by lightning, he is hardly surprised. He has long suspected he is the unluckiest of all of Paradise Beach's residents. *Of course* he would be struck by lightning, and *of course* it would happen on his birthday. But after Nate recovers, strange things start to happen—strange, *good* things. The bread toaster suddenly works—every slice browns to perfection—and now, in baseball, he hits home runs when he used to always strike out. It's like everything he touches turns to good fortune. Nate's "Midas touch" brings him newfound popularity, which threatens his longtime friendship with Gen. While he admits that Gen is the smartest girl in town, she insists that "luck" isn't a real thing. But Nate *knows* something has changed even though he can't explain it. Is it possible that the lightning changed his luck?

Funny, fast paced, and filled with quirky, memorable characters, this story reinforces the importance of friendship and community. Helping to drive this point, the story is set in a small coastal Florida town during the 1990s, which allows young readers to glimpse how friendships and community are built in real life instead of online. Gen's devotion to the beach's loggerhead turtle population expand this sense of community to the Ecosystem as well. Especially in the face dramatic climate change, stories like this one, which focus on our interconnectedness, will become essential.

For those coping with: being an outsider/misfit, being gifted, broken friendships/growing apart, bullying, change, cliques, lack of friends, village/small-town life

For those drawn to: character-driven novels, humor, likeable/relatable characters, mystery/suspense, Realistic Fiction, sea adventures

Themes/subjects: birthdays, Christianity, class/socioeconomic differences, cliques, community, ecosystems, family, Florida, friendship, problem-solving, science versus magic, seaside towns, self-esteem, teamwork/cooperation, village/small-town life

Read-alikes: Magic powers and strange weather are also unleashed on a memorable birthday in Ingrid Law's Newbery-winning *Savvy*. The luckless protagonist calls to mind Susan Patron's *The Higher Power of Lucky*, about the protagonist's resilience after a lightning storm changes her life.

Resau, Laura. *The Lightning Queen*. Grades 3–6. 🎧.

Every summer since Mateo can remember, he has abandoned his Xbox and his comfortable life in Maryland for the dusty hills of rural Oaxaca, Mexico, where he visits his Grandpa Teo. Grandpa Teo, a doctor to some, a "healer" to others, has lived in Oaxaca for his entire life; so, unlike his grandson, he is accustomed to living without electricity or running water. Once Mateo arrives, his grandpa invites him into his healing hut and begins to share a story that Mateo has never heard before, about his grandpa's childhood best friend, Esma, a Romani "Gypsy" girl who arrived with her family in a caravan and dazzled his entire village with their traveling outdoor cinema. As Grandpa Teo tells the story, Mateo becomes entranced, as if he is inside the movie of his grandfather's youth. In this way, he discovers the many heartaches his grandfather endured as a boy: the sudden death of his younger sister, his mother's incurable grief, and prejudice as an Indigenous person. At the same time, Mateo learns how his grandfather's special connection with Esma gave him the strength to flourish despite these difficulties. So, when Mateo learns that Grandpa Teo and Esma have lost touch over the years, he makes it his mission to help them reconnect.

Teo and Esma's friendship, representative of two persecuted cultures that have embraced each other, opens into a larger, multilayered story about the history of Indigenous peoples, the role of colonialism, and the need for critical consciousness. While the ideas are complex, Resau's crisp sentences and straightforward narrative invite easy discussion.

For those coping with: being an outsider/misfit, disability, distant/ uncommunicative parent, domineering relatives, forgiving others, grieving parent, mentally ill family member, recognizing privilege in oneself

For those drawn to: culturally responsive literature, early twentieth century settings, Historical Fiction, idealized village settings, likeable/relatable characters, simplified lifestyles

Themes/subjects: ambitions, authoritarian figures, class/socioeconomic differences, community, country versus city, courage, cultural differences, disfigurement, education/learning, farm life, film/film history, friendship, gender roles (twentieth century), grief/loss, healing/healers, heritage/ancestry, immigrants, Indigenous peoples (Mexico), learning a new language, literacy/illiteracy, racism, Romani, teachers, village/small-town life

Read-alikes: Lindsay Eagar's *Hour of the Bees* also takes place during summer vacation and uses Magical Realism to tell an intergenerational story about a girl and her grandfather. Veera Hiranandani's *The Night Diary* examines religious tensions, this time between Hindus and Muslims during India's early independence.

Sedgwick, Marcus. *Midwinterblood*. Grades 9+. 🎧.

According to the rumors, a rare orchid grows on Blessed Island that is capable of curing all ills and may even have the power to extend life. Eric Seven, a journalist working in the year 2073, travels to the remote and secretive Nordic isle to investigate. At first, he finds the island as idyllic as its name implies. Pretty colored houses line little lanes, trees and flowers everywhere. The people, too, greet him with warmth and generosity. One of them, Merle, offers to be his guide, and it is like love at first sight. No, more than that, it's like he knows her from somewhere, or some time, before. But how? He has never been to Blessed Island before . . . or has he?

A novel in short stories, each part introduces a new character—an archaeologist, a World War II fighter pilot, a painter, a ghost, a vampire, a Viking—digging deeper and deeper into the island's history. Together they reveal a literal story about reincarnation (Eric and Merle as father and daughter, mother and son, brother and sister, etc.). But as each story also riffs on themes of love and sacrifice, cumulatively they tell a larger story about the transcendent power of love. Mysterious and haunting, this novel will have readers thinking long after they put it down.

For those coping with: betrayal, evil/manipulative adults, family conflict, forgiving others, loneliness, moral dilemmas

For those drawn to: Horror elements, multiple intertwined storylines, mystery/suspense, ominous atmosphere, postmodern stories, romance, time travel

Themes/subjects: archaeologists/archaeology, artists, civilization, death, dreams/nightmares, forgiveness, free will, grief/loss, immortality, islands, LGBTQIA, myths/legends, rescues, supernatural beings, wars/battles

Read-alikes: Those drawn to Historical Fiction and how past generations affect the present may also like Leslye Walton's *The Strange and Beautiful Sorrows of Ava Lavender*. In Alexandra Bracken's *Passenger*, fate brings two characters together, again and again, also throughout history.

Suma, Nova Ren. *The Walls Around Us*. Grades 9+. 🎧📖.

It's August, and Violet is packing up for New York City and her first semester at Julliard. She can't wait: her lifelong dream of becoming a prima ballerina is about to come true. It's hard to rejoice, though, knowing that her best friend, Ori, should be in her place instead—since she was always the better dancer. But three years ago, Ori was convicted of a double murder and sent to Aurora Hills, an upstate detention center for girls. But just one month into her sentence, Ori dies, along with several other inmates, of food poisoning. Violet didn't kill Ori, but should she feel guilty? After all, it's not her fault that she is the next-best ballet dancer.

Amber, who was Ori's cellmate, recalls her last days at Aurora Hills. Incarcerated a year before Ori's arrival, Amber was able to help Ori get along inside the prison walls. For example, she could tell her how many peanut butter cups it would take to curry a certain favor and which plants in the prison yard could be sold for drugs.

Intricately plotted, this gradually unfolding ghost story will leave readers haunted for days. Layered moral dilemmas and complex characters evoke nuanced discussions about the criminal justice system and the limits of restorative justice. More philosophical than political, this novel does not sensationalize these problems but clarifies them.

For those coping with: being wealthy or privileged, being wronged, betrayal by a friend, bullying, false accusations, recognizing privilege in oneself

For those drawn to: alternating perspectives, ghost stories, gradually unfolding stories, moral dilemmas, multiple intertwined storylines, mystery/suspense, ominous atmosphere, secret codes/clues, supernatural stories

Themes/subjects: ballet/ballerinas, books (love of), bullies, class/socioeconomic differences, cliques, failings of the legal

CHAPTER 6 | Magical Realism for Children and Young Adults

system, friendship, gender roles (twenty-first century), gifted children or teens, guilt, imprisonment/entrapment, jealousy, murder, poisoning/poisons, prisons/jails, racism, secrets, sex, trauma (emotional or physical), violence/abuse, wealthy girls, wrongfully accused

Read-alikes: Both Walter Dean Myers's classic *Monster* and Jason Reynolds and Brendan Kiely's *All American Boys* are multilayered stories that ask complex questions about guilt and innocence.

Walton, Leslye. *The Strange and Beautiful Sorrows of Ava Lavender.* Grades 9+. 🎧.

Although the doctors were bewildered by Ava's birth—why was she born with bird's wings while her twin brother, Henry, was not?— they needed only to dig a little further into her family history, and they would have discovered she comes from a long line of inexplicable relatives. Ava's story really begins at the turn of the twentieth century, when her great-grandparents emigrate from France to New York with their four young children. While the family arrives safely, without a hitch, in New York City, only heartache awaits them. In fact, by the time Ava's grandmother, Emilienne, is nineteen, her heart has been broken three times. Shattered by so much loss, Ava's grandmother gives up on love and marries for convenience. She follows her husband to Seattle, where they settle into a slightly haunted house the color of faded periwinkles. There, she gives birth to one child, Viviane, who grows up, falls in love, and, on the first of March in 1944, becomes Ava's and Henry's mother. Now comes Ava's story, which is a story about the beauty and danger of living with wings.

Walton's magical elements make reading this novel a complete sensual experience. It is also a complex story about coming-of-age, sexual violence (a neighbor stalks Ava, believing she is an angel, and attempts to take her wings), and generational trauma—how grief is not always one's own, but inherited. This is a story that can be a source of both comfort and strength.

For those coping with: being a victim of gossip/slander, being an outsider/misfit, being different, betrayal, distant/ uncommunicative parent, jealousy, sexual assault, village/small-town life

For those drawn to: arresting/original settings, coming-of-age stories, eccentric characters, gradually unfolding stories, Historical Fiction, mid-twentieth-century settings, multiple intertwined storylines, poetic language

Themes/subjects: community, crushes, death, deceptiveness of appearances, disability (cognitive), disfigurement, dreams/nightmares, family, gender roles (twentieth century), ghosts, grief/loss, haunted houses, heritage/ancestry, psychic ability, resilience, Seattle, sex, sexual violence, shyness, twins, women in business

Read-alikes: Both Francesca Lia Block's lyrical novel *I Was a Teenage Fairy* and Laura Ruby's *Bone Gap* use magical elements to examine sexual abuse place but take place in more contemporary settings.

Wolitzer, Meg. *Belzhar.* Grades 9+. 🎧.

Reeve, the first boy Jam ever really loved, is dead, and, a year later, she still can't bring herself to leave her bedroom. Worried, her parents send her to the Wooden Barn, a boarding school for "emotionally fragile, highly intelligent children" in rural Vermont, where she is placed in a Special Topics English Course. This course, as Jam's roommate explains, is shrouded in mystery. Students are personally selected by Mrs. Quenell, the instructor, but no one knows why or how they are chosen. Inevitably, these students become an exclusive, tightly knit group. Every year the course focuses on a different writer; this year, she and four other students study the works of Sylvia Plath, starting with her famous novel, *The Bell Jar*.

As part of the course, Mrs. Quenell gives them a notebook and asks them to keep a personal journal for the semester. When Jam starts to write, however, something miraculous happens. She is suddenly transported to another dimension where she is reunited with her beloved Reeve. Jam learns from her classmates that their journal experiences have been similar, and before the end of the semester, each of them have to choose to remain either in this world or forever in the magical realm of Belzhar.

This is a remarkable story about grief and the transcendent power of art. In this case, the act of journaling is what allows the characters to enter Belzhar, the experience of which helps them come to terms with their loss, accept it, and find the strength to move on. Those struggling with depression may especially find comfort in this story, as it is a reminder to readers that they are not alone. For English teachers, assigning this novel alongside Plath's *The Bell Jar* would make for an engaging lesson in intertextuality; it would also make the perfect segue into a freewriting/journaling assignment.

For those coping with: change, death's finality, emotional detachment or avoidance, fear of facing one's past, rejection, shame, traumatic memories

For those drawn to: boarding-school stories, character-driven novels, gradually unfolding stories, romance

Themes/subjects: anger, art as coping strategy, boarding schools, bullies, cliques, crushes, depression, disability (paralysis), friendship, grief/loss, high school life, literary allusions, missing persons, self-esteem, Sylvia Plath, teachers, trauma (emotional or physical)

Read-alikes: Plath's *The Bell Jar* is a must–companion read. Jam's struggle with self-acceptance recalls Stephen Chbosky's *The Perks of Being a Wallflower* and also E. Lockhart's unreliable narrator in *We Were Liars*.

Read On: Matching Readers and Magical Realism

Children

Author	Title	For those coping with
King, A. S.	*Everybody Sees the Ants*	bullying, emotional detachment or avoidance, family conflict, powerlessness, preoccupied/busy parents
King, A. S.	*Please Ignore Vera Dietz*	broken friendships/growing apart, feeling ashamed of family, guilt, past wrongdoing, strained relationship with father
King, A. S.	*Still Life with Tornado*	domestic violence, family conflict, ostracism/rejection, powerlessness, self-doubt, traumatic memories
Mabry, Samantha	*All the Wind in the World*	climate change, distrust of others, emotional detachment or avoidance, exploitation of one's poverty, finding employment

Mabry, Samantha	*Tigers, Not Daughters*	death of a sibling, domestic violence, emotional detachment or avoidance, family conflict, jealousy, parental neglect, sexual assault, sibling issues/rivalry, strained relationship with a father, village/small-town life
Mason-Black, Jennifer	*Devil and the Bluebird*	death of a parent, domestic violence, finding a purpose/ direction in life, homelessness, jealousy, powerlessness, sibling issues/rivalry, trusting instincts, worry/anxiety about a loved one
McLemore, Anna-Marie	*Wild Beauty*	being an outsider/misfit, death of a loved one, family conflict, (the) immigrant experience, loneliness, sexual identity
Medina, Meg	*The Girl Who Could Silence the Wind*	false accusations, gender inequality, guilt, sexual harassment in the workplace, worry/anxiety about a loved one
Parks, Kathy	*Notes from My Captivity*	death's finality, forgiving others, questioning one's faith, recognizing privilege in oneself, trusting instincts
Wallach, Tommy	*Thanks for the Trouble*	death of a parent, emotional detachment or avoidance, finding a purpose/direction in life, lack of friends, sense of inferiority

NOTES

1. Sharon Sieber, "Magical Realism," in *The Cambridge Companion to Fantasy Literature*, ed. Edward James and Farah Mendlesohn (Cambridge: Cambridge University Press, 2012), 170.
2. Brenda Cooper, *Magical Realism in West African Fiction: Seeing with a Third Eye* (London: Routledge, 1998), 216.
3. Wendy B. Faris, *Ordinary Enchantments: Magical Realism and the Remystification of Narrative* (Nashville: Vanderbilt University Press, 2004), 7.
4. Isabel Allende, "The Shaman and the Infidel," interview by Marilyn Berlin Snell, *New Perspectives Quarterly* 8, no. 1 (Winter 1991): 54.
5. Maggie Ann Bowers, *Magic(al) Realism* (London: Routledge, 2004), 21.
6. Ibid., 67.
7. Ibid., 68.
8. Rudine Sims Bishop, "Mirrors, Windows, and Sliding Glass Doors," *Perspectives* 6, no. 3 (1990): ix–xi.

7

Steampunk Fiction for Children and Young Adults

Introduction to the Genre

Part of a larger subculture that encompasses music, art, fashion, film, video games, gadgetry, and the do-it-yourself (DIY) movement, Steampunk novels combine Historical Fiction with Science Fiction, the past with the future. Influential precursors such as Jules Verne's *Twenty Thousand Leagues under the Sea*, H. G. Wells's *The Time Machine*, and Mary Shelley's *Frankenstein* introduced the use of imaginary technology to fiction, shaping the direction of the genre.

Technology, and especially steam-driven technology, is the basis of Steampunk Fiction. The majority of novels are set in the Victorian era, and many of these in London—a time and place representing the Industrial Revolution at its peak. Steampunk authors take readers back to the roots of the modern world, offering both a critique of the impact of technology and a reimagined depiction of the past. Machines, vehicles, and gadgets—both real and imaginary—dominate the novels. An airship as an espionage school for females, cities on wheels that prey on smaller cities for fuel and resources, a futuristic prison controlling its inmates through artificial intelligence, and a biological airship that functions as its own ecosystem are a few examples of the startlingly innovative uses of technology in Steampunk novels. Redressing the imbalance of novels that glorify nature and the countryside, Steampunk works depict exhilarating new inventions and reenvisioned urban landscapes.

Engineers, mechanics, scientists, and inventors populate these novels. Such characters are the makers and creators of their worlds, designing a new way of living and being. An air of promise, possibility, and unprecedented opportunity characterize Steampunk Fiction. Set during a time of uncharted territories and expanding frontiers, Steampunk also captures the excitement of extraordinary inventions and mechanical wonders. With a view of technology from a fresh perspective, readers marvel at its potential or fear its unforeseen impact. And no technology embodies the sense of soaring possibilities better than the dirigible, the quintessential Steampunk vehicle. The potential for a more holistic relationship with technology is a strong appeal in Steampunk.

But not all Steampunk writers depict technology's potential and promise. Many portray its negative effects, made all the more striking through the powerful combination of a Historical and Science Fiction lens. The unintended consequences of technology gone wrong, the disastrous effects of technology in the wrong hands, the damaging impact of industrialization on the environment and on marginalized peoples compel readers to reexamine their assumptions about technological progress. In fact, the *punk* in *Steampunk* highlights the challenging of authority and the status quo that is central to these works. As a countercorporate and anti–mass production philosophy, steampunk culture tries to reclaim a more harmonious, less complicated relationship with technology.[1]

Philip Reeve, Gail Carriger, and Scott Westerfeld dominate the Steampunk genre in terms of imaginative power as well as number of novels. Steampunk series fans will also find the novels of Kenneth Oppel, Colleen Gleason, and Cassandra Clare addictive.

Matching Readers and Steampunk Fiction: Appeal Factors as Bridges

As readers discuss what they've read and enjoyed, be alert to both Science Fiction fans and Historical Novel enthusiasts who are open to new directions in reading or would just like something more from their favorite genre. Moving beyond a discussion of book favorites to general interests can help you discover fans of steampunk culture—its art, fashion, films, or gadgetry. Individuals with a DIY propensity will be attracted to the many inventors, creators, and mechanics in the novels. Asking about readers' hobbies and interests will identify individuals with a penchant for technology, an interest in science, or a general appreciation of STEM fields. Steampunk novels explore society's inequalities; hence, thought-provoking depictions of marginalized peoples will appeal to disenfranchised readers as well as teachers in search of curriculum tie-ins. Those who thrive on all things Victorian; anyone who delights in cities; those in search of an empowering novel for misfits and outsiders; readers who enjoy wildly imaginative world building—all will fall in love with Steampunk novels.

The wide range of subgenres within Steampunk ensures enough choice to suit a variety of tastes. Readers who are drawn to characters from the lower rungs of society's ladder will enjoy Boilerpunk stories such as Stefan Bachmann's *The Peculiar*. Clockpunk novels such as Philip Pullman's *Clockwork* favor clockwork over steam-driven technology, while Dieselpunk Fiction like Scott Westerfeld's Leviathan Trilogy depicts diesel or nuclear technology. Gail Carriger's Finishing School books are a good example of Mannerpunk, a type of Steampunk that highlights elaborate social hierarchies.

Key Novels/Sure Bets

Carriger, Gail. *Etiquette & Espionage*. 📕. Grades 6–9. 🎧.

> The first novel in Carriger's spirited Finishing School series, *Etiquette & Espionage* opens with fourteen-year-old Sophronia spying on others from the dumbwaiter in her Victorian house. Much to Sophronia's chagrin, her exasperated mother packs her off and sends her to finishing school. But upon arrival at Mademoiselle Geraldine's Finishing Academy for Young Ladies of Quality, Sophronia is shocked to discover the school housed in a massive dirigible floating in the sky. Even more surprising is the nature of the school: although it "finishes," or polishes, young ladies for entrance into polite society, it also trains them in the art of "finishing off" enemies.
>
> Witty banter and a humorous tone combine with intrigue to create a sparkling, derring-do novel featuring female spies. The genius of the finishing school is in exploiting the conventions of Victorian women in the service of espionage. Rather than bemoan gender inequality, the school celebrates the opportunities that femininity provides for covert deeds. It is at this school that Sophronia reframes her unconventionality as a strength rather than a weakness. The book will appeal to readers who wish they were more like others or those who feel as if they do not meet parental or societal expectations. Sophronia's story will also resonate with readers who believe that their parents favor their siblings.

🎧 available as an audiobook   📕 part of a larger series

For those coping with: being different, favoritism, gender inequality

For those drawn to: arresting/original settings, strong female characters, Victorian settings, witty tone

Themes/subjects: airships/dirigibles, boarding schools, deception and disguise, education/learning, England (Victorian era), etiquette, inventions/inventors, spies/spying, steam-driven technology

Read-alikes: Kathleen Baldwin's *A School for Unusual Girls* depicts another intriguing school that is a front for spy training. Like Sophronia, spirited Ella in Gail Carson Levine's novel *Ella Enchanted* is forced to attend a finishing school and cope with parental favoritism.

Fisher, Catherine. *Incarceron*. 🖥. Grades 7+. 🎧.

After the Years of Rage, the colossal prison Incarceron was created to contain "the scum of humanity." The prison was then sealed shut permanently, its location known only to the Warden of Incarceron. One of the inmates, Finn the Starseer, recalls flashes of a time when he lived in the Outside. No one believes him, because the futuristic prison brainwashes inmates to think there is no Outside. Meanwhile, the Warden's daughter, Claudia, lives in a fairy tale–like past on the Outside. Claudia and Finn both find a magical crystal key that allows them to communicate with each other. Each of them is trapped in inescapable situations and neither knows whom to trust. The reader, too, is forced to continually reassess characters as more information is revealed. Nothing is what it seems.

From the very first page, this fast-moving story contains strange twists and turns that rivet the reader. No one who reads it will forget the larger-than-life prison with its mesmerizing artificial intelligence. This *New York Times* best seller will appeal equally to fans of Science Fiction, Steampunk, Dystopia, Mystery, Fantasy, and Adventure. It will also appeal to readers who feel overwhelmed by a seemingly hopeless situation.

For those coping with: abuse (emotional), cruelty, change, powerlessness

For those drawn to: arresting/original settings, dual intertwined storylines, Dystopias, futuristic settings, ominous atmosphere, unexpected plot twists

Themes/subjects: amnesia, appearance versus reality, arranged marriages, artificial intelligence, brainwashing/indoctrination,

CHAPTER 7 | Steampunk Fiction for Children and Young Adults 113

captives, deception and disguise, escapes, far future, father-daughter relationships, imprisonment/entrapment, political corruption, prisoners, underground

Read-alikes: Artificial intelligence, surveillance, and entrapment also dominate Erin Bow's *The Scorpion Rules*. Marie Lu's dystopian *Legend* is another story about deception on a mass scale.

Johnson, Jaleigh. *The Mark of the Dragonfly.* 🔖. Grades 4–8. 🎧.

Piper, a thirteen-year-old orphan who lives in Scrap Town Number Sixteen, makes her living by scavenging the nearby meteor fields for objects she can fix and sell. She discovers Anna, a brilliant but strange girl who is injured during a meteorite shower. Anna's dragonfly tattoo marks her as an important person of the Dragonfly Territories, but she cannot remember anything about herself. The girls flee from a stranger who calls himself Anna's father, escaping as stowaways on the 401, a powerful steam-engine train that travels to the Dragonfly Territories. Combining elements of Dystopia, Adventure, and Steampunk, this best seller is set in a captivatingly strange otherworld in which meteor storms shower artifacts, trinkets, and machines on Piper's world.

Piper must come to terms with her unconventional abilities and new responsibilities. As a synergist and healer of machines, she is symbolic of a reimagined past, one in which nature and technology coexist in a harmonious relationship. Characters such as Anna and Jeyne Steel who are part mechanical and part human suggest a symbiosis that is promising for the future. Readers who feel unusual or unlike their friends will find Piper's story a source of comfort and inspiration.

For those coping with: being different, death of a parent, moral dilemmas, orphanhood, poverty

For those drawn to: Dystopias, mystery/suspense, romance

Themes/subjects: amnesia, females in unconventional roles/occupations, friendship, gifted children or teens, healing/healers, machinists/mechanics, political oppression, pollution, trains

Read-alikes: Jeanne DuPrau's *City of Ember* is set in a similarly bleak but arresting world that endangers survival. Readers who enjoy books about cyborgs and strong female characters in untraditional occupations will like Marissa Meyer's *Cinder*.

Oppel, Kenneth. *Airborn.* 📖. Grades 6–10. 🎧.

Fifteen-year-old cabin boy Matt Cruse has a driving passion: to become junior sail maker of the luxury airship, the Aurora. While traveling to Australia, Matt meets Kate DeVries, a teen passenger from a wealthy family. Kate persuades him to help look for a flying mammal that no one except her late grandfather believes existed. But once the Aurora takes flight, it is fatally damaged in a storm, rerouted to a desert island, and captured by pirates.

Although the fast-faced plot will keep readers engrossed, its astute psychological portraits will keep them hooked. Matt does not fully understand his fear of being landlocked but knows that his passion for the Aurora is connected with his father, a sailmaker who died onboard. Kate is an intrepid explorer who ignores not only her uncommunicative parents but also all society's rules and conventions. The novel will appeal to readers who must come to terms with the death of a loved one or those who feel isolated because they are unconventional. A Michael L. Printz Honor book, *Airborn* will make readers yearn for all things skyward.

For those coping with: anxiety/fear, being different, being wealthy or privileged, death of a parent, gender inequality, injustice, jealousy, poverty

For those drawn to: dangerous adventures, likeable/relatable characters, mystery/suspense, strong female characters

Themes/subjects: airships/dirigibles, class/socioeconomic differences, desert islands, driving force/passion, fantastical or folklore animals, pirates, scientific exploration, wealthy girls

Read-alikes: The pure joy of flight is a theme that also dominates Eoin Colfer's *Airman* and Philip Reeve's *A Web of Air*.

Reeve, Philip. *Mortal Engines.* 📖. Grades 6+. 🎧.

Fifteen-year-old apprentice-historian Tom Natsworthy lives in thirtieth-century London. Like many places in this postapocalyptic world, seven-tiered London is a Traction City—a place that rolls on huge caterpillar tracks, surviving by devouring the fuel and resources of smaller places. When a veiled girl named Hester tells Tom that a respected historian murdered her parents and disfigured her, he does not believe her. But when the historian pushes him into a waste chute, he and Hester must survive together in the dangerous Out-Country.

The opening novel in the Hungry City Chronicles does not minimize the horrors of this out-of-control world. Because the Sixty

CHAPTER 7 | Steampunk Fiction for Children and Young Adults

Minute War left survivors without technological knowledge, people considered it natural that "cities ate towns, just as the towns ate smaller towns." Dazzlingly inventive and deeply thought provoking, this winner of the Nestlé Smarties Gold Award will appeal to readers who enjoy exciting survival stories set in the far future.

As Tom faces lethal cyborgs and a conspiracy involving a weapon of mass destruction, he makes a series of difficult choices. Readers who lack confidence in their abilities will be reassured by Tom's story. And those who are preoccupied with body image will find Hester's example reassuring.

For those coping with: corrupt or criminal parent, disfigurement, moral dilemmas, poor body image, self-doubt, sense of inferiority

For those drawn to: arresting/original settings, dual intertwined storylines, Dystopias, futuristic settings, survival stories

Themes/subjects: airships/dirigibles, class/socioeconomic differences, cyborgs, far future, historians, museums, political corruption, postapocalyptic world, weapons of mass destruction/bombs

Read-alikes: Scott Westerfeld's Leviathan books take place in a bleak Darwinian-influenced world, while James Dashner's *The Maze Runner* is a gripping survival story set in a bleak, brutal future.

Westerfeld, Scott. *Leviathan.* 📗. Grades 7+. 🎧.

On the cusp of World War I, Alek, Archduke Ferdinand's fifteen-year-old son, is whisked away in the middle of the night. Believing that he has been kidnapped, he subsequently learns that his parents have been assassinated. Meanwhile, fifteen-year-old Deryn Sharp, disguised as a boy and flying a covert mission on a biologically engineered airship, crosses paths with Prince Alek. Disguising their identities and situated on different sides of the war, the pair face a series of tough moral dilemmas. In this alternative history, countries are either Clankers, that rely on mechanical technology, or Darwinists, that use biologically engineered vehicles.

As royalty, Alek has been kept apart from others outside court and knows little of everyday life. Deryn's passion is flying; she has little in common with other females her age. Readers who feel as if they do not belong or those who have experienced the death of a parent will find inspiration in their stories. Winner of the Locus Award for Young Adult Novel and the Aurealis Award for Excellence in Speculative

Fiction, *Leviathan* will give readers a new perspective on the moral complexities of wartime existence.

For those coping with: being an outsider/misfit, death of a parent, feeling entitled, finding a direction/purpose in life, gender inequality, moral dilemmas, needing to prove oneself

For those drawn to: dangerous adventures, dual intertwined storylines, war stories

Themes/subjects: airships/dirigibles, genetic engineering, girls disguised as boys, orphans, pilots, princes, secrets, steam-driven technology, teamwork/cooperation, wars/battles, warships, World War I

Read-alikes: Maddie in Elizabeth E. Wein's Historical Novel, *Code Name Verity*, is another fearless pilot in a world war. In Wendy Spinale's Steampunk novel, *Everland*, teenagers fight for survival as global powers seek world domination.

More Excellent Steampunk Novels

Alexander, William. *Goblin Secrets*. **Grades 4–7.** 🎧

Rownie escapes from Graba, an evil witch with gearwork legs who owns a magical, movable shack. The witch collects stray vagabond children, forcing them to work for her and leaving them perpetually hungry. In constant fear of meeting Graba after escaping from her, Rownie joins a theater group of goblins and searches for his missing older brother. Rownie is careful to avoid the Guard, a strange gearwork security force that works for the Lord Mayor of Zombay.

Almost everything in Rownie's life has been taken away from him, but he learns to regain agency as an actor. Using a variety of masks and acting in different roles embolden his actions and help him cope with his fears. Readers who feel anxious, frightened of others, or inadequate can gain insight in coping skills from Rownie's story.

Death is presented in the story as an integral part of a continuum, a natural and inevitable component of life. Readers who must come to terms with the death of a loved one will view it in a different light after reading this novel. Winner of the National Book Award for Young People's Literature, *Goblin Secrets* will appeal to readers who enjoy books with a menacing atmosphere, offbeat characters, and whimsical humor.

For those coping with: abuse (emotional), death, death's finality, self-doubt, sense of inferiority

CHAPTER 7 | Steampunk Fiction for Children and Young Adults 117

For those drawn to: eccentric characters, humor, witty tone

Themes/subjects: actors/acting, goblins, mechanical or clockwork creatures, missing persons, orphans, witches

Read-alikes: Laura Amy Schlitz's Historical Fantasy, *Splendors and Gloom*, is also about a manipulative villain, a group of entertainers, and a missing child. Readers interested in humorous books about goblins will also enjoy Neil Gaiman's award-winning Fantasy *The Graveyard Book*.

Bachmann, Stefan. *The Peculiar.* ▣. Grades 5–8. ⌒.

The mechanical Age of Smoke emerged after fairies invaded England and lost a war with humans. Clockwork, iron, mechanical inventions, and industry became an antidote to fairy magic, repressing the fay. Living in one of the fairy slums of Bath, Bartholomew Kettle witnesses the strange disappearance of a neighborhood friend. Although his mother warns him that, as a "Peculiar" (a part-human, part-fairy creature), he needs to avoid unwanted attention, Bartholomew knows that he must investigate the disappearance.

Readers who are attracted to the bizarre, the unusual, and the strange will not want to miss Bachmann's *The Peculiar*. Although Bartholomew and a man named Jelliby team up to rescue Peculiars in danger, neither is a likely candidate for heroic action. Bartholomew feels "small and ugly and different from everyone else," while Jelliby is timid, unadventurous, and unassertive. Their stories of courage will embolden readers who lack assertiveness and self-confidence. Readers who have faced prejudice will also identify with the plight of the Peculiars.

For those coping with: being an outsider/misfit, poor body image, powerlessness, racism, unassertiveness/timidity

For those drawn to: arresting/original settings, dual intertwined storylines, eccentric characters, sinister atmosphere, Victorian settings, witty tone

Themes/subjects: brother-sister relationships, captives, fairies, kidnapping, mechanical or clockwork creatures, missing persons, political corruption, slums

Read-alikes: Edward Carey's *Heap House* is another deliciously offbeat story about a timid protagonist and an array of wildly eccentric characters. Although more serious in tone and theme, J. R. R. Tolkien's *The Hobbit* presents another unlikely hero who acts courageously despite his fears and lack of confidence.

Clare, Cassandra. *Clockwork Angel.* Grades 9+. 🎧.

After sixteen-year-old Tessa spends the last of her money on a funeral for her guardian aunt, she leaves New York to live with her brother in London. But when she arrives in port, her brother is not there. Instead, a servant with odd bulging eyes directs her into a carriage containing two odious women, Mrs. Black and Mrs. Dark. Although they produce a letter from her brother, they take her to a place called the Dark House, torture her, and force her to practice her hitherto unknown talent for shapeshifting. These Dark Sisters threaten to kill Tessa's brother if she does not cooperate with all their demands. Two months later, a stranger breaks into Tessa's room, fights the horrifying sisters, and takes Tessa to a place called the Institute. Although the Institute people appear friendly, she does not know who to trust or what to believe.

The haunting settings, unsettling events, and menagerie of strange, grotesque characters are strong appeals in this *New York Times* best seller. Inside the eerie world of Downworlders is a group of demon killers who form their own family and act as a counterbalance to the automatons, villains, and murderers in the novel. Readers who have been betrayed by someone they trust and those who feel alone in the world will be drawn to this addictive novel.

For those coping with: ambivalence about romantic feelings, being an outsider/misfit, betrayal, corrupt or criminal sibling, fear of facing one's past, orphanhood

For those drawn to: arresting/original settings, dangerous adventures, grotesque/bizarre characters, Horror elements, nineteenth-century settings, richly detailed descriptions, romance, supernatural stories

Themes/subjects: automatons, brother-sister relationships, demons, family (nontraditional), London (Victorian era), missing persons, secret societies, shapeshifters, vampires, warlocks

Read-alikes: In Gwendolyn Clare's *Ink, Iron, and Glass*, another sixteen-year-old girl with magical ability searches for a missing family member. Set in Victorian England, Libba Bray's *A Great and Terrible Beauty* features a lonely, vulnerable teenager who discovers her magical ability.

Colfer, Eoin. *Airman.* Grades 7–10. 🎧.

Set in the late nineteenth century on the Saltee Islands off the Irish coast, *Airman* is the story of the surprising fate of a teenage boy. One of

CHAPTER 7 | Steampunk Fiction for Children and Young Adults **119**

the three thousand subjects of the progressive King Nicholas, Conor is beloved by his parents and a good friend of the king's daughter, Isabella. Tutored by the visionary, Victor Vigny, Conor views himself as a scientist-in-training. But at the age of fourteen, he accidently witnesses the betrayal and assassination of the king and the murder of Victor Vigny.

Conor's life is dramatically changed in an instant. Forced to mine diamonds in treacherous conditions, he loses family, friends, and reputation. He is befriended by another inmate and learns how to survive the torture of gang members. But when the other inmate disappears, Conor joins the gang and becomes as corrupt as his fellow Battering Ram members. Surprising twists and turns in the plot provide plenty of drama in this intense story. It will especially appeal to readers who believe they have lost their moral compass. Celebrating visionaries, inventors, and scientists, the novel will also inspire those who are intellectually curious or love to imagine new ideas or inventions.

For those coping with: change, evil/manipulative adults, injustice/unfairness

For those drawn to: dangerous adventures, nineteenth-century settings, survival stories

Themes/subjects: airships/dirigibles, escapes, exile/banishment, gangs, imprisonment/entrapment, inventions/inventors, islands, mines/mining, princesses, prisoners, revenge, robbery/thieves, scientists, spies/spying

Read-alikes: William Pène du Bois's *The Twenty-One Balloons* is a Historical Fantasy about a hot-air balloonist who lands on a remote island in the nineteenth century. Like Conor, Matt in Kenneth Oppel's Airborn series is passionate about flying machines.

Cornwell, Betsy. *Mechanica.* 🖥. Grades 6–10.

A *New York Times* best seller, *Mechanica* is a highly original variation of the Cinderella story. Mechanica leads a grim life after her father remarries and then dies. Stepmother and her two daughters are cruel, selfish, and unjust, turning Mechanica into an unpaid servant for the family. But on her sixteenth birthday, Mechanica reads a letter from her deceased mother. The letter leads her to a hidden basement workshop that contains tools and magical gadgets belonging to her mechanic/inventor mother. Inheriting her mother's love of creating and fixing objects, Mechanica is delighted to find a host of mechanized marvels and a part mechanical, part natural horse named Jules. But just as Mechanica forms a plan for a better life, her worst nightmare comes true.

In her role as dogged inventor and lonely, persecuted teen, the reimagined Cinderella figure forges ahead despite her insecurities and fears. Readers coping with the loss of a parent, those facing cruel or unjust treatment by others, or anyone feeling deep loneliness will find that Mechanica's story resonates with their experiences. Despite the fact that "few people thought a woman capable of mechanical brilliance," Mechanica does not let such prejudices prevent her from building a better life for herself.

For those coping with: cruelty, death of a parent, favoritism, injustice/unfairness, females in unconventional roles/occupations, loneliness, racism

For those drawn to: Fairy Tale–inspired stories, romance, strong female characters

Themes/subjects: class/socioeconomic differences, friendship, inventions/inventors, machinists/mechanics, mechanical or clockwork creatures, mechanical or electronic devices, orphans, perseverance/determination, princes, steam-driven technology, stepmothers, stepsisters

Read-alikes: Readers who enjoy Cinderella-inspired stories will also like Margaret Peterson Haddix's *Just Ella*. Caitlin Kittredge's *The Iron Thorn* is the story of a mechanically gifted teenage girl trying to survive in a steampunk world.

Gleason, Colleen. *The Clockwork Scarab*. 📖. Grades 7+. 🎧.

In 1889, Mina (niece of Sherlock Holmes) and Eveline (sister of Bram Stoker) are invited to a mysterious midnight meeting at the British Museum. These seventeen-year-olds are asked to undertake a secret mission to find a missing young woman. While in the museum, they hear a door closing and, upon exploration, discover a woman's corpse. As Mina and Eveline investigate further, they begin to suspect a serial killer.

Cameo appearances by Sherlock Holmes and Bram Stoker remind readers of the dark and mysterious elements of this Victorian world. Clockwork gears and cogs power devices and even add decorative accessories for dresses and hair, balancing Victorian darkness with playful and ingenious creations.

Descendants of famous families, both girls have impossibly high expectations to meet. In addition, both of them have an inflated

CHAPTER 7 | Steampunk Fiction for Children and Young Adults **121**

opinion of themselves and are used to working solo. But as the girls experience setbacks and failures, they gradually learn the value of working together. Mina's story will resonate with readers whose parent is distant, uncommunicative, or absent. And anyone who has failed at something will look upon this experience with fresh insight after reading the novel.

For those coping with: abandonment/desertion, being unloved by a parent, failure, gender inequality, idolized or famous parents, inability to cooperate/work with others, living up to high expectations

For those drawn to: alternating perspectives, detective novels, nineteenth-century settings, time travel

Themes/subjects: clockwork devices/inventions, detectives (child/teen), Egyptology, missing persons, murder investigation, museums, secret societies, serial killer investigation, teamwork/cooperation, vampire slayers

Read-alikes: Readers who enjoy Victorian-era novels featuring intrepid female detectives coping in a world that favors males will be drawn to Philip Pullman's Sally Lockart series and William Ritter's Jackaby novels.

Johnson, Jaleigh. *The Quest to the Uncharted Lands.* 🔖. **Grades 4–8.**

After Stella Glass discovers that her scientist parents must leave her at home when they undertake a dangerous expedition to the Uncharted Lands, she devises a daring plan to sneak aboard the airship Iron Glory as a stowaway. Once in hiding, she meets another stowaway who is trying to return home. Although they are deeply suspicious of each other's differences, Stella and Cyrus learn to work together to defeat the Faceless man, a creature who can adopt the appearance of anyone he chooses. Intent on destroying the airship and defeating the mission, the Faceless man is a formidable enemy.

A companion to *The Mark of the Dragonfly*, *The Quest to the Uncharted Lands* is set in the same world but with a new cast of characters. The Uncharted Lands themselves suggest the exhilaration of a historical time when unexplored places still existed as well as the anticipation of a future in which possibilities seem endless. The olarans that Stella meet are half-human/half-machine creatures, embodying a prototype of unified opposites. This story about healing and wholeness will appeal to readers who are resistant to change and those who find it challenging to cooperate with others.

For those coping with: betrayal, change, evil/manipulative adults, inability to cooperate/work with others

For those drawn to: dangerous adventures, romance

Themes/subjects: airships/dirigibles, cultural differences, exploration of unknown lands/places, friendship, healing/healers, invisibility, journeys/quests, mechanical or clockwork creatures, scientists, stowaways

Read-alikes: Karen Hesse's *Stowaway* is a derring-do adventure story about a stowaway sailing to uncharted lands. A daring adolescent girl must try to prevent sabotage of an airship in Gail Carriger's *Manners & Mutiny*.

Kristoff, Jay. *Stormdancer.* 📖. Grades 9+. 🎧.

This first novel in the Lotus War Trilogy is the story of a sixteen-year-old girl growing up in a deteriorating Japanese feudal society on the brink of environmental collapse. People wear kerchiefs over their mouths and goggles over their eyes to protect themselves from the toxic smoke of refinery chimney stacks. Fumes from the fuel, chi, cause people to die from the dreaded black lung disease.

After the shogun hears about a sighting of an extinct Thunder Tiger, he orders Yukiko's father to find it. Although the father believes he is doomed to fail, he and Yukiko board an airship and unexpectedly find the animal. Once captured, the powerful Thunder Tiger threatens to burst through its cage. Lightning hits the ship and everyone except Yukiko and the Thunder Tiger escapes on a lifeboat.

A finalist for the Aurealis Award for Excellence in Speculative Fiction, *Stormdancer* is an intense, dramatic story of survival. Yukiko does not know who will betray her in this totalitarian society. Her ideas change as she gradually discovers the truth behind a web of lies and deceit. Readers who must face painful truths, make a difficult change in their lives, or battle against injustice will find in Yukiko an inspiring role model.

For those coping with: betrayal, injustice/unfairness, poverty, revenge (desire for)

For those drawn to: Asian-inspired novels, Dystopias, richly detailed descriptions, strong female characters, survival novels

Themes/subjects: addiction (drugs/alcohol), airships/dirigibles, brainwashing/indoctrination, demons, environmentalism, father-daughter relationships, fantastical or folklore animals, feudalism, honor, hunting/hunters, Japanese feudal culture, Japanese

CHAPTER 7 | Steampunk Fiction for Children and Young Adults

mythology/legends, lotus flowers, pollution, samurai, slums, telepathy (human-animal), totalitarianism, women warriors

Read-alikes: Living in a corrupt and oppressive industrialized city, a teenage girl does not know whom she can trust in A. J. Hartley's Steampunk Adventure *Steeplejack*. Forced to land in the Ice Wastes of a postplague continent, Hester and Tom face betrayal and danger in Philip Reeve's *Predator's Gold*.

McQuerry, Maureen. *The Peculiars*. Grades 9+.

Growing up, Lena always knew she was different than others. Ashamed of her unusual hands, she tries to hide them by wearing gloves. Lena's grandmother tells her that her hands are a sure sign of goblin blood, likely inherited from her father. When Lena turns eighteen, she receives a letter and a small inheritance from her father, the man who abandoned her thirteen years previously because he had "no talent for ordinary life." Despite her mother's objections, Lena decides to travel north to the wild province of Scree to find him. Her journey to the wildlands in search of her father and clues to her identity is risky physically and psychologically.

Like Stefan Bachmann's *The Peculiar*, Maureen McQuerry's similarly named novel focuses on the unusual, the abnormal, the out-of-the-ordinary. Anyone who feels inferior because of their appearance, or those who have been abandoned by or let down by a parent, will find a better way of reframing their challenges after reading Lena's story.

Although the plot draws readers in with its many secrets, its exploration of issues such as colonialism, nature versus nurture, and scientific inquiry versus faith will appeal to readers who enjoy thought-provoking novels and teachers looking for curriculum tie-ins.

For those coping with: abandonment/desertion, being an outsider/misfit, corrupt or criminal parent, desire to find absent parent, moral dilemmas, poor body image

For those drawn to: dangerous adventures, romance

Themes/subjects: airships/dirigibles, colonialism, goblins, inventions/inventors, libraries/librarians, mines/mining, nature versus nurture, perseverance/determination, scientific inquiry, spies/spying, steam-driven technology

Read-alikes: A teenage girl who also feels unsure of herself in Garth Nix's *Lirael* works in a highly unusual library, one mile below the earth. Feeling out of place cataloging magical creatures in a museum, Vespa, in Tiffany Trent's *The Unnaturalists*, does not initially realize she is a witch.

Oppel, Kenneth. *The Boundless.* Grades 5–8. 🎧.

After attending the last-spike ceremony of the Canadian Pacific Railway, Will survives both an avalanche and an attack by a sasquatch. During the avalanche, his father saves the life of the rail baron Van Horne, a feat that earns him a promotion. Three years later, Will joins his general manager father on the maiden journey of the Boundless, an immense train that stretches seven miles long. While on this trip, Will witnesses a murder, is pursued by the murderer, and is double-crossed by those he trusts.

Set against the backdrop of Western expansion, nation building, and unprecedented opportunities, the story gives readers a sense of what it was like to have lived in the 1880s. The train itself, from its luxurious first-class cars to its wretched colonist-class section, reflects the deep divisions of late nineteenth-century society. Ironically, the railway, which Van Horne says would "connect our new dominion from sea to sea," reflects the racial and class divisions of the era.

Will's father expects his son to join the railway business when he finishes school. But Will is an artist and would rather go to art school in San Francisco. Readers who believe that their parents do not understand them or have unrealistic expectations will identify with Will's struggles.

For those coping with: being misunderstood by a parent, parental disapproval

For those drawn to: dangerous adventures, eccentric characters, nineteenth-century settings

Themes/subjects: artists, Canada (nineteenth century), circuses/circus performers, father-son relationships, railway travel, robbery/thieves, steam-driven technology, trains

Read-alikes: Laurence Yep's stirring Historical Novel, *Dragon's Gate*, is about a boy who joins his father to help build the North American transcontinental railway. Gary Paulsen's *Hatchet* is a high-stakes Adventure story about a boy who must crash land a bush plane and then learn to survive after the pilot suddenly dies.

Pullman, Philip. *Clockwork, or All Wound Up.* Grades 5–8. 🎧.

Pullman's Gothic Horror story begins on a blustery winter evening in a German inn. The clockmaker apprentice Karl sits in the corner,

CHAPTER 7 | Steampunk Fiction for Children and Young Adults

humiliated that he has failed to make the village tower's clockwork figure for the following day's ceremony. Meanwhile Fritz, a local novelist, reads his latest story to the tavern dwellers. *Clockwork* is about a prince who is dying, discovered to have a clockwork heart. The renowned clockmaker Dr. Kalmenius is summoned to help. Fritz breaks off the story because someone is at the door of the inn. To the horror of the villagers, it is Dr. Kalmenius himself. The strange come-to-life clockmaker offers to solve Karl's problem by giving him a cursed clockwork knight for the village tower.

This is a story about agency and control. The novelist Fritz admits that he has lost control of his story; Karl, his work; and the prince, his life. Each element in the book is interconnected like clockwork and tied to this theme. Older readers will appreciate the philosophical ideas that are presented in an accessible manner. Pullman explores the nature of humanity, reality, time, and stories. Younger readers will enjoy the bizarre and scary story. Those who feel powerless in their own lives will find hope and reassurance in the ending of the novel.

For those coping with: powerlessness

For those drawn to: Gothic settings/atmosphere, postmodern stories, sinister atmosphere, supernatural stories

Themes/subjects: apprentices, clock- and watchmakers, inns/ taverns, knights, mechanical or clockwork creatures, princes, stories

Read-alikes: John Bellairs's *The House with a Clock in Its Walls* is a sinister story about a mysterious clock. In Cornelia Funke's vividly imagined Fantasy *Inkheart*, characters from a book also unexpectedly appear in the real world.

Pullman, Philip. *The Golden Compass.* 📗. Grades 7+. 🎧.

Twelve-year-old Lyra lives in an Oxford college under the guardian-ship of her uncle, Lord Asriel. A man who has little time for her, he travels back and forth to the far north, engaging in secret exploits. Mrs. Coulter, a woman introduced to her by the Oxford scholars, adopts her and takes her on a trip to the far north. Once she arrives in the inhospitable landscape, she is horrified at what is taking place in a strange experimental station.

Into the old world of Victorian-style colleges, Pullman introduces fantastic creatures such as armored bears, a futuristic compass called an alethiometer, and mysterious human experimentation. In true Steampunk fashion, he reimagines the late nineteenth century as a time when such imaginary inventions existed.

Lyra learns to cope with the treachery and deceit of those closest to her. She also learns to accept circumstances that she is powerless to change. Her story will resonate with readers who have suffered neglect or have experienced betrayal by people whom they trust. Winner of the Carnegie Medal, the *Guardian* Fiction Prize, and the "Carnegie of Carnegies" 70th Anniversary Award, *The Golden Compass* will appeal to readers who enjoy exhilarating adventures and richly imagined fantasy worlds.

For those coping with: betrayal, parental neglect

For those drawn to: arresting/original settings, dangerous adventures, richly detailed descriptions

Themes/subjects: captives, class/socioeconomic differences, experiments, fantastical or folklore animals, father-daughter relationships, free will, imprisonment/entrapment, kidnapping, missing persons, political corruption, prophecies/omens, witches

Read-alikes: Sophia's quest for a missing loved one in S. E. Grove's *The Glass Sentence* is epic in scale and consequence. Tilja journeys into an evil, dangerous empire in Peter Dickinson's adventure-filled Fantasy, *The Ropemaker*.

Reeve, Philip. *Fever Crumb*. 📖. Grades 6–9. 🎧.

Abandoned at birth, fourteen-year-old Fever is raised by Dr. Crumb. An apprentice engineer living in an engineering complex, Fever is trained to prioritize rational thought and scientific thinking. Emotions are considered vestiges of a primitive past. Londoners suspect that she is a Scrivener—a person who is not "exactly human." Then, everything changes for Fever. Stalked by people who want to kill her, introduced to a hidden passage beneath London that holds an important secret, abandoned by her parents, and lied to by her guardian, Fever has no one to turn to.

When she discovers that everything she has believed about herself is a lie, she has no idea how to cope. Readers who have been abandoned by a parent, those who are unable to express their emotions, and others who have been rejected or ostracized will find strength in Fever's experience. An exciting story involving dangerous pursuits by killers, the novel also introduces the idea of traction castles—castles that run on motorized wheels and are forerunners to the traction cities of the Hungry City Chronicles. The first of a trio of prequels to these chronicles, *Fever Crumb* can be read without knowing the other books in the companion series.

CHAPTER 7 | Steampunk Fiction for Children and Young Adults   **127**

For those coping with: abandonment/desertion, being an outsider/ misfit, emotional detachment or avoidance, ostracism/rejection, racism

For those drawn to: arresting/original settings, futuristic settings, killer stalking a character, unusual/unconventional characters

Themes/subjects: abandoned children, apprentices, brainwashing/ indoctrination, cyborgs, engineers/engineering, far future, females in unconventional roles/occupations, human experimentation, London, mechanical or electronic devices, reason/scientific thinking

Read-alikes: An enterprising teenage girl stumbles upon horrifying human experimentation in Alisa Kwitney's *Cadaver & Queen*. Gifted with machines but awkward around people, Poe must also outsmart the enemies who wish to kill her in Allie Condie's gripping dystopian novel, *The Last Voyage of Poe Blythe*.

Reeve, Philip. *Larklight.* 📖. Grades 6–10. 🎧.

The first novel in Reeve's Larklight series opens in "a shapeless, ramshackle, drafty, lonely sort of house" drifting in outer space "a terribly long way from anywhere." Art Mumby and his sister, Myrtle, await their father's guest from the Royal Xenological Society. But when Mr. Webster appears, he is a monstrous white spider that suddenly captures and kills their father. Escaping to the moon, the children are captured by giant moths, then rescued by the infamous pirate Jack Havock and his crew of ostracized crustaceans. Meanwhile, a race of spiders is intent on destroying the British Empire and its outer-space territories.

Larklight house is a characteristic Reeve structure—huge, mobile, and out of the ordinary. As the children travel throughout outer space, they encounter a series of surprises that prompt them to reconsider their earlier ideas. Readers who feel left out or ostracized will be reassured of their value after reading *Larklight*. Jack's cruel treatment by supposedly learned people will resonate with readers who have suffered bullying, injustice, or abuse. A novel of high adventure and derring-do, *Larklight* will appeal to readers who enjoy imaginative stories with a witty twist.

For those coping with: abuse (emotional), being different, bullying, cruelty, racism

For those drawn to: arresting/original settings, humor, outer-space settings, survival stories

Themes/subjects: aliens, brother-sister relationships, captives, England (Victorian era), imperialism, kidnapping, outer space, pirates, rescues, robbery/thieves, space vehicles, spiders

Read-alikes: Matt faces a series of unexpected disasters when he travels to outer space in Kenneth Oppel's *Starclimber*. Twins travel by sky ship to an unexplored continent to find their scientist father in Vashti Hardy's Steampunk novel, *Brightstorm*.

Read On: Matching Readers and Steampunk Novels

Children

Author	Title	For those coping with
Bachmann, Stefan	*The Whatnot*	lack of confidence, manipulation by adults, poverty, powerlessness, racism
Carriger, Gail	*Curtsies & Conspiracies*	being different, loneliness, ostracism/rejection, self-doubt, unpopularity
Hardy, Vashti	*Brightstorm*	death of a parent, disability, evil/manipulative adults, financial loss of parents, injustice/unfairness
Kirby, Matthew J.	*The Clockwork Three*	desire to find birth parent, disabled parent, distrust of others, exploitation of one's poverty, financial loss of parents
Oppel, Kenneth	*Skybreaker*	being an outsider/misfit, gender inequality, jealousy, poverty, racism
Oppel, Kenneth	*Starclimber*	failing to achieve a goal, jealousy, self-doubt, sense of inferiority
Reeve, Philip	*Predator's Gold*	betrayal, disfigurement, jealousy, poor body image
Reeve, Philip	*A Web of Air*	being different, emotional detachment or avoidance, evil/manipulative adults, underutilizing one's talents

CHAPTER 7 | Steampunk Fiction for Children and Young Adults **129**

Westerfeld, Scott	*Behemoth*	being an outsider/misfit, feeling entitled, gender inequalities, moral dilemmas, needing to prove oneself
Westerfeld, Scott	*Goliath*	being an outsider/misfit, feeling entitled, gender inequalities, guilt, needing to prove oneself

Teens

Author	Title	For those coping with
Bailey, Kristin	*Legacy of the Clockwork Key*	ambivalence about romantic feelings, death of parents, evil/manipulative adults, financial loss of parents, poverty
Clare, Gwendolyn	*Ink, Iron, and Glass*	abandonment/desertion, being gifted, corrupt/criminal parent, distrust of others, inability to cooperate/work with others
Cornwell, Betsy	*Venturess*	absent parent, deception, secretive adults, troubled relationship with a mother
Cremer, Andrea R.	*The Inventor's Secret*	ambivalence about romantic feelings, betrayal, sibling issues/ rivalry
Dolamore, Jaclyn	*Magic under Glass*	entrapment in a hopeless situation, financial loss of parents, powerlessness
Hartley, A. J.	*Steeplejack*	feeling unprepared for roles/ responsibilities, lack of confidence, poverty, racism
Kirby, Matthew J.	*The Clockwork Three*	desire to find birth parent, disabled parent, distrust of others, exploitation of one's poverty, financial loss of parents
Kittredge, Caitlin	*The Iron Thorn*	abandonment/desertion, betrayal, fear of a hereditary disease, mentally ill family member

Kwitney, Alisa	*Cadaver & Queen*	ambivalence about romantic feelings, being underestimated by others, being wronged, betrayal, gender inequality
Lee, Mackenzi	*This Monstrous Thing*	death of a sibling, guilt, moral dilemmas
Spinale, Wendy	*Everland*	absent parent, epidemic/pandemic threat, feeling unprepared for roles/responsibilities, orphanhood

NOTE

1. For more information on the role of technology in Steampunk Fiction and culture, see David Beardsley, "Introduction: A Rhetoric of Steam," in *Clockwork Rhetoric: The Language and Style of Steampunk*, ed. Barry Brummett (Jackson: University Press of Mississippi, 2014): xiv–xxxii; Rachel A. Bowser and Brian Croxall, "Introduction: Industrial Evolution," *Neo-Victorian Studies* 3, no. 1 (2010): 1–45; and Rebecca Onion, "Reclaiming the Machine: An Introductory Look at Steampunk in Everyday Practice," *Neo-Victorian Studies* 1, no. 1 (2008): 138–63.

8

Verse Novels for Children and Young Adults

Introduction to the Genre

Verse Novels are not a blended genre, but a blended format combining the elements of the poetic line with those of the traditional plot-driven novel. Like novels, they tell a story—complete with a beginning, middle, and end—but they are written in mostly nonrhyming free verse.

Verse differs from prose in that it is written in lines that deliberately ignore the margins on the page. As the poet Mary Oliver explains, the word *verse* derives from the Latin for "to turn," and "turning the line"— that is, determining where a line begins and ends—is the major project of the poet's work.[1] The line matters to the Verse novelist as well. Free verse is "free" because it is not constrained by strict, metrical design (in contrast to, say, a Shakespearean sonnet written in iambic pentameter). But that does not mean there is no design at all. Sound, line length, and rhythm pattern still matter in free verse and are used for emphasis, just as in speech. Indeed, free verse is meant to sound like natural speech—conversational, intimate—rather than formal and composed.

Each section of a Verse Novel is short, usually a page or less, but sections can be as long as three pages. Each section is also usually titled in order to provide context, indicate a speaker, or announce a theme. The visual layout varies from section to section, too. For example, one poem may be in abecedarian, followed by a shape poem, a catalog poem, and a prose poem. The form shifts with the subject, but a connecting plot emerges through their sequence and arrangement.

131

It's important to note that Verse Novels are crafted not only to be *seen* but also to be *heard*. Repetition, alliteration, caesura, enjambment, and other poetic devices are used to make music out of speech—as in a monologue in a play or voiceover narration in a film. In this way, Verse Novels follow in the oral poetic tradition. They beg to be read aloud. For this reason, too, they can make great audiobooks.

The scholar Joy Alexander argues that in activating readers' visual and aural imaginations, the Verse Novel may reflect a revival of orality—but a secondary orality, one created and served by digital technologies.[2] In fact, Verse Novels for children did not begin to appear in the publishing market until the 1990s, just as the Digital Revolution was building momentum. Major breakout titles in the United States included Virginia Euwer Wolff's *Make Lemonade* and Karen Hesse's *Out of the Dust*. But by the early 2000s, the Verse Novel had established its prominence—perhaps not coincidentally—as mobile devices and social networking were by then disrupting and transforming the way we write and communicate. Certainly, the Verse Novel is here to stay; but its definition will continue to evolve as writers use the possibilities of technology to experiment with structure and presentation in novel ways.

Matching Readers and Verse Novels: Appeal Factors as Bridges

Emotion is what poetry, and the Verse Novel, are all about. The vast majority of Verse Novels are first-person narratives, written in the present tense. These novels center around a significant emotional event, which prompts the speaker or speakers into dramatic monologue. Thus, readers are drawn into the immediacy of the moment, as if they are eavesdropping on the speaker's thoughts. While this confessional style can lend itself to angsty outpourings, especially in young adult novels, the best examples distinguish themselves with well-crafted language and memorable storytelling.

Family conflict, grief, death, abandonment, and loss are frequent themes in Verse Novels. In portraying ordinary life, the format lends itself to Realistic Fiction, including the related genres Historical Fiction (fictional stories that take place in a real past), Biography, and Memoir. The difference is that Verse Novels do not center so much on the typical, everyday problems of growing up, but rather the extraordinary, difficult ones. In these stories, characters frequently endure wrongful accusations, unexpected tragedies, or premature losses. For example, Jeannine Atkins's *Stone Mirrors*, a biographical account of nineteenth-century African

CHAPTER 8 | Verse Novels for Children and Young Adults

American artist Edmonia Lewis, describes the incredible obstacles she overcomes after her classmates falsely accuse her of attempted murder.

As in *Stone Mirrors*, loss frequently becomes the central motivator for personal growth. Sometimes the loss is also the catalyst that enables the protagonist to recognize the power of artistic creation and to pursue their art as an act of healing. In these kinds of Verse Novels, protagonists are often shown to benefit from reading and writing poetry. The Verse Novel itself, as a created artifact, conveys the power of poetry to offer permanence and comfort in an unpredictable world. As the protagonists learn to use their poetic sensibilities to express their emotions, they also become models/mentors for readers outside of the text. This is true of Jack in *Love That Dog*, Xiomara in *The Poet X*, Nick in *Booked*, and Jacqueline Woodson in her Verse Novel/Memoir *Brown Girl Dreaming*. While poetry dominates, Verse Novels may portray other kinds of art as coping mechanisms: sculpture in *Stone Mirrors*, music in *Out of the Dust*, drama in *Under the Mesquite*, drawing in *The Red Pencil*. In any case, the protagonists discover how the act of creation helps them heal. By giving them a means of making meaning of their loss, the loss no longer has to define them.

This isn't to say that Verse Novels cannot be fun or celebratory. For example, Marion Dane Bauer's *Little Cat's Luck* celebrates the birth of a litter of kittens as well as a surprising new friendship. And although the narrators in Sharon Creech's *Love That Dog* and Janice N. Harrington's *Catching a Storyfish* both deal with a loss (the death of a pet, moving away), their tone is lighthearted and full of amusement.

In other words, while Verse Novels often take up difficult topics, they are nonetheless life-affirming stories. Readers who are feeling lonely, neglected, or bereft can find comfort and reassurance, connection with others, and models for identity. The intimate, first-person narration of these novels reads much like a conversation with a good friend.

In addition, this format may also appeal to readers looking for an escape from the present world. Immigration stories such as Thanhhà Lại's *Inside Out & Back Again*, Katherine Applegate's *Home of the Brave*, and Ann E. Burg's *All the Broken Pieces* describe what it feels like to be an outsider in America. Historical Fiction in this format also provides an escape to the past: Helen Frost's *Salt*, about the War of 1812, Burg's *Unbound*, about fugitive slaves who find freedom in Virginia's Great Dismal Swamp, and Hesse's *Out of the Dust* are just a few of the outstanding Historical Fiction novels included in this chapter.

Finally, because of their breezy, conversational style and abundance of white space, Verse Novels may also appeal to reluctant readers. While such readers may initially be put off by the poetry-like appearance, if they are encouraged to try to read just a few pages, they may become hooked.

Key Novels/Sure Bets

Sharon Creech, Ann E. Burg, and Kwame Alexander are some of the most recognized writers in this genre, having contributed several works that will appeal to children and middle readers. For young adults, there is no contest: Elizabeth Acevedo leads the genre.

Acevedo, Elizabeth. *The Poet X.* Grades 7+. 🎧.

Xiomara (pronounced see-oh-MAH-ruh) would like to keep a low profile, cause "no waves," but it seems her body does not want to cooperate. Over the summer, she has grown in both height and curves, which has been drawing unwanted attention from some of the men in her Harlem neighborhood. But once sophomore year starts, she realizes that she might not mind the attention of one boy: her new biology partner, Aman. A boyfriend, though, would be impossible. Her mother forbids it and demands that Xiomara spend all her free time at church with her. Sharing a bedroom with her twin brother, Xavier, in their cramped New York City apartment also means she has no space of her own, no freedom—except within the pages of a journal her brother has given her. And as she writes, she begins to find her voice and the courage to use it.

Each verse chronicles a moment or collection of significant moments—a first kiss, a first date, a major fight with her mother—of Xiomara's coming-of-age. The prose is crisp and deceptively simple as the sights and sounds Acevedo creates linger long after the novel is finished. Those who have also felt their dreams discouraged will find comfort in Xiomara's story and a model of strength. Teachers can use this novel to introduce students to slam poetry.

For those coping with: being misunderstood by parents, family conflict, gender inequality, moral dilemmas, questioning one's faith, self-doubt, troubled relationship with a mother

For those drawn to: character-driven novels, coming-of-age stories, romance, strong female characters, urban settings

Themes/subjects: art as coping strategy, artists, brother-sister relationships, class/socioeconomic differences, community, courage, crushes, Dominican Americans, gender roles (twenty-first century), high school life, mother-daughter relationships,

🎧 available as an audiobook   📚 part of a larger series

CHAPTER 8 | Verse Novels for Children and Young Adults

music, New York City, perseverance/determination, poetry, teachers as mentors, twins

Read-alikes: Acevedo's lyricism and Xiomara's coming-of-age call to mind Sandra Cisneros's Esperanza in the classic *The House on Mango Street*. Those who enjoy the novel's diary style and emotional intensity should also try NoNieqa Ramos's Verse Novel *The Disturbed Girl's Dictionary*.

Alexander, Kwame. *The Crossover.* 📖. Grades 5–8. 🎧.

Josh, who goes by J.B. and is better known as "Filthy McNasty," and his identical twin brother, Jordan, have been playing basketball since they were literally in diapers. Their dad, a former professional NBA player, has been taking them to the court and teaching them the "Rules of Basketball" all their life. The most talented players on the team, the twins are posed to lead Reggie Lewis Junior High's Wildcats team to the county championships. But then, in walks a pair of pink Reeboks, and suddenly Jordan never has time to practice free throws with Josh. Unable to contain his resentment, Josh takes out his anger on Jordan during a game—and gets suspended from the team. Now Josh must find a way to repair his relationship with his brother in order to bring his family and his team back together again.

The rapid rhythm of Alexander's verse calls to mind the jazzy energy of Langston Hughes's poetry. A story about basketball as much as a story about the importance of family and nurturing familial bonds, *The Crossover* captures those first growing pains—the transition from childhood to adulthood. As word definitions play an important role in the novel's structure, assignments modeled on Alexander's could help students gain an appreciation for words and precision. Note: a graphic-novel adaptation is also available.

For those coping with: broken friendships/growing apart, change, death of a parent, family conflict, jealousy, sibling issues/rivalry

For those drawn to: character-driven novels, coming-of-age stories, Realistic Fiction, romance, witty tone

Themes/subjects: African Americans, ambitions, anger, basketball, death, driving force/passion, family, grief/loss, illness, middle school life, music, twins

Read-alikes: *Rebound* is Alexander's must-read follow-up/prequel to *The Crossover*. Readers who are drawn to Alexander's language should also check out his *Booked*, about a soccer fanatic who reluctantly discovers his love of poetry.

136   PART II | Annotations

Burg, Ann E. *All the Broken Pieces.* Grades 6–8. 🎧.

Born during the early stages of the Vietnam War to a Vietnamese mother and an American father, Matt Pinn's entire childhood has been shadowed by violence and sadness. His father leaves, promising to return, but never does. Then, his younger brother is badly wounded—maimed—and Matt blames himself. His mother, scared for Matt's life, takes the opportunity to send him to America, where he will be safe with an adopted family. Although Matt adjusts to his "now" family, as he calls them, in a quiet existence of baseball practice and music lessons, he is still wracked with guilt: If his new family knew where he came from, what he saw, what he did and didn't do, how could they love him? And how could his biological family love him after he left?

A compelling story about trauma and healing, *All the Broken Pieces* is a comfort to any reader who has ever struggled with guilt or self-blame. As Matt finds love and acceptance in his new community and builds confidence in his own abilities (he learns to play the piano and is also a gifted pitcher), Matt begins to see that beauty exists not in spite of, but because of tragedy, and he begins the process of loving and forgiving himself. The rhythm of this Verse Novel matches the unfolding of the narrative. Once started, it's hard to put down.

For those coping with: biracialism, desire to find absent parent, disabled loved ones, emotional detachment or avoidance, self-blame, war trauma

For those drawn to: character-driven novels, gradually unfolding stories, Historical Fiction, mid-twentieth-century settings, psychological focus, suburban settings, war stories

Themes/subjects: art as coping strategy, Asian Americans, baseball, bullies, community, depression, disability (paralysis), father-son relationships, immigration, music, racism, refugees, secrets, teachers as mentors, teamwork/cooperation, Vietnam War, war veterans

Read-alikes: Companion reads include Thanhhà Lại's *Inside Out & Back Again*, about a girl fleeing the Vietnam War, and Ching Yeung Russell's *House without Walls*, about a Chinese Vietnamese girl who travels with her brother to America in 1979 during the Boat People Exodus.

Creech, Sharon. *Love That Dog.* 📕. Grades 4–8. 🎧.

It's September, a new school year, and Jack's teacher has just assigned the entire class to write a poem. At first, Jack can't disguise his disgust:

CHAPTER 8 | Verse Novels for Children and Young Adults **137**

"I don't want to / because boys / don't write poetry. // Girls do." But as time goes on, and with the help of a patient teacher, Jack finds he rather enjoys *thinking* about poems—the images they conjure in his mind—even when he doesn't particularly like the poems themselves. He begins to imitate some of his favorites, by William Carlos Williams and Walter Dean Myers, and soon discovers he has a knack for language, too. He turns to his favorite subject, his yellow dog, Sky, and begins to tell another story about a man and his best friend.

Written in language that is both fun and accessible, this series is a great way to introduce poetry to young people. The poems to which Jack alludes in the story are also included, which can facilitate discussions about intertextuality. But it's Jack's writing—specifically, how he uses writing to grieve and memorialize his dead dog—that speaks to poetry's power as a mode of self-expression.

For those coping with: concern with what others think, death's finality, self-doubt, unassertiveness/timidity, underutilizing one's talents

For those drawn to: animal stories, humor, likeable/relatable characters, multiple intertwined storylines

Themes/subjects: art as coping strategy, boy artists, education/ learning, heroes/mentors, literary allusions, pets, poetry, self-esteem, teachers as mentors, writers (aspiring)

Read-alike: Jack's story continues in *Hate That Cat*. Creech's *Heartbeat*, about a twelve-year-old girl dealing with the arrival of her first sibling, and *Moo*, about a girl's move from the big city to rural Maine, are also excellent Verse Novels.

More Excellent Verse Novels

Applegate, Katherine. *Home of the Brave*. Grades 5–7.

After first losing his father and his brother to Sudan's violent civil war, ten-year-old Kek becomes separated from his mother. Although he is able to reunite with his aunt and cousin, who have also been displaced by the war's violence, they now live far away in the United States, in Minneapolis. For Kek, who has never experienced a life outside his family's African village and understands wealth only in terms of the number of cows one has, not dollars, the Midwest is a strange and confusing place. But it is also sometimes enchanting, with its winter snows, enormous schools, and grocery stores full of food. Still, Kek longs for news of his mother, even when his aunt warns him not to "hope too hard." He finds solace in friends: a neighbor, Hannah, a foster child who can relate to his feelings of loss and alienation, and an elderly woman, Lou, whom he is drawn to because of her small farm and the cow grazing on it. The cow is a comfort, a symbol of home, as he waits for word, any word, about his mother.

Despite the novel's heavy subject matter, it is filled with warmth and humor. Kek's puzzled-outsider status leads to several comic episodes (using the washing machine as a dishwasher, for example) that serve to deepen the reader's understanding of cultural differences and to expand their empathy for the immigrant experience.

For those coping with: absent parent, being different, death of a parent, desire to find absent parent, feeling entitled, homesickness, guilt, recognizing privilege, (the) immigrant experience, loneliness, moving/relocating, war trauma

For those drawn to: humor, likeable/relatable characters, Realistic Fiction, war stories

Themes/subjects: Africa (Sudan), civil wars, community, cultural differences, disfigurement, family, farm life, foster children, friendship, immigration, learning a new language, (the) Midwest (United States), missing persons, refugees

Read-alike: Jasmine Warga's *Other Words for Home* is also a story about the immigrant experience/acculturation from the perspective of a young girl from Syria.

Atkins, Jeannine. *Stone Mirrors: The Sculpture and Silence of Edmonia Lewis.* **Grades 9+.**

Edmonia Lewis, who is half black, half Ojibwe, is an outsider at her almost all-white Oberlin prep school. But, given that it is one of the few interracial schools that exist in nineteenth-century America, Edmonia must make do if she wants to continue her education and attend art school. But when her classmates—supposed friends—accuse her of attempted murder, Edmonia's dreams are ruined. Although she is acquitted, no one believes her, or *wants* to believe her, so she is kidnapped, violently attacked, and punished anyway. Wanting to bury the memory of this pain, Edmonia accepts an offer from an abolitionist in Boston to work as a domestic. Though her dream of becoming a sculptor seems as far away as ever, Edmonia is both patient and tenacious. With the help of friends and teachers, she finds other ways to hone her skills, which eventually lead her to her own studio in Rome, where, finally, through sculpture, she can make her voice heard.

Filled with beautiful, lyrical sentences and gorgeous imagery, *Stone Mirrors* offers comfort to anyone who has felt powerless in the

CHAPTER 8 | Verse Novels for Children and Young Adults

face of injustice or whose voice has been silenced. Atkins's portrayal of Edmonia can also awaken readers to alternative perspectives and models for identity, as Edmonia uses her art not only to cope with trauma but also to find the courage to make herself seen and heard.

For those coping with: betrayal by a friend, injustice/unfairness, loneliness, moving/relocating, powerlessness, prejudice, recognizing privilege, sense of inferiority, sexual assault

For those drawn to: biographical novels, character-driven novels, culturally responsive literature, Historical Fiction, nineteenth-century settings, richly detailed descriptions, strong female characters

Themes/subjects: African Americans, art as coping strategy, artists, being wrongfully accused, boarding schools, driving force/ passion, exile/banishment, Indigenous peoples (United States), literary allusions, (the) Midwest (United States), perseverance/ determination, racism, secrets, sexual violence

Read-alike: Margarita Engle's *With a Star in My Hand*, about the Nicaraguan poet Rubén Darío, is also a tale of someone rising above his circumstances.

Bauer, Marion Dane. *Little Cat's Luck*. Grades 2–5.

Patches, an orange-and-black calico cat, finds herself suddenly overwhelmed with longing for a snug room of her own. Though she loves her human family (her little girl, in particular), there is nowhere in the house where she can be alone. But one day, while looking out of her watching window, she notices of a golden leaf drifting down from a tree in the front yard. Enchanted, Patches chases after it, breaking through the watching window's screen. But then she loses sight of it . . . and her way home. As she wanders, she crosses paths with Gus, a very vocal and famously mean dog. While the two do not initially hit it off, a surprise arrival—*kittens!*—draws them together. With Gus's help, she safely delivers her babies, but still she worries: How will she ever get back home?

Told with warmth and filled with quirky humor, *Little Cat's Luck* is a book for all animal lovers. Emphasizing the importance of listening, having tolerance, and helping others, it is a refreshing contrast to the present realities of political polarization and a sincere reminder to everyone to be kind to each other. Bauer's visual use of words (font size and pictorial arrangement) introduces young readers to the pleasure of playing with words and thus would make a great segue to a classroom unit on writing poetry.

For those coping with: change, homesickness, inability to cooperate/ work, jealousy

For those drawn to: Animal Fantasies, humor, likeable/relatable characters, suburban settings

Themes/subjects: birth/life cycle, cats (talking), dogs (talking), instinct, jealousy, journeys/quests, mice/rodents (talking), pets, stealing, teamwork/cooperation

Read-alikes: This is a companion to Bauer's Verse Novel *Little Dog, Lost,* but for those interested in another animal story that emphasizes cooperation, check out Dodie Smith's classic *The Hundred and One Dalmatians.*

Burg, Ann E. *Serafina's Promise.* Grades 5–8.

After her brother dies of disease and hunger just weeks after he is born, young Serafina is determined to become a doctor so she can save children like him. But in Haiti, education is not a given. There are few public schools, so families must pay for their children's tuition. Most families, though, are struggling just to survive. They not only can't afford tuition but also must rely on their children to work and help bring in income. In addition, natural disasters—floods, earthquakes—are a constant threat to their homes and livelihood. When Serafina's family loses their house in a flood, she must stay at home to help her mother, who is pregnant again, and her aging grandmother while her father goes to Port-au-Prince during the day to work in the market. Still, Serafina is determined. She finds a way to make her own money and attend school. But as soon as she does, guilt sets in: Why should she go to school when others can't and when her family needs her so much?

Haitian Creole and French phrases are woven throughout the verse to remind readers of the language difference and also to reveal colonial tensions. For instance, once in school, Serafina is confused and frustrated by the fact that she must learn French, rather than her native Creole, in order to succeed in the school system. While offering readers a glimpse into Haitian culture and the effects of extreme poverty, as well as the potential to expand their capacity for empathy, this novel also provides models for identity, as Serafina, who has so little, makes the most of her creativity, courage, and determination.

For those coping with: financial loss of parents, finding employment, guilt, jealousy, lack of control over events, moral dilemmas, recognizing privilege, self-doubt, sense of inferiority, snobbery/elitism

CHAPTER 8 | Verse Novels for Children and Young Adults

For those drawn to: character-driven novels, culturally responsive literature, psychological focus, Realistic Fiction, strong female characters, survival stories

Themes/subjects: ambitions, child labor, colonialism, courage, doctors/medicine, driving force/passion, earthquakes, education/learning, family, friendship, grief/loss, Haiti, homelessness, islands, jealousy, learning a new language, literacy/illiteracy, missing persons, saving and investment, perseverance/determination, poverty

Read-alike: Jewell Parker Rhodes's *Ninth Ward*, the first book in the Louisiana Girls Trilogy, is a lyrical novel about resilience and survival in the face of Hurricane Katrina.

Burg, Ann E. *Unbound*. Grades 4–8. 🎧.

For all of her nine years, Grace has known life only as a slave, working the tobacco plantation alongside her mother, stepfather, and younger brothers. But when Master Allen and his wife send for her to come work as a servant, Grace must move to their estate and live separately from her family. The master and his wife live in an enormous house in a lifestyle of comfort and luxury: their stomachs are never empty. But still they are cruel and entitled, full of religious hypocrisy. After trying very hard to ignore their heartlessness, Grace slips and snaps back at the missus. Soon after, she learns that the master plans to sell her mother and brothers on the auction block. Grace runs away to warn her family, and together they form a plan of escape. But Grace worries: If her family knew she was the reason they must flee, could they ever forgive her?

Expertly researched, this novel describes the little-known Great Dismal Swamp "maroons"—escaped slaves who founded their own communities in the hidden marshlands of Virginia and North Carolina. But, even without this history lesson, this novel stands on its beautiful, evocative language and psychological focus. Young readers can appreciate Grace's urge to blame herself for her family's troubles, but as the story unfolds, it becomes clear that only because she stands up for herself and challenges the status quo is her family able to find freedom. Those who struggle to speak their mind can find courage in Grace's example.

For those coping with: anxiety/fear, biracialism, bullying, compliant/docile personality, evil/manipulative adults, homesickness, injustice/unfairness, moral dilemmas, recognizing privilege, self-blame

For those drawn to: character-driven novels, culturally responsive literature, Historical Fiction, psychological focus, seventeenth-century settings, survival stories

Themes/subjects: African Americans, anger, appearance versus reality, child labor, class/socioeconomic differences, community, courage, disfigurement, escapes, family, freedom, literacy/illiteracy, lying, racism, slavery/slaves, violence/abuse

Read-alikes: The protagonist of Christopher Paul Curtis's novel *The Journey of Little Charlie* faces similar obstacles after his sharecropper father dies. Sharon Lovejoy's *Running Out of Night* is about a friendship that develops between two girls, one an escaped slave, the other an abused white girl, as they seek freedom.

Crowder, Melanie. *Audacity*. Grades 7+. 🎧.

Clara dreams of books—poetry and literature, Chekhov and Tolstoy—but she lives in Russia at the turn of the twentieth century, and her orthodox Jewish family forbids her to read them. But when anti-Semitism sweeps their town, ending in massacre, Clara vows to never bow down to anyone again—to always fight back. She and her family flee to safety in America, where Clara must work to support her family. In New York City's garment district, Clara is literally locked inside a sweatshop with several other young immigrant women, sewing ten or more hours per day. Although Clara tries to inure herself to the tedium of this work, she cannot stand by as she and her coworkers endure terrible working conditions and harassment for fear of dismissal. She discovers a union office and decides to form a union for women garment workers—even though she can barely speak English and every man in the union office laughs in her face and tells her to go away.

Based on the real-life story of Clara Lemlich, Crowder's beautiful verse captures the imagination of the young labor activist who led the Uprising of 20,000, a massive strike of shirtwaist workers in NYC's garment industry. While educating readers about early twentieth-century gender roles and the discrimination young immigrant women faced, this story is also a call to action to resist complacency and stand up for the rights of others.

For those coping with: being an outsider/misfit, being underestimated by others, evil/manipulative adults, exploitation of one's poverty, moral dilemmas, parental disapproval, recognizing privilege

CHAPTER 8 | Verse Novels for Children and Young Adults **143**

For those drawn to: character-driven novels, coming-of-age, culturally responsive literature, Historical Fiction, psychological focus

Themes/subjects: ambitions, anger, anti-Semitism, books (love of), capitalism, courage, crushes, factories/factory workers, family, fashion industry, labor exploitation, labor unions, gender roles (twentieth century), immigration, Jewish descent, learning a new language, libraries/librarians, literacy/illiteracy, New York (early twentieth century), poverty, rebellions, saving and investment, slums

Read-alike: Jan Andrews's *To See the Stars* continues this history, as the protagonist is another immigrant worker who witnesses the Triangle shirtwaist factory fire of 1911.

Frost, Helen. *Salt: A Story of Friendship in a Time of War.* **Grades 5–7.** 🎧.

James Gray is twelve years old in 1812 and has lived in Fort Wayne, Indiana Territory, his entire life. When he isn't helping his father at the trading post, he is exploring the forests, trapping rabbits for his mother, or fishing with his best friend, Anikwa. Anikwa, who is also twelve, is a member of the Miami (also spelled Myaamia) tribe in Kekionga—the same region that the Americans call Fort Wayne. Although James speaks mostly English and Anikwa speaks mostly Miami, the two communicate through smiles and gestures, bird calls, and whistles. Growing up together, their families have always been warm neighbors to each other; but the Miami must defend themselves as Americans threaten to take their land and their way of life. So divided, how can James and Anikwa's friendship survive?

Carefully constructed, this novel alternates between James's and Anikwa's perspectives, which are signified through their visual arrangement. James's poems are bands of prose, like stripes of the American flag, which are woven through the pulsing, drumbeat shape of Anikwa's poems. Short verses about the origins of salt are also sprinkled throughout, symbolizing the object of colonial interests, the source of conflict and division. While alone, each poem is simply told, full of concrete imagery, together they offer a complex understanding of the tensions that led to the War of 1812. An often never-told chapter of the American past, this novel is a must-read for any student of our country's history.

For those coping with: feeling entitled, moral dilemmas, recognizing privilege, revenge (desire for)

For those drawn to: alternating perspectives, culturally responsive literature, Historical Fiction, homefront stories, seventeenth-century settings, survival stories, war stories

Themes/subjects: appearance versus reality, colonialism, community, cultural differences, family, friendship, hunting/hunters, Indigenous peoples (United States), (the) Midwest (United States), soldiers, War of 1812, wrongfully accused

Read-alike: Louise Erdrich's classic *The Birchbark House*, about the Ojibwa, will appeal to readers who wonder what it would have been like to be an Indigenous child in nineteenth-century America.

Grimes, Nikki. *Garvey's Choice*. Grades 4–8.

Garvey is all about books, math and science, starry nights, and *Star Trek*. His dad, though, doesn't get it—or him. He wants a son who plays football, not chess. It doesn't help that Garvey is also over-weight, making him the constant butt of jokes at home and at school. Garvey wants to please his father. He tries to conform. He runs. He tries crash diets. But he fails and fails again, leaving him to conclude that he will never live up to his father's expectations. Fortunately, his friends keep him in good company, encouraging him to just con-centrate on being himself. Heeding their advice, Garvey decides he will stop worrying about making others happy and instead do what makes him happy: singing and R&B. He joins the chorus and slowly realizes that he no longer has to *try* to fit in . . . because he already does.

Although this is a short, breezy read, each verse is actually a care-fully constructed tanka. Teachers could easily adapt this novel into a lesson on form poetry. While it deals with body issues, it is more about building self-esteem and finding ways to nurture and love one-self outside of familial networks. Any child who struggles with self-esteem, or feels undervalued by their loved ones, can relate to Garvey and learn from his example.

For those coping with: being misunderstood by parents, being underestimated by others, bullying, concern with what others think, disapproval, lack of confidence, poor body image, unpopularity

For those drawn to: humor, likeable/relatable characters, Realistic Fiction, suburban settings

Themes/subjects: African Americans, appearance versus reality, art as coping strategy, body image, books (love of), boy artists,

CHAPTER 8 | Verse Novels for Children and Young Adults **145**

bullies, courage, family, father-son relationships, friendship, gender roles (twenty-first century), music, self-esteem

Read-alike: Sherri Winston's novel *The Sweetest Sound* is similarly plotted, but instead follows a shy, female protagonist who is also a secretly talented singer.

Harrington, Janice N. *Catching a Storyfish*. Grades 4–7.

Back in Alabama, everyone called Kathryn "Keet Keet Parakeet" because she always had something to say and always had a story to tell. But after her parents move her and her little brother, Noah (nicknamed Nose because he is so nosy), to Illinois, Keet feels like a fish out of water. On the first day at her new school, her classmates laugh at her southern accent—*Alabama*, not *Alabamer*, they cackle—and Keet never wants to open her mouth again. Yep, as far as she's concerned, the only good thing about moving to Illinois is being closer to her grandpa, who teaches her how to fish—and also how to tell a good fish story. With his example and a little nudging from a new friend, Keet begins to find her voice again.

Harrington, a masterful poet, plays with all kinds of forms in this Verse Novel, including abecedarian, blues, and haiku; yet each poem reads as naturally and effortlessly as conversation. This novel is an ideal introduction to poetry, as it demonstrates the pleasure of language for language's sake. Keet's humor and singular perception also set this novel apart—she is an unforgettable character who not only models accepting herself but also takes pride in her roots.

For those coping with: being an outsider/misfit, being different, change, concern with what others will think, homesickness, lack of confidence, moving/relocating, worry/anxiety about a loved one

For those drawn to: character-driven novels, humor, likeable/ relatable characters, multiple perspectives, Realistic Fiction, strong female characters, suburban settings

Themes/subjects: accents (language), African Americans, appearance versus reality, art as coping strategy, courage, family, fishing, friendship, grandfathers, libraries/librarians, (the) Midwest (United States), shyness, stories, poetry

Read-alikes: Job struggles are also what causes the protagonist and her family to move in Eileen Spinelli's Verse Novel *Where I Live*, and Nikki Grimes's Verse Novel *Words with Wings* is also about a girl struggling to cope at a new school after her parents' divorce.

Hesse, Karen. *Out of the Dust.* **Grades 6+. 🎧.**

First drought, then dust: it's 1934, and Billie Jo and her parents don't know that the Dust Bowl has only just begun. As she watches their wheat crop die, Billie Jo sweeps the dust of the windowsills off the parlor floor, but her efforts are futile—she no sooner finishes cleaning when another dust storm comes to carry dirt everywhere. She can't even drink a glass of milk without the taste of grit in her mouth. She does find solace in school (she is a top student) and her piano. But then, just before her fourteenth birthday, tragedy strikes. First, a terrible fire leaves Billie Jo and her mother severely scarred. Billie Jo's hands are so blistered with burns that she is unable to play her piano. And, although the fire was an accident, Billie Jo blames herself. Overcome with grief, she and her father barely speak to each other, and the sight of the blighted, windswept land just compounds her sadness. Billie Jo decides she must leave, must get out of the dust, to recover her spirit, to recover hope.

Hesse's stunning, vivid language sets this Verse Novel apart. Expertly researched, it will bring the Great Depression to life for students, but this story will appeal to anyone who has struggled through hardship and who has struggled to hope.

For those coping with: death of a parent, death's finality, depression, disfigurement, distant/uncommunicative parent, grieving parent, guilt, hopelessness, loneliness, self-blame, troubled relationship with a mother

For those drawn to: character-driven novels, early twentieth-century settings, Historical Fiction, psychological focus, Realistic Fiction

Themes/subjects: art as coping strategy, community, death, disfigurement, dreams/nightmares, (the) Dust Bowl, forgiveness, grief/loss, music, Oklahoma, poverty

Read-alike: Historical Fiction fans should also check out Hesse's *Witness*, about the arrival of the KKK in a small Vermont town.

Lại, Thanhhà. *Inside Out & Back Again.* **Grades 4–6. 🎧.**

In Vietnamese, the name Kim Hà means "golden river," but in America, it just means "haha," bullying, and embarrassment. Hà, her mother, and her three older brothers move to Alabama in 1975, fleeing just before the war ends at home in Saigon. Now in Alabama, there are new challenges. Hà cannot understand English or why the white children in her fourth-grade class sit separately from the black children. To make matters worse, a pink-faced bully torments her daily, making fun of her name, her accent, her clothes, and the way

CHAPTER 8 | Verse Novels for Children and Young Adults

she looks. Naturally, Hà wonders if the journey was worth it. She longs for her father, missing in action, and the tastes of home.

Written as a diary in four parts, *Inside Out & Back Again* charts each phase of Hà's journey: the poverty she experiences in war-torn Vietnam, the dehumanizing conditions she endures in order to flee, culture shock, and adaptation. Lại's language and unforgettable images set this novel apart. Semiautobiographical, this novel translates historical fact into concrete experience. It would be hard to read this story and not feel in awe of Hà, who bears the emotional toll of being an outcast with strength, wisdom, and humor beyond her years.

For those coping with: being an outsider/misfit, bullying, (the) immigrant experience, injustice/unfairness, loneliness, poverty, racism, recognizing privilege, village/small-town life

For those drawn to: character-driven novels, Memoir, psychological focus, Realistic Fiction, survival stories, war stories

Themes/subjects: accents (language), Alabama, Asian Americans, anger, bullies, community, cultural differences, death, escapes, family, grief/loss, immigration, learning a new language, missing persons, poverty, racism, refugees, saving and investment, Vietnam War

Read-alikes: Ching Yeung Russell's *House without Walls* also recounts the journey from Vietnam to America; Jasmine Warga's *Other Words for Home* also addresses cultural differences, but from a Syrian perspective.

McCall, Guadalupe Garcia. *Under the Mesquite*. Grades 7+.

Lupita has lived her entire life on the borderlands of Mexico and Texas. When she is six, she and her family move to Eagle Pass, Texas, where they settle into a comfortable suburban life. Mami, who adores being the mother of eight "bebés," stays at home, managing the household, while Papi spends the day working construction jobs. Life in Eagle Pass is pretty picturesque as Mami prepares homemade tortillas and tends to their rose garden—a beautiful sight, despite the pesky mesquite tree that is determined to grow between the bushes. But when Lupita is just seventeen years old, Mami is diagnosed with cancer. Now, as her mother endures painful treatments, Lupita, the oldest, must take care of the house and her siblings on her behalf. She does so happily, willingly—anything for her Mami—but what to do about all the grief that weighs so heavily on her heart? How can she go on with this huge void, knowing it can never be filled?

Largely autobiographical, this Verse Novel is a poignant meditation on loss. After Mami dies, Lupita finds solace in her studies (she is a hardworking student) and, more importantly, art. She writes poems in her journal, acts in her high school's drama program, and eventually finds the courage to un-pause and continue her life by leaving home and enrolling in college. McCall weaves Spanish words and allusions to Mexican culture (Pedro Infante, Selena) to emphasize Lupita's dual identity as Mexican and American. While certainly serving children's literature in representing this less-heard voice, this novel is primarily written for those who have lost much, especially at a young age.

For those coping with: change, death of a parent, death's finality, grieving parent, poor body image, poverty

For those drawn to: character-driven novels, coming-of-age stories, Memoir, Realistic Fiction, strong female characters, suburban settings

Themes/subjects: accents (language), actors/acting, ambitions, art as coping strategy, body image, community, cultural differences, family, gardens, gender roles (twentieth century), grief/loss, high school life, illness (terminal), Latino/a Americans, poetry, poverty, saving and investment, self-reliance, Texas

Read-alike: Familial love, loss, and coming-of-age are also central themes in Margarita Engle's Historical Novel in verse about the Zoot Suit Riots, *Jazz Owls*.

Pinkney, Andrea Davis. *The Red Pencil*. Grades 5–7. 🎧📖.

Growing up in Southern Darfur, twelve-year-old Amira has only known life on her family's quiet farm. Along with her little sister, she helps her parents milk cows, pick melons and okra, and tend to their sheep. But when war breaks out in early 2003, the life Amira has always known comes to an end. Her father dies; her hut is destroyed; and now she must travel to safety, by foot, with her mother, her sister, and other survivors. They reach a relocation camp in Kalma, but the conditions are so cramped and food is so scarce that the camp brings little comfort. Overwhelmed by grief, Amira can't speak. A camp volunteer gifts her with a red pencil, which she uses to express herself through drawing. Slowly, she begins to dream again: of learning to read, of going to school. But her mother is still attached to the old ways—fearful that if Amira gets an education, she will become unmarriageable—and so Amira must find the courage and determination to follow a new path.

CHAPTER 8 | Verse Novels for Children and Young Adults

Pinkney's novel is a standout in that it offers an accessible and realistic account of the war in Darfur by conveying its horror without resorting to gratuitous details of violence. And, though the ending is hopeful, neither does it gloss over the survivors' emotional trauma or pretend a resolution to the conflict. At the same time, Amira offers a model for identity as she pulls away from her family's traditions and realizes her own agency by choosing to empower herself through literacy and education. Any child who has felt torn between loyalty to self and loyalty to family will appreciate Amira's boldness and resolve.

For those coping with: being misunderstood by parents, change, death of a parent, disability, family conflict, homelessness, moral dilemmas, parental disapproval, recognizing privilege, war trauma

For those drawn to: character-driven novels, coming-of-age, culturally responsive literature, disability (mutism), disfigurement, psychological focus, Realistic Fiction, survival stories, war stories

Themes/subjects: Africa (Sudan), art as coping strategy, community, courage, escapes, family, farm life, gender roles (twenty-first century), genocide, grief/loss, Islam, literacy/illiteracy, mother-daughter relationships, pets, poverty, refugees, religious faith, sisters, wars/battles

Read-alike: Victoria Jamieson and Omar Mohamed's Graphic Novel *When Stars Are Scattered* also describes refugee life, but in Kenya.

Reynolds, Jason. *Long Way Down*. Grades 8+. 🎧.

Will's brother has just died—someone shot him. Will is devastated, heartbroken, but he knows that crying is against "The Rules." The Rules, which have been passed onto Will from his brother, who passed them on from his father, also dictate: no snitching, just revenge. It's not the first time Will has lost someone he loves to gun violence, but it is the first time he plans to do something about it. He finds his brother's gun in the drawer where he left it, tucks it in his jeans, and heads for the person he thinks killed his brother. But when Will gets in his elevator, something strange happens: He sees a ghost. And then another. One by one, every friend he lost to a gun appears, making him think twice about pulling the trigger.

In this cautionary tale about vengeance, Reynolds relies on realism rather than excessive moralizing to express why breaking the cycle of violence is the only way to restore justice. For readers who have experienced such violence, this novel may offer a mirror to remind them that they are not alone. However, teachers may use this novel with students who have lived a more sheltered experience to discuss (1) how not all childhoods are the same, and (2) the institutional structures (for example, poverty induced by segregation/redlining) that contribute to patterns of violence.

For those coping with: being wealthy or privileged, feeling entitled, injustice/unfairness, recognizing privilege, revenge (desire for)

For those drawn to: culturally responsive literature, gradually unfolding stories, ghost stories, multiple perspectives, Realistic Fiction, streetwise characters

Themes/subjects: anger, avenging a death, ghosts, grief/loss, gun violence, murder, revenge

Read-alike: *Punching the Air* by writer Ibi Zoboi and Yusef Salaam, one of the Exonerated Five in the Central Park Jogger case, is a novel-in-verse that responds to Reynolds's novel with an examination of the prison industrial complex.

Walrath, Dana. *Like Water on Stone*. Grades 8+.

Before 1914, when the country now known as Turkey was still the Ottoman Empire, Christian Armenians were able to live in relative peace under Turkish rule, despite their inferior status as "gavours," the Turkish word for a non-Muslim. But as World War I breaks out, Ottoman rulers want to eliminate any potential threat to their empire—including Armenians. When soldiers march into Palu, thirteen-year-old twins Shahen and Sosi, brother and sister, flee with their little sister—the only family they have left—to the mountains. For months, they hide by day and travel by night toward Aleppo, hoping to find passage to America, where they can reunite with their uncle. But the journey is fraught, as they must not only escape the violence but also survive in the wilderness.

Alternating perspectives between Shahen and Sosi provide a gendered and therefore broader understanding of the danger. (At one point, Shahen dresses as a girl in order to spare his life, only to learn other ways his disguise makes him and his sister vulnerable to sexual violence.) Extremely well researched and one of the only novels of its kind, it should be required reading in high school history classes, especially since few here have heard of the Armenian genocide. To this day, Turkey continues to deny this state-sanctioned murder of at least one million Armenians.

CHAPTER 8 | Verse Novels for Children and Young Adults — 151

For those coping with: (the) immigrant experience, lack of control over events, religious intolerance or persecution, strained relationship with a father, war trauma

For those drawn to: alternating perspectives, culturally responsive literature, early twentieth-century settings, Historical Fiction, multiple perspectives, survival stories, war stories

Themes/subjects: appearance versus reality, Armenians, Christianity, class/socioeconomic differences, courage, escapes, family, genocide, grief/loss, homelessness, immigration, music, political oppression, sexual violence, Turkey, twins, World War I

Read-alike: Ruta Sepetys's *Between Shades of Gray* is another expertly researched novel about a seldom-told history: families deported to Siberia and forced to labor in Stalin's work camps during World War II.

Warga, Jasmine. *Other Words for Home*. Grades 4–8. 🎧.

Twelve-year-old Jude and her best friend, Fatima, love American movies, especially romantic comedies, and together they dream of one day becoming famous actresses. But when civil unrest breaks out near their home in Syria, Jude's and Fatima's dreams are forever altered. While Jude and her pregnant mother are able to flee to America, Fatima, and also her Baba and her older brother, Issa, must remain in war-torn Syria. Jude and her mother land in Cincinnati, Ohio, where Jude's uncle, a physician, and his family live. While both her uncle and her American aunt embrace Jude with open arms, their home, with its all-white décor and pancake-batter smells, feel so foreign to her—not like *home* at all. Sarah, Jude's cousin, is no help, either; barely acknowledging her presence, Sarah just makes her feel even more like a stranger. Invisibility follows her at school, too. She used to sparkle in her Syrian classrooms, but now she won't even raise her hand for fear of revealing her accent. But when tryouts begin for the school musical, Jude remembers her love of acting and for the first time in a while feels a flash of hope. Acting is just the motivation she needs to reclaim her confidence—and dreams.

While a tender, moving story about a girl's resilience in the face of violence and loss, this novel also taps into more universal themes about loneliness and the human need for belonging. Although Jude's voice drives the novel, the other characters also have dimension so that their interactions with one another highlight their intersectionality without feeling contrived. It would be hard for readers to finish this novel and not recognize our connection with others.

For those coping with: concern with what others think, homesickness, (the) immigrant experience, lack of confidence, recognizing privilege, snobbery/elitism, worry/anxiety about a loved one

For those drawn to: character-driven novels, humor, Realistic Fiction, strong female characters

Themes/subjects: accents (language), actors/acting, ambitions, art as coping strategy, biracialism, brother-sister relationships, class/socioeconomic differences, courage, cultural differences, family, friendship, influence of popular culture, jealousy, learning a new language, middle school life, (the) Midwest (United States), racism

Read-alike: Reem Faruqi's *Unsettled* is also a Verse Novel about a Muslim girl immigrating to America, but her protagonist experiences a different cultural change as she immigrates from Pakistan to the American South.

Woodson, Jacqueline. *Brown Girl Dreaming*. Grades 4–7. 🎧.

For better or worse, Jacqueline is always getting called out for "making up stories." Born in 1963 in Columbus, Ohio, she is still an infant when her mother leaves her father and brings her and her older brother and sister to the South to live with her parents in Greenville, South Carolina. Living in Greenville means learning how to grow sweet peas and peaches and summer nights rocking on the porch swing with her grandfather telling her stories. Her house is always bustling with cousins and neighbors and conversations about marching and standing up for what's right. Jacqueline loves Greenville, the smell of rain and pine trees, and her grandmother's cooking, but her mother has her heart set on New York City, where "diamonds" are supposed to speckle the sidewalks and "money falls from the sky." So, just before first grade, Jacqueline and her siblings move to Brooklyn. But once they arrive, Jacqueline wonders if it wasn't "another New York City" the southerners were talking about because life in the North is not exactly easy, either.

Part Memoir, part Artist's Novel, Woodson draws from her own experience to make the history of the African American experience come alive. While she recounts the treatment of African Americans in the North and the South during the 1960s and '70s, Woodson also focuses on personal struggles, like what it's like for Jacqueline to live in the shadow of her bookish older sister, Odell. Whether readers want to gain an understanding of this history or are looking for comfort and reassurance of self-worth, this National Book Award winner

CHAPTER 8 | Verse Novels for Children and Young Adults **153**

delivers. It's the kind of story one can return to and gain something new again and again.

For those coping with: absent parent, change, homesickness, jealousy, moving/relocating, racism, recognizing privilege, sense of inferiority

For those drawn to: coming-of-age stories, culturally responsive literature, likeable/relatable characters, Memoir, urban settings

Themes/subjects: African Americans, ambitions, art as coping strategy, books (love of), community, country versus city, death, family, friendship, grandfathers, poetry, racial segregation, racism, religious faith, stories, words (power of)

Read-alike: Margarita Engle's *Enchanted Air: Two Cultures, Two Wings* describes her growing up between her mother's native Cuba and Los Angeles in the aftermath of the Cuban missile crisis.

NOTES

1. Mary Oliver, *A Poetry Handbook* (Boston: Houghton Mifflin Harcourt, 1994), 35.
2. Joy Alexander. "The Verse-Novel: A New Genre," *Children's Literature in Education* 36, no. 3 (2005): 270.

Subject/Theme/Appeals Index

A

abandoned children
Bone Gap (Ruby), 90
Fever Crumb (Reeve), 127
Ghostopolis (TenNapel), 38
Hey, Kiddo (Krosoczka), 33
Thornhill (Smy), 37
abuse. *See* violence/abuse
accents (language)
American Street (Zoboi), 91
Catching a Storyfish (Harrington), 145
Inside Out & Back Again (Lai), 147
Other Words for Home (Warga), 152
Under the Mesquite (McCall), 148
actors/acting
Goblin Secrets (Alexander), 117
Other Words for Home (Warga), 152
Under the Mesquite (McCall), 148
addiction (drugs/alcohol)
American Street (Zoboi), 91
Hey, Kiddo (Krosoczka), 33
Release (Ness), 99
Swing It, Sunny (Holm & Holm), 31
Africa (Ghana), 31
Africa (Sudan)
Home of the Brave (Applegate), 138
The Red Pencil (Pinkney), 149
African Americans
American Street (Zoboi), 91
Brown Girl Dreaming (Woodson), 153
Catching a Storyfish (Harrington), 145
The Crossover (Alexander), 135
Dread Nation (Ireland), 57
Garvey's Choice (Grimes), 144
New Kid (Craft), 27
Stone Mirrors: The Sculpture and

Silence of Edmonia Lewis (Atkins), 139
Unbound (Burg), 142
afterlife, 38
airships/dirgibles
Airborn (Oppel), 114
Airman (Colfer), 119
Etiquette & Espionage (Carriger), 112
Leviathan (Westerfeld), 116
Mortal Engines (Reeve), 115
The Peculiars (McQuerry), 123
The Quest to the Uncharted Lands (Johnson), 122
Alabama, 147
aliens, 128
alternating perspectives
Bone Gap (Ruby), 90
The Clockwork Scarab (Gleason), 121
Like Water on Stone (Walrath), 151
Pablo and Birdy (McGhee), 88
Release (Ness), 98
Salt: A Story of Friendship in a Time of War (Frost), 144
The Walls Around Us (Suma), 104
When the Moon Was Ours (McLemore), 96
ambitions
American Street (Zoboi), 91
Audacity (Crowder), 143
Brown Girl Dreaming (Woodson), 153
The Crossover (Alexander), 135
Hey, Kiddo (Krosoczka), 33
The Lightning Queen (Resau), 103
Other Words for Home (Warga), 152
Roller Girl (Jamieson), 32

155

156   SUBJECT/THEME/APPEALS INDEX

ambitions *(continued)*
   Serafina's Promise (Burg), 141
   Under the Mesquite (McCall), 148
amnesia
   Incarceron (Fisher), 112
   The Mark of the Dragonfly (Johnson),
     113
amulets, 59
ancestry. *See* heritage/ancestry
ancient Rome, 59
ancient world settings, 59
angels, 98
anger
   American Street (Zoboi), 91
   Audacity (Crowder), 143
   Belzhar (Wolitzer), 107
   The Crossover (Alexander), 135
   Inside Out & Back Again (Lai), 147
   Long Way Down (Reynolds), 150
   A Monster Calls (Ness), 89
   Pablo and Birdy (McGhee), 88
   Release (Ness), 99
   Unbound (Burg), 142
Animal Fantasies
   The Book of Boy (Murdock), 97
   Crenshaw (Applegate), 92
   Hamster Princess: Harriet the Invincible
     (Vernon), 40
   Little Cat's Luck (Bauer), 140
   Me and Marvin Gardens (King), 94
   Pablo and Birdy (McGhee), 88
   Secrets at Sea (Peck), 50
animal stories
   El Deafo (Bell), 26
   Love That Dog (Creech), 137
anti-Semitism, 143
appearance versus reality
   The Astonishing Color of After (Pan),
     100
   Bone Gap (Ruby), 90
   Catching a Storyfish (Harrington), 145
   Garvey's Choice (Grimes), 144
   Incarceron (Fisher), 112
   Like Water on Stone (Walrath), 151
   The Nest (Oppel), 100
   Salt: A Story of Friendship in a Time of
     War (Frost), 144

Thornhill (Smy), 37
Unbound (Burg), 142
appearances. *See* deceptiveness of
   appearances
apprentices
   Clockwork, or All Wound Up
     (Pullman), 125
   Fever Crumb (Reeve), 127
   The Inquisitor's Apprentice (Moriarty),
     58
archaeologists/archaeology
   The Lie Tree (Hardinge), 48
   Midwinterblood (Sedgwick), 104
aristocracy/upper classes, 50
Armenians, 151
arranged marriages, 112
arresting/original settings
   The Astonishing Color of After (Pan),
     100
   Clockwork Angel (Clare), 118
   Etiquette & Espionage (Carriger), 112
   Fever Crumb (Reeve), 127
   The Golden Compass (Pullman), 126
   Heap House (Carey), 47
   Incarceron (Fisher), 112
   Larklight (Reeve), 127
   Mortal Engines (Reeve), 115
   The Peculiar (Bachmann), 117
   The Strange and Beautiful Sorrows of
     Ava Lavender (Walton), 105
   The Thief Lord (Funke), 93
   Thornhill (Smy), 37
   When the Moon Was Ours
     (McLemore), 96
   Wonderstruck (Selznick), 36
art as coping strategy
   All the Broken Pieces (Burg), 136
   The Astonishing Color of After (Pan),
     100
   Belzhar (Wolitzer), 107
   Brown Girl Dreaming (Woodson), 153
   Catching a Storyfish (Harrington), 145
   The Collected Essex County (Lemire),
     34
   Garvey's Choice (Grimes), 144
   Hey, Kiddo (Krosoczka), 33
   Illegal (Eoin & Donkin), 31

SUBJECT/THEME/APPEALS INDEX

Love That Dog (Creech), 137
New Kid (Craft), 27
Other Words for Home (Warga), 152
Out of the Dust (Hesse), 146
The Poet X (Acevedo), 134
The Red Pencil (Pinkney), 149
Speak: The Graphic Novel (Anderson & Carroll), 30
Stone Mirrors: The Sculpture and Silence of Edmonia Lewis (Atkins), 139
Thornhill (Smy), 37
Under the Mesquite (McCall), 148
Wonderstruck (Selznick), 36
A Year without Mom (Tolstikova), 39
artificial intelligence, 112
artists
    The Astonishing Color of After (Pan), 100
    The Boundless (Oppel), 124
    Midwinterblood (Sedgwick), 104
    Pashmina (Nidhi), 35
    The Poet X (Acevedo), 134
    Speak: The Graphic Novel (Anderson & Carroll), 30
    Stone Mirrors: The Sculpture and Silence of Edmonia Lewis (Atkins), 139
    A Year without Mom (Tolstikova), 39
    See also boy artists
Asian Americans
    All the Broken Pieces (Burg), 136
    American Born Chinese (Yang), 29
    The Astonishing Color of After (Pan), 100
    Inside Out & Back Again (Lai), 147
    New Kid (Craft), 27
Asian-inspired novels
    American Born Chinese (Yang), 29
    Stormdancer (Kristoff), 122
assassins, 49
assertiveness, 30
authoritarian figures
    The Lightning Queen (Resau), 103
    Release (Ness), 99
automatons, 118
avenging a death, 150

B

ballet/ballerinas, 104
baseball, 136
basketball, 135
beauty, 90
bees
    Bone Gap (Ruby), 90
    The Nest (Oppel), 100
being wrongfully accused, 139
Belle Époque, 53
biblical allusions, 98
biographical novels, 139
biracialism
    The Astonishing Color of After (Pan), 100
    Other Words for Home (Warga), 152
birds
    Pablo and Birdy (McGhee), 88
    Summer of Salt (Leno), 95
birthdays
    Lucky Strike (Pyron), 101
    Pablo and Birdy (McGhee), 88
    Summer of Salt (Leno), 95
birth/life cycle, 140
Blitz, 54
boarding school stories
    Belzhar (Wolitzer), 107
    A Great and Terrible Beauty (Bray), 46
    Thornhill (Smy), 37
boarding schools
    Belzhar (Wolitzer), 107
    The Charmed Children of Rookskill Castle (Fox), 54
    Etiquette & Espionage (Carriger), 112
    A Great and Terrible Beauty (Bray), 46
    Stone Mirrors: The Sculpture and Silence of Edmonia Lewis (Atkins), 139
body image
    American Street (Zoboi), 91
    Bone Gap (Ruby), 90
    The Book of Boy (Murdock), 98
    Garvey's Choice (Grimes), 144
    Under the Mesquite (McCall), 148
    When the Moon Was Ours (McLemore), 97

158   SUBJECT/THEME/APPEALS INDEX

books (love of)
  Audacity (Crowder), 143
  Brown Girl Dreaming (Woodson), 153
  Garvey's Choice (Grimes), 144
  The Walls Around Us (Suma), 104
boy artists
  The Astonishing Color of After (Pan),
    100
  The Collected Essex County (Lemire),
    34
  Garvey's Choice (Grimes), 144
  Hey, Kiddo (Krosoczka), 33
  Love That Dog (Creech), 137
  New Kid (Craft), 27
brainwashing/indoctrination
  Fever Crumb (Reeve), 127
  Grave Mercy (LaFevers), 49
  Incarceron (Fisher), 112
Brittany (fifteenth century), 49
brothers
  The Collected Essex County (Lemire),
    34
  The Gilded Wolves (Chokshi), 53
brother-sister relationships
  Clockwork Angel (Clare), 118
  Crenshaw (Applegate), 92
  Larklight (Reeve), 128
  Mark of the Thief (Nielsen), 59
  Me and Marvin Gardens (King), 94
  Other Words for Home (Warga), 152
  The Peculiar (Bachmann), 117
  The Poet X (Acevedo), 134
  Swing It, Sunny (Holm & Holm), 31
bullies
  All the Broken Pieces (Burg), 136
  American Born Chinese (Yang), 29
  American Street (Zoboi), 91
  Belzhar (Wolitzer), 107
  Bone Gap (Ruby), 90
  Garvey's Choice (Grimes), 145
  Inside Out & Back Again (Lai), 147
  Me and Marvin Gardens (King), 94
  A Monster Calls (Ness), 89
  New Kid (Craft), 27
  Smile (Telgemeier), 28
  Speak: The Graphic Novel (Anderson &
    Carroll), 30

Spinning (Walden), 41
Thornhill (Smy), 37
The Walls Around Us (Suma), 104
When the Moon Was Ours (McLemore),
  97

C

California, 28
camping, 39
Canada (nineteenth century), 124
Canada (twentieth century), 34
cancer, 89
capitalism
  American Street (Zoboi), 91
  Audacity (Crowder), 143
  Me and Marvin Gardens (King), 94
captives
  The Golden Compass (Pullman), 126
  Incarceron (Fisher), 113
  Larklight (Reeve), 128
  The Peculiar (Bachmann), 117
(the) Caribbean, 88
castles, 54
Catholicism, 98
cats (talking)
  Crenshaw (Applegate), 92
  Little Cat's Luck (Bauer), 140
character-driven novels
  All the Broken Pieces (Burg), 136
  American Born Chinese (Yang), 29
  The Astonishing Color of After (Pan),
    100
  Audacity (Crowder), 143
  Belzhar (Wolitzer), 107
  Catching a Storyfish (Harrington), 145
  The Collected Essex County (Lemire),
    34
  The Crossover (Alexander), 135
  Dragon's Keep (Carey), 52
  El Deafo (Bell), 26
  Hey, Kiddo (Krosoczka), 33
  Honor Girl (Thrash), 38
  Inside Out & Back Again (Lai), 147
  Lucky Strike (Pyron), 101
  Me and Marvin Gardens (King), 94
  The Nest (Oppel), 99
  New Kid (Craft), 27

SUBJECT/THEME/APPEALS INDEX

Other Words for Home (Warga), 152
Out of the Dust (Hesse), 146
The Poet X (Acevedo), 134
The Red Pencil (Pinkney), 149
Serafina's Promise (Burg), 141
Smile (Telgemeier), 28
Speak: The Graphic Novel (Anderson & Carroll), 30
Stone Mirrors: The Sculpture and Silence of Edmonia Lewis (Atkins), 139
Swing It, Sunny (Holm & Holm), 31
Unbound (Burg), 142
Under the Mesquite (McCall), 148
When the Moon Was Ours (McLemore), 96
chase stories
Ghostopolis (TenNapel), 38
Pablo and Birdy (McGhee), 88
The Thief Lord (Funke), 93
Chicago (mid-twentieth century), 60
child labor
Serafina's Promise (Burg), 141
Sweep: The Story of a Girl and Her Monster (Auxier), 46
Unbound (Burg), 142
children. *See* abandoned children; gifted children or teens; orphans
chimney sweeps, 46
China (twenty-first century), 100
Christianity
Like Water on Stone (Walrath), 151
Lucky Strike (Pyron), 101
circuses/circus performers, 124
city. *See* country versus city
civil wars, 138
civilization, 104
classics-inspired fiction
Bone Gap (Ruby), 90
Ghostopolis (TenNapel), 38
Thornhill (Smy), 37
class/socioeconomic differences
Airborn (Oppel), 114
American Street (Zoboi), 91
Bone Gap (Ruby), 90
Crenshaw (Applegate), 92
The Golden Compass (Pullman), 126
The Lightning Queen (Resau), 103

Like Water on Stone (Walrath), 151
Lucky Strike (Pyron), 101
Me and Marvin Gardens (King), 94
Mechanica (Cornwell), 120
Mortal Engines (Reeve), 115
New Kid (Craft), 27
Other Words for Home (Warga), 152
The Poet X (Acevedo), 134
Release (Ness), 99
Secrets at Sea (Peck), 50
Unbound (Burg), 142
The Walls Around Us (Suma), 104
climate change, 94
cliques
American Born Chinese (Yang), 29
American Street (Zoboi), 91
Belzhar (Wolitzer), 107
Honor Girl (Thrash), 39
Lucky Strike (Pyron), 101
Smile (Telgemeier), 28
Spinning (Walden), 41
Thornhill (Smy), 37
The Walls Around Us (Suma), 104
A Year without Mom (Tolstikova), 39
clock- and watchmakers, 126
clockwork creatures. *See* mechanical or clockwork creatures
clockwork devices/inventions, 121
codes/ciphers, 54
collectors/collections, 36
colonialism
The Gilded Wolves (Chokshi), 53
The Peculiars (McQuerry), 123
Salt: A Story of Friendship in a Time of War (Frost), 144
Serafina's Promise (Burg), 141
comic adventures
The Book of Boy (Murdock), 97
Hamster Princess: Harriet the Invincible (Vernon), 40
comics (love of)
The Collected Essex County (Lemire), 34
Hey, Kiddo (Krosoczka), 33
New Kid (Craft), 27
Pashmina (Nidhi), 35

160 SUBJECT/THEME/APPEALS INDEX

coming-of-age stories
    American Born Chinese (Yang), 29
    Audacity (Crowder), 143
    Brown Girl Dreaming (Woodson), 153
    The Crossover (Alexander), 135
    Hey, Kiddo (Krosoczka), 33
    The Lie Tree (Hardinge), 48
    The Poet X (Acevedo), 134
    The Red Pencil (Pinkney), 149
    Spinning (Walden), 41
    *The Strange and Beautiful Sorrows of
       Ava Lavender* (Walton), 105
    *Thirteen Doorways, Wolves behind Them
       All* (Ruby), 60
    Under the Mesquite (McCall), 148
community
    All the Broken Pieces (Burg), 136
    Brown Girl Dreaming (Woodson), 153
    Crenshaw (Applegate), 92
    Home of the Brave (Applegate), 138
    Illegal (Eoin & Donkin), 31
    Inside Out & Back Again (Lai), 147
    The Lightning Queen (Resau), 103
    Lucky Strike (Pyron), 101
    Out of the Dust (Hesse), 146
    Pablo and Birdy (McGhee), 88
    The Poet X (Acevedo), 134
    The Red Pencil (Pinkney), 149
    *Salt: A Story of Friendship in a Time of
       War* (Frost), 144
    *The Strange and Beautiful Sorrows of
       Ava Lavender* (Walton), 106
    Unbound (Burg), 142
    Under the Mesquite (McCall), 148
competitions/testing
    Honor Girl (Thrash), 39
    Roller Girl (Jamieson), 32
    Spinning (Walden), 41
convents, 49
corruption, 98
country versus city
    Brown Girl Dreaming (Woodson), 153
    The Collected Essex County (Lemire),
       34
    The Lightning Queen (Resau), 103
courage
    American Street (Zoboi), 91

The Astonishing Color of After (Pan),
    100
Audacity (Crowder), 143
Bone Gap (Ruby), 90
Catching a Storyfish (Harrington), 145
Garvey's Choice (Grimes), 145
Honor Girl (Thrash), 39
The Lightning Queen (Resau), 103
Like Water on Stone (Walrath), 151
Me and Marvin Gardens (King), 94
The Nest (Oppel), 100
Other Words for Home (Warga), 152
Pablo and Birdy (McGhee), 88
The Poet X (Acevedo), 134
The Red Pencil (Pinkney), 149
Release (Ness), 99
Serafina's Promise (Burg), 141
Speak: The Graphic Novel (Anderson &
    Carroll), 30
Spinning (Walden), 41
Unbound (Burg), 142
When the Moon Was Ours
    (McLemore), 97
court/palace settings, 49
courts/courtiers, 49
creationism versus evolution, 48
crushes
    American Born Chinese (Yang), 29
    American Street (Zoboi), 91
    The Astonishing Color of After (Pan),
       100
    Audacity (Crowder), 143
    Belzhar (Wolitzer), 107
    Bone Gap (Ruby), 90
    The Collected Essex County (Lemire),
       34
    Honor Girl (Thrash), 39
    The Poet X (Acevedo), 134
    Release (Ness), 99
    Smile (Telgemeier), 28
    Spinning (Walden), 41
    *The Strange and Beautiful Sorrows of
       Ava Lavender* (Walton), 106
    Summer of Salt (Leno), 95
    A Year without Mom (Tolstikova),
       39
cults (religious), 51

SUBJECT/THEME/APPEALS INDEX

cultural differences
American Born Chinese (Yang), 29
American Street (Zoboi), 91
The Astonishing Color of After (Pan),
100
Bone Gap (Ruby), 90
Home of the Brave (Applegate), 138
Inside Out & Back Again (Lai), 147
The Lightning Queen (Resau), 103
Other Words for Home (Warga), 152
Pashmina (Nidhi), 35
The Quest to the Uncharted Lands
(Johnson), 122
*Salt: A Story of Friendship in a Time of
War* (Frost), 144
Under the Mesquite (McCall), 148
A Year without Mom (Tolstikova), 39
culturally responsive literature
American Born Chinese (Yang), 29
The Astonishing Color of After (Pan),
100
Audacity (Crowder), 143
Brown Girl Dreaming (Woodson), 153
El Deafo (Bell), 26
Honor Girl (Thrash), 38
The Lightning Queen (Resau), 102
Like Water on Stone (Walrath), 151
Long Way Down (Reynolds), 150
Me and Marvin Gardens (King), 94
New Kid (Craft), 27
The Red Pencil (Pinkney), 149
Release (Ness), 98
*Salt: A Story of Friendship in a Time of
War* (Frost), 144
Serafina's Promise (Burg), 141
*Stone Mirrors: The Sculpture and
Silence of Edmonia Lewis* (Atkins),
139
Unbound (Burg), 142
When the Moon Was Ours
(McLemore), 96
curses/hexes, 97
cyborgs
Fever Crumb (Reeve), 127
Mortal Engines (Reeve), 115

D

dangerous adventures
Airborn (Oppel), 114
Airman (Colfer), 119
The Boundless (Oppel), 124
Clockwork Angel (Clare), 118
The Golden Compass (Pullman), 126
Illegal (Eoin & Donkin), 30
The Inquisitor's Apprentice (Moriarty),
58
Leviathan (Westerfeld), 116
The Peculiars (McQuerry), 123
The Quest to the Uncharted Lands
(Johnson), 122
daughters. *See* father-daughter
relationships; mother-daughter
relationships
death
The Astonishing Color of After (Pan),
100
Brown Girl Dreaming (Woodson),
153
The Collected Essex County (Lemire),
34
The Crossover (Alexander), 135
Grave Mercy (LaFevers), 49
Inside Out & Back Again (Lai), 147
Midwinterblood (Sedgwick), 104
A Monster Calls (Ness), 89
Out of the Dust (Hesse), 146
*The Strange and Beautiful Sorrows of
Ava Lavender* (Walton), 106
deception and disguises
Etiquette & Espionage (Carriger), 112
Incarceron (Fisher), 113
Murder, Magic, and What We Wore
(Jones), 58
deceptiveness of appearances
The Astonishing Color of After (Pan),
100
The Book of Boy (Murdock), 98
*The Strange and Beautiful Sorrows of
Ava Lavender* (Walton), 106
demons
Clockwork Angel (Clare), 118
Ghostopolis (TenNapel), 38
dental work, 28

162   SUBJECT/THEME/APPEALS INDEX

depression
  All the Broken Pieces (Burg), 136
  The Astonishing Color of After (Pan),
    100
  Belzhar (Wolitzer), 107
  Speak: The Graphic Novel (Anderson &
    Carroll), 30
  Thornhill (Smy), 37
desert islands, 114
deserts, 31
detective novels
  The Clockwork Scarab (Gleason), 121
  Ghostopolis (TenNapel), 38
determination. *See* perseverance/
    determination
Dickinson, Emily, 100
dirigibles. *See* airships/dirigibles
disability (cognitive)
  Bone Gap (Ruby), 90
  *The Strange and Beautiful Sorrows of
    Ava Lavender* (Walton), 106
disability (deafness)
  El Deafo (Bell), 26
  Wonderstruck (Selznick), 36
disability (mutism)
  The Red Pencil (Pinkney), 149
  Thornhill (Smy), 37
disability (paralysis)
  All the Broken Pieces (Burg), 136
  Belzhar (Wolitzer), 107
disfigurement
  Home of the Brave (Applegate), 138
  The Lightning Queen (Resau), 103
  Out of the Dust (Hesse), 146
  The Red Pencil (Pinkney), 149
  *The Strange and Beautiful Sorrows of
    Ava Lavender* (Walton), 106
  Unbound (Burg), 142
divorce, 39
doctors/medicine, 141
dogs, 88
dogs (talking), 140
Dominican Americans, 134
dragons, 52
dreams/nightmares
  The Astonishing Color of After (Pan),
    100

Bone Gap (Ruby), 90
The Book of Boy (Murdock), 98
Hey, Kiddo (Krosoczka), 33
Midwinterblood (Sedgwick), 104
A Monster Calls (Ness), 89
The Nest (Oppel), 100
Out of the Dust (Hesse), 146
Pablo and Birdy (McGhee), 88
*The Strange and Beautiful Sorrows of
    Ava Lavender* (Walton), 106
Wonderstruck (Selznick), 36
dressmaking, 58
driving force/passion
  Airborn (Oppel), 114
  The Crossover (Alexander), 135
  Serafina's Promise (Burg), 141
  *Stone Mirrors: The Sculpture and
    Silence of Edmonia Lewis* (Atkins), 139
dual intertwined storylines
  *The Charmed Children of Rookskill
    Castle* (Fox), 54
  Illegal (Eoin & Donkin), 30
  Incarceron (Fisher), 112
  Leviathan (Westerfeld), 116
  Mortal Engines (Reeve), 115
  Pablo and Birdy (McGhee), 88
  The Peculiar (Bachmann), 117
  *Thirteen Doorways, Wolves behind Them
    All* (Ruby), 60
  Thornhill (Smy), 37
  Wonderstruck (Selznick), 36
(the) Dust Bowl, 146
dysfunctional families, 30
Dystopias
  Incarceron (Fisher), 112
  The Mark of the Dragonfly (Johnson),
    113
  Mortal Engines (Reeve), 115
  Stormdancer (Kristoff), 122

E

early twentieth-century settings
  The Diviners (Bray), 51
  The Inquisitor's Apprentice (Moriarty),
    58
  The Lightning Queen (Resau), 102
  Like Water on Stone (Walrath), 151

SUBJECT/THEME/APPEALS INDEX **163**

Out of the Dust (Hesse), 146
earthquakes
    Serafina's Promise (Burg), 141
    Smile (Telgemeier), 28
eccentric characters
    Bone Gap (Ruby), 90
    The Boundless (Oppel), 124
    Crenshaw (Applegate), 92
    Ghostopolis (TenNapel), 38
    Goblin Secrets (Alexander), 117
    Heap House (Carey), 47
    Pablo and Birdy (McGhee), 88
    The Peculiar (Bachmann), 117
    The Strange and Beautiful Sorrows of
      Ava Lavender (Walton), 105
ecosystems
    Lucky Strike (Pyron), 101
    Me and Marvin Gardens (King), 94
Edison (Thomas), 58
education/learning
    Crenshaw (Applegate), 92
    El Deafo (Bell), 26
    Etiquette & Espionage (Carriger), 112
    The Lightning Queen (Resau), 103
    Love That Dog (Creech), 137
    New Kid (Craft), 27
    Serafina's Promise (Burg), 141
Egyptology, 121
engineers/engineering, 127
England (post-World War I), 56
England (Regency period), 58
England (twenty-first century), 89
England (Victorian era)
    Etiquette & Espionage (Carriger), 112
    Larklight (Reeve), 128
    The Lie Tree (Hardinge), 48
entrapment. *See* imprisonment/
    entrapment
environmental justice, 94
epic/grand-scale stories, 52
escapes
    Airman (Colfer), 119
    The Book of Boy (Murdock), 98
    Ghostopolis (TenNapel), 38
    Illegal (Eoin & Donkin), 31
    Incarceron (Fisher), 113
    Inside Out & Back Again (Lai), 147

Like Water on Stone (Walrath), 151
    The Red Pencil (Pinkney), 149
    Unbound (Burg), 142
etiquette, 112
exile/banishment
    Airman (Colfer), 119
    Stone Mirrors: The Sculpture and
      Silence of Edmonia Lewis (Atkins), 139
experiments, 126
exploration of unknown lands/places
    The Book of Boy (Murdock), 98
    The Quest to the Uncharted Lands
      (Johnson), 122
Exposition Universelle (Paris, 1889), 53

F

factories/factory workers
    Audacity (Crowder), 143
    Pashmina (Nidhi), 35
failings of the legal system
    American Street (Zoboi), 91
    The Walls Around Us (Suma), 104–105
fairy tale-inspired stories
    Hamster Princess: Harriet the Invincible
      (Vernon), 40
    Mechanica (Cornwell), 120
    The Peculiar (Bachmann), 117
    When the Moon Was Ours (McLemore),
      96
family
    American Street (Zoboi), 91
    The Astonishing Color of After (Pan),
      100
    Audacity (Crowder), 143
    Brown Girl Dreaming (Woodson), 153
    Catching a Storyfish (Harrington), 145
    The Collected Essex County (Lemire),
      34
    Crenshaw (Applegate), 92
    The Crossover (Alexander), 135
    Garvey's Choice (Grimes), 145
    Home of the Brave (Applegate), 138
    Illegal (Eoin & Donkin), 31
    Inside Out & Back Again (Lai), 147
    Like Water on Stone (Walrath), 151
    Lucky Strike (Pyron), 101
    The Nest (Oppel), 100

164 SUBJECT/THEME/APPEALS INDEX

family *(continued)*
    Other Words for Home (Warga), 152
    The Red Pencil (Pinkney), 149
    Salt: A Story of Friendship in a Time of War (Frost), 144
    Serafina's Promise (Burg), 141
    The Strange and Beautiful Sorrows of Ava Lavender (Walton), 106
    Unbound (Burg), 142
    Under the Mesquite (McCall), 148
    A Year without Mom (Tolstikova), 39
family (extended), 33
family (nontraditional), 118
family secrets
    Pashmina (Nidhi), 35
    When the Moon Was Ours (McLemore), 97
    Wonderstruck (Selznick), 36
fantastical or folklore animals
    Airborn (Oppel), 114
    The Golden Compass (Pullman), 126
far future
    Fever Crumb (Reeve), 127
    Incarceron (Fisher), 113
    Mortal Engines (Reeve), 115
farm life
    Bone Gap (Ruby), 90
    Home of the Brave (Applegate), 138
    The Lightning Queen (Resau), 103
    The Red Pencil (Pinkney), 149
    When the Moon Was Ours (McLemore), 97
fashion industry, 143
fashion/dress, 58
father-daughter relationships
    The Astonishing Color of After (Pan), 100
    The Golden Compass (Pullman), 126
    Incarceron (Fisher), 113
    The Lie Tree (Hardinge), 48
father-son relationships
    All the Broken Pieces (Burg), 136
    The Boundless (Oppel), 124
    Garvey's Choice (Grimes), 145
    A Monster Calls (Ness), 89
female characters. *See* strong female characters

females in unconventional roles/ occupations, 113, 127
feudalism, 98
film/film history
    The Lightning Queen (Resau), 103
    Wonderstruck (Selznick), 36
fishing, 145
flappers, 51
Florida, 101
forgiveness
    The Book of Boy (Murdock), 98
    The Collected Essex County (Lemire), 34
    Midwinterblood (Sedgwick), 104
    A Monster Calls (Ness), 89
    Out of the Dust (Hesse), 146
    Release (Ness), 99
    When the Moon Was Ours (McLemore), 97
foster children, 138
France (medieval period)
    The Book of Boy (Murdock), 98
    The Inquisitor's Tale, or, The Three Magical Children and Their Holy Dog (Gidwitz), 55
    The Passion of Dolssa (Berry), 50
France (nineteenth century), 53
free will
    Ghostopolis (TenNapel), 38
    The Golden Compass (Pullman), 126
    Midwinterblood (Sedgwick), 104
freedom, 142
friars, 50
friendship
    American Born Chinese (Yang), 29
    The Astonishing Color of After (Pan), 100
    Belzhar (Wolitzer), 107
    Brown Girl Dreaming (Woodson), 153
    Catching a Storyfish (Harrington), 145
    The Collected Essex County (Lemire), 34
    Crenshaw (Applegate), 92
    Dragon's Keep (Carey), 52
    Dread Nation (Ireland), 57
    El Deafo (Bell), 26
    Garvey's Choice (Grimes), 145

SUBJECT/THEME/APPEALS INDEX

A Great and Terrible Beauty (Bray), 46
Hey, Kiddo (Krosoczka), 33
Home of the Brave (Applegate), 138
Honor Girl (Thrash), 39
*The Inquisitor's Tale, or, The Three
    Magical Children and Their Holy Dog*
    (Gidwitz), 55
The Lightning Queen (Resau), 103
Lucky Strike (Pyron), 101
The Mark of the Dragonfly (Johnson),
    113
Me and Marvin Gardens (King), 94
Mechanica (Cornwell), 120
New Kid (Craft), 27
Other Words for Home (Warga), 152
The Quest to the Uncharted Lands
    (Johnson), 122
Release (Ness), 99
Roller Girl (Jamieson), 32
*Salt: A Story of Friendship in a Time of
    War* (Frost), 144
Serafina's Promise (Burg), 141
Smile (Telgemeier), 28
Speak: The Graphic Novel (Anderson &
    Carroll), 30
Summer of Salt (Leno), 95
Swing It, Sunny (Holm & Holm), 31
The Walls Around Us (Suma), 105
When the Moon Was Ours (McLemore),
    97
Wonderstruck (Selznick), 36
A Year without Mom (Tolstikova), 39
future. *See* far future
futuristic settings
    Fever Crumb (Reeve), 127
    Incarceron (Fisher), 112
    Mortal Engines (Reeve), 115

G

gangs, 119
garbage/junk
    Heap House (Carey), 47
    Me and Marvin Gardens (King), 94
gardens
    Thornhill (Smy), 37
    Under the Mesquite (McCall), 148

gender identity, 97
gender roles (nineteenth century), 48
gender roles (twentieth century)
    Audacity (Crowder), 143
    Honor Girl (Thrash), 39
    The Lightning Queen (Resau), 103
    Pashmina (Nidhi), 35
    *The Strange and Beautiful Sorrows of
        Ava Lavender* (Walton), 106
    Under the Mesquite (McCall), 148
gender roles (twenty-first century)
    American Street (Zoboi), 91
    Bone Gap (Ruby), 90
    Garvey's Choice (Grimes), 145
    The Poet X (Acevedo), 134
    The Red Pencil (Pinkney), 149
    Roller Girl (Jamieson), 32
    Spinning (Walden), 41
    The Walls Around Us (Suma), 105
    When the Moon Was Ours (McLemore),
        97
genetic engineering, 116
genocide
    Like Water on Stone (Walrath), 151
    The Red Pencil (Pinkney), 149
gentrification, 27
ghost stories
    American Street (Zoboi), 91
    The Astonishing Color of After (Pan),
        100
    *The Charmed Children of Rookskill
        Castle* (Fox), 54
    Ghostopolis (TenNapel), 38
    Long Way Down (Reynolds), 150
    Pashmina (Nidhi), 35
    The Poisoned House (Ford), 54
    Release (Ness), 98
    Thornhill (Smy), 37
    The Walls Around Us (Suma), 104
ghosts
    The Astonishing Color of After (Pan),
        100
    *The Charmed Children of Rookskill
        Castle* (Fox), 54
    Ghostopolis (TenNapel), 38
    Long Way Down (Reynolds), 150
    Pashmina (Nidhi), 35

166   SUBJECT/THEME/APPEALS INDEX

ghosts *(continued)*
The Poisoned House (Ford), 54
Release (Ness), 99
The Strange and Beautiful Sorrows of
   Ava Lavender (Walton), 106
Thirteen Doorways, Wolves behind Them
   All (Ruby), 60
Thornhill (Smy), 37
gifted children or teens
The Astonishing Color of After (Pan),
   100
The Mark of the Dragonfly (Johnson),
   113
The Walls Around Us (Suma), 105
girls disguised as boys, 116
goblins
Ghostopolis (TenNapel), 38
Goblin Secrets (Alexander), 117
The Peculiars (McQuerry), 123
Gothic settings/atmosphere
Bone Gap (Ruby), 90
The Charmed Children of Rookskill
   Castle (Fox), 54
Clockwork, or All Wound Up
   (Pullman), 125
The Poisoned House (Ford), 54
Splendors and Glooms (Schlitz), 61
Thornhill (Smy), 37
gradually unfolding stories
All the Broken Pieces (Burg), 136
American Street (Zoboi), 91
Belzhar (Wolitzer), 107
The Book of Boy (Murdock), 97
The Diviners (Bray), 51
Long Way Down (Reynolds), 150
The Nest (Oppel), 99
The Strange and Beautiful Sorrows of
   Ava Lavender (Walton), 105
The Thief Lord (Funke), 93
The Walls Around Us (Suma), 104
When the Moon Was Ours
   (McLemore), 96
grandfathers
Brown Girl Dreaming (Woodson), 153
Catching a Storyfish (Harrington), 145
Hey, Kiddo (Krosoczka), 33
Swing It, Sunny (Holm & Holm), 31

grandmothers, 89
grief/loss
The Astonishing Color of After (Pan),
   100
Belzhar (Wolitzer), 107
The Book of Boy (Murdock), 98
The Collected Essex County (Lemire),
   34
The Crossover (Alexander), 135
Inside Out & Back Again (Lai), 147
The Lightning Queen (Resau), 103
Like Water on Stone (Walrath), 151
Long Way Down (Reynolds), 150
Midwinterblood (Sedgwick), 104
A Monster Calls (Ness), 89
Out of the Dust (Hesse), 146
Pablo and Birdy (McGhee), 88
The Red Pencil (Pinkney), 149
Serafina's Promise (Burg), 141
The Strange and Beautiful Sorrows of
   Ava Lavender (Walton), 106
Under the Mesquite (McCall), 148
grotesque/bizarre characters, 118
guilt
The Astonishing Color of After (Pan),
   100
The Book of Boy (Murdock), 98
The Collected Essex County (Lemire), 34
A Monster Calls (Ness), 89
Release (Ness), 99
The Walls Around Us (Suma), 105
gun violence
American Street (Zoboi), 91
Illegal (Eoin & Donkin), 31
Long Way Down (Reynolds), 150

H

Haiti, 141
haunted houses
The Poisoned House (Ford), 54
The Strange and Beautiful Sorrows of
   Ava Lavender (Walton), 106
Thornhill (Smy), 37
healing/healers
The Lightning Queen (Resau), 103
The Mark of the Dragonfly (Johnson),
   113

SUBJECT/THEME/APPEALS INDEX 167

The Quest to the Uncharted Lands
(Johnson), 122
When the Moon Was Ours
(McLemore), 97
heist stories
The Gilded Wolves (Chokshi), 53
The Thief Lord (Funke), 93
heritage/ancestry
The Astonishing Color of After (Pan),
101
The Lightning Queen (Resau), 103
Pablo and Birdy (McGhee), 88
*The Strange and Beautiful Sorrows
of Ava Lavender* (Walton), 106
Summer of Salt (Leno), 95
heroes/mentors
Dragon's Keep (Carey), 52
Love That Dog (Creech), 137
Roller Girl (Jamieson), 32
Spinning (Walden), 41
high school life
American Street (Zoboi), 91
The Astonishing Color of After (Pan),
101
Belzhar (Wolitzer), 107
The Poet X (Acevedo), 134
Speak: The Graphic Novel (Anderson
& Carroll), 30
Under the Mesquite (McCall), 148
historians, 115
Historical Fiction
All the Broken Pieces (Burg), 136
Audacity (Crowder), 143
The Book of Boy (Murdock), 97
The Lightning Queen (Resau), 102
Like Water on Stone (Walrath), 151
Out of the Dust (Hesse), 146
*Salt: A Story of Friendship in a Time of
War* (Frost), 144
*Stone Mirrors: The Sculpture and
Silence of Edmonia Lewis* (Atkins),
139
*The Strange and Beautiful Sorrows of
Ava Lavender* (Walton), 105
Swing It, Sunny (Holm & Holm),
31
Unbound (Burg), 142

Wonderstruck (Selznick), 36
homefront stories
*The Charmed Children of Rookskill
Castle* (Fox), 54
*Salt: A Story of Friendship in a Time of
War* (Frost), 144
*Thirteen Doorways, Wolves behind Them
All* (Ruby), 60
homelessness
Crenshaw (Applegate), 92
Like Water on Stone (Walrath), 151
Serafina's Promise (Burg), 141
homosexuality
Honor Girl (Thrash), 39
Spinning (Walden), 41
Horror elements
Clockwork Angel (Clare), 118
Midwinterblood (Sedgwick), 103
The Nest (Oppel), 99
human experimentation, 127
humor
The Book of Boy (Murdock), 97
Catching a Storyfish (Harrington),
145
Crenshaw (Applegate), 92
El Deafo (Bell), 26
Garvey's Choice (Grimes), 144
Ghostopolis (TenNapel), 38
Goblin Secrets (Alexander), 117
Hamster Princess: Harriet the Invincible
(Vernon), 40
Home of the Brave (Applegate), 138
Honor Girl (Thrash), 38
Larklight (Reeve), 127
Little Cat's Luck (Bauer), 140
Love That Dog (Creech), 137
Lucky Strike (Pyron), 101
Me and Marvin Gardens (King), 94
New Kid (Craft), 27
Other Words for Home (Warga), 152
Pablo and Birdy (McGhee), 88
Secrets at Sea (Peck), 50
Smile (Telgemeier), 28
*Sweep: The Story of a Girl and Her
Monster* (Auxier), 46
Swing It, Sunny (Holm & Holm), 31
The Thief Lord (Funke), 93

SUBJECT/THEME/APPEALS INDEX

hunger/food insecurity, 92
hunting/hunters, 144

I

ice-skating, 41
idealized village settings
    The Lightning Queen (Resau), 102
    Pablo and Birdy (McGhee), 88
illiteracy. *See* literacy/illiteracy
illness
    The Crossover (Alexander), 135
    Illegal (Eoin & Donkin), 31
    The Nest (Oppel), 100
illness (terminal)
    The Collected Essex County (Lemire), 34
    Ghostopolis (TenNapel), 38
    A Monster Calls (Ness), 89
    Under the Mesquite (McCall), 148
imaginary friends, 92
immigration
    All the Broken Pieces (Burg), 136
    Audacity (Crowder), 143
    Home of the Brave (Applegate), 138
    Illegal (Eoin & Donkin), 31
    Inside Out & Back Again (Lai), 147
    The Lightning Queen (Resau), 103
    Like Water on Stone (Walrath), 151
    Pablo and Birdy (McGhee), 88
    A Year without Mom (Tolstikova), 39
immortality, 104
imperialism, 128
imprisonment/entrapment
    Airman (Colfer), 119
    Bone Gap (Ruby), 90
    The Golden Compass (Pullman), 126
    Incarceron (Fisher), 113
    The Walls Around Us (Suma), 105
India, 35
Indigenous peoples (Mexico), 103
Indigenous peoples (United States)
    Me and Marvin Gardens (King), 94
    Salt: A Story of Friendship in a Time of War (Frost), 144
    Stone Mirrors: The Sculpture and Silence of Edmonia Lewis (Atkins), 139
influence of popular culture

American Born Chinese (Yang), 29
Other Words for Home (Warga), 152
inns/taverns
    Clockwork, or All Wound Up (Pullman), 125
    The Inquisitor's Tale, or, The Three Magical Children and Their Holy Dog (Gidwitz), 55
    The Passion of Dolssa (Berry), 50
Inquisition
    The Inquisitor's Tale, or, The Three Magical Children and Their Holy Dog (Gidwitz), 55
    The Passion of Dolssa (Berry), 50
instinct, 140
inventions/inventors
    Airman (Colfer), 119
    Etiquette & Espionage (Carriger), 112
    The Inquisitor's Apprentice (Moriarty), 58
    Mechanica (Cornwell), 120
    The Peculiars (McQuerry), 123
invisibility, 122
Islam, 149
islands
    Airman (Colfer), 119
    Dragon's Keep (Carey), 52
    The Lie Tree (Hardinge), 48
    Midwinterblood (Sedgwick), 104
    Serafina's Promise (Burg), 141

J

jealousy
    The Collected Essex County (Lemire), 34
    Ghostopolis (TenNapel), 38
    Honor Girl (Thrash), 39
    Little Cat's Luck (Bauer), 140
    Other Words for Home (Warga), 152
    Roller Girl (Jamieson), 32
    Serafina's Promise (Burg), 141
    The Walls Around Us (Suma), 105
    A Year without Mom (Tolstikova), 39
Jewish boys, 58
Jewish descent, 143
Jews, 55

SUBJECT/THEME/APPEALS INDEX

journeys/quests
  The Book of Boy (Murdock), 98
  Ghostopolis (TenNapel), 38
  Little Cat's Luck (Bauer), 140
  The Quest to the Uncharted Lands
    (Johnson), 122
  Wonderstruck (Selznick), 36

K
kidnapping
  Bone Gap (Ruby), 90
  The Golden Compass (Pullman), 126
  Larklight (Reeve), 128
  The Peculiar (Bachmann), 117
  Splendors and Glooms (Schlitz), 61
  When the Moon Was Ours (McLemore),
    97
killer stalking a character, 127
knights, 125

L
labor exploitation, 143
labor unions, 143
language. *See* accents (language);
    learning a new language
Latino/a Americans
  New Kid (Craft), 27
  Under the Mesquite (McCall), 148
learning. *See* education/learning
learning a new language
  The Astonishing Color of After (Pan),
    101
  Audacity (Crowder), 143
  Home of the Brave (Applegate), 138
  Inside Out & Back Again (Lai), 147
  The Lightning Queen (Resau), 103
  Other Words for Home (Warga), 152
  Serafina's Promise (Burg), 141
LGBTQIA
  Midwinterblood (Sedgwick), 104
  Release (Ness), 99
  Summer of Salt (Leno), 95
  When the Moon Was Ours (McLemore),
    97
libraries/librarians
  Audacity (Crowder), 143
  Catching a Storyfish (Harrington), 145

The Peculiars (McQuerry), 123
likeable/relatable characters
  Airborn (Oppel), 114
  Brown Girl Dreaming (Woodson), 153
  Catching a Storyfish (Harrington), 145
  Crenshaw (Applegate), 92
  El Deafo (Bell), 26
  Garvey's Choice (Grimes), 144
  Home of the Brave (Applegate), 138
  The Lightning Queen (Resau), 102
  Little Cat's Luck (Bauer), 140
  Love That Dog (Creech), 137
  Lucky Strike (Pyron), 101
  Mark of the Thief (Nielsen), 59
  Murder, Magic, and What We Wore
    (Jones), 58
  New Kid (Craft), 27
  The Passion of Dolssa (Berry), 50
  Release (Ness), 98
  Roller Girl (Jamieson), 32
  Secrets at Sea (Peck), 50
  Smile (Telgemeier), 28
  Summer of Salt (Leno), 95
  *Sweep: The Story of a Girl and Her
    Monster* (Auxier), 46
  *Thirteen Doorways, Wolves behind Them
    All* (Ruby), 60
  A Year without Mom (Tolstikova), 39
literacy/illiteracy
  Audacity (Crowder), 143
  The Book of Boy (Murdock), 98
  The Lightning Queen (Resau), 103
  The Red Pencil (Pinkney), 149
  Serafina's Promise (Burg), 141
  Unbound (Burg), 142
literary allusions
  The Astonishing Color of After (Pan),
    101
  Belzhar (Wolitzer), 107
  Bone Gap (Ruby), 90
  Crenshaw (Applegate), 92
  Love That Dog (Creech), 137
  *Stone Mirrors: The Sculpture and
    Silence of Edmonia Lewis* (Atkins), 139
  Summer of Salt (Leno), 95
  When the Moon Was Ours (McLemore),
    97

London, 127
London (Victorian era)
Clockwork Angel (Clare), 118
Heap House (Carey), 47
Splendors and Glooms (Schlitz), 61
Sweep: The Story of a Girl and Her Monster (Auxier), 46
loss. *See* grief/loss
lying
Crenshaw (Applegate), 92
The Lie Tree (Hardinge), 48
Roller Girl (Jamieson), 32
Unbound (Burg), 142
lyrical prose, 48

M

machinists/mechanics
The Mark of the Dragonfly (Johnson), 113
Mechanica (Cornwell), 120
magical trees
The Lie Tree (Hardinge), 48
A Monster Calls (Ness), 89
magicians, 61
mansions, 47
materialism, 47
mechanical or clockwork creatures
The Charmed Children of Rookskill Castle (Fox), 54
Clockwork, or All Wound Up (Pullman), 125
Goblin Secrets (Alexander), 117
Mechanica (Cornwell), 120
The Peculiar (Bachmann), 117
The Quest to the Uncharted Lands (Johnson), 122
mechanical or electronic devices
Fever Crumb (Reeve), 127
Mechanica (Cornwell), 120
media influence on identity
Honor Girl (Thrash), 39
New Kid (Craft), 27
Roller Girl (Jamieson), 32
Swing It, Sunny (Holm & Holm), 31
medieval settings
Dragon's Keep (Carey), 52
Grave Mercy (LaFevers), 49

The Inquisitor's Tale, or, The Three Magical Children and Their Holy Dog (Gidwitz), 55
The Passion of Dolssa (Berry), 50
Memoir
Brown Girl Dreaming (Woodson), 153
El Deafo (Bell), 26
Hey, Kiddo (Krosoczka), 33
Honor Girl (Thrash), 38
Inside Out & Back Again (Lai), 147
Smile (Telgemeier), 28
Spinning (Walden), 41
Under the Mesquite (McCall), 148
A Year without Mom (Tolstikova), 39
mice, 50
mice/rodents (talking), 140
Middle Ages, 98
middle school life
The Crossover (Alexander), 135
New Kid (Craft), 27
Other Words for Home (Warga), 152
Roller Girl (Jamieson), 32
Smile (Telgemeier), 28
A Year without Mom (Tolstikova), 39
mid-twentieth-century settings
All the Broken Pieces (Burg), 136
The Strange and Beautiful Sorrows of Ava Lavender (Walton), 105
(the) Midwest (United States)
Bone Gap (Ruby), 90
Catching a Storyfish (Harrington), 145
Home of the Brave (Applegate), 138
Other Words for Home (Warga), 152
Salt: A Story of Friendship in a Time of War (Frost), 144
Stone Mirrors: The Sculpture and Silence of Edmonia Lewis (Atkins), 139
mines/mining
Airman (Colfer), 119
The Peculiars (McQuerry), 123
miracles
The Book of Boy (Murdock), 98
The Inquisitor's Tale, or, The Three Magical Children and Their Holy Dog (Gidwitz), 55
The Passion of Dolssa (Berry), 50

SUBJECT/THEME/APPEALS INDEX

missing persons
Belzhar (Wolitzer), 107
The Charmed Children of Rookskill Castle (Fox), 54
Clockwork Angel (Clare), 118
The Clockwork Scarab (Gleason), 121
Goblin Secrets (Alexander), 117
The Golden Compass (Pullman), 126
Home of the Brave (Applegate), 138
Inside Out & Back Again (Lai), 147
The Peculiar (Bachmann), 117
Serafina's Promise (Burg), 141
Splendors and Glooms (Schlitz), 61
monsters
A Monster Calls (Ness), 89
Sweep: The Story of a Girl and Her Monster (Auxier), 46
moral dilemmas, 104
mother-daughter relationships
American Street (Zoboi), 91
The Astonishing Color of After (Pan), 101
Dragon's Keep (Carey), 52
A Great and Terrible Beauty (Bray), 46
The Lie Tree (Hardinge), 48
Pashmina (Nidhi), 35
The Poet X (Acevedo), 134
The Red Pencil (Pinkney), 149
Roller Girl (Jamieson), 32
A Year without Mom (Tolstikova), 39
moving/relocating, 39
multiple intertwined storylines
American Born Chinese (Yang), 29
American Street (Zoboi), 91
The Astonishing Color of After (Pan), 100
The Diviners (Bray), 51
Ghostopolis (TenNapel), 38
Love That Dog (Creech), 137
Midwinterblood (Sedgwick), 103
The Passion of Dolssa (Berry), 50
Splendors and Glooms (Schlitz), 61
The Strange and Beautiful Sorrows of Ava Lavender (Walton), 105
The Walls Around Us (Suma), 104
multiple perspectives
Catching a Storyfish (Harrington), 145

The Gilded Wolves (Chokshi), 53
The Inquisitor's Tale, or, The Three Magical Children and Their Holy Dog (Gidwitz), 55
Like Water on Stone (Walrath), 151
Long Way Down (Reynolds), 150
The Passion of Dolssa (Berry), 50
The Thief Lord (Funke), 93
murder
The Lie Tree (Hardinge), 48
Long Way Down (Reynolds), 150
Release (Ness), 99
The Walls Around Us (Suma), 105
murder investigation
The Clockwork Scarab (Gleason), 121
Murder, Magic, and What We Wore (Jones), 58
museums
The Clockwork Scarab (Gleason), 121
Mortal Engines (Reeve), 115
Wonderstruck (Selznick), 36
music
All the Broken Pieces (Burg), 136
The Crossover (Alexander), 135
Garvey's Choice (Grimes), 145
Illegal (Eoin & Donkin), 31
Like Water on Stone (Walrath), 151
Out of the Dust (Hesse), 146
The Poet X (Acevedo), 135
mystery/suspense
Airborn (Oppel), 114
American Street (Zoboi), 91
Bone Gap (Ruby), 90
The Book of Boy (Murdock), 97
The Inquisitor's Apprentice (Moriarty), 58
The Lie Tree (Hardinge), 48
Lucky Strike (Pyron), 101
The Mark of the Dragonfly (Johnson), 113
Midwinterblood (Sedgwick), 103
A Monster Calls (Ness), 89
The Nest (Oppel), 99
Summer of Salt (Leno), 95
Thornhill (Smy), 37
The Walls Around Us (Suma), 104

172   SUBJECT/THEME/APPEALS INDEX

mystery/suspense *(continued)*
> *When the Moon Was Ours* (McLemore),
> 96
> *Wonderstruck* (Selznick), 36

myths/legends
> *American Born Chinese* (Yang), 29
> *Midwinterblood* (Sedgwick), 104

N

nature versus nurture, 123
New York City, 135
New York City (twenty-first century), 27
New York (early twentieth-century)
> *Audacity* (Crowder), 143
> *The Diviners* (Bray), 51
> *The Inquisitor's Apprentice* (Moriarty),
> 58

New York (post-World War II), 36
nightmares. *See* dreams/nightmares
nineteenth-century settings
> *Airman* (Colfer), 119
> *The Boundless* (Oppel), 124
> *Clockwork Angel* (Clare), 118
> *The Clockwork Scarab* (Gleason), 121
> *Dread Nation* (Ireland), 57
> *The Gilded Wolves* (Chokshi), 53
> *A Great and Terrible Beauty* (Bray), 46
> *Heap House* (Carey), 47
> *Murder, Magic, and What We Wore*
> (Jones), 58
> *The Poisoned House* (Ford), 54
> *Stone Mirrors: The Sculpture and Silence*
> *of Edmonia Lewis* (Atkins), 139
> *Sweep: The Story of a Girl and Her*
> *Monster* (Auxier), 46

nontraditional families, 88
nuns, 49

O

oceans, 31
offbeat stories, 47
Oklahoma, 146
ominous atmosphere
> *American Street* (Zoboi), 91
> *Incarceron* (Fisher), 112
> *Midwinterblood* (Sedgwick), 103
> *A Monster Calls* (Ness), 89

> *The Nest* (Oppel), 99
> *Release* (Ness), 98
> *The Walls Around Us* (Suma), 104
> *When the Moon Was Ours* (McLemore),
> 96

Oregon, 32
orphanages, 60
orphans
> *Goblin Secrets* (Alexander), 117
> *Leviathan* (Westerfeld), 116
> *Mechanica* (Cornwell), 120
> *Thirteen Doorways, Wolves behind Them*
> *All* (Ruby), 60
> *Thornhill* (Smy), 37
> *Wonderstruck* (Selznick), 36

outer space, 127

P

passion. *See* driving force/passion
peasants, 55
perseverance/determination
> *Mechanica* (Cornwell), 120
> *The Peculiars* (McQuerry), 123
> *The Poet X* (Acevedo), 135
> *Serafina's Promise* (Burg), 141
> *Stone Mirrors: The Sculpture and Silence*
> *of Edmonia Lewis* (Atkins), 139

perspectives. *See* alternating perspectives;
> multiple perspectives

pets
> *Crenshaw* (Applegate), 92
> *Little Cat's Luck* (Bauer), 140
> *Love That Dog* (Creech), 137
> *The Red Pencil* (Pinkney), 149

pilots, 116
pirates
> *Airborn* (Oppel), 114
> *Larklight* (Reeve), 128

Plague, 98
plot twists. *See* unexpected plot twists
poetic language
> *The Astonishing Color of After* (Pan),
> 100
> *Bone Gap* (Ruby), 90
> *The Collected Essex County* (Lemire), 34
> *A Monster Calls* (Ness), 89
> *The Nest* (Oppel), 99

SUBJECT/THEME/APPEALS INDEX

Speak: The Graphic Novel (Anderson & Carroll), 30
The Strange and Beautiful Sorrows of Ava Lavender (Walton), 105
poetry
  The Astonishing Color of After (Pan), 101
  Brown Girl Dreaming (Woodson), 153
  Catching a Storyfish (Harrington), 145
  Love That Dog (Creech), 137
  The Poet X (Acevedo), 135
  Under the Mesquite (McCall), 148
poisoning/poisons
  Grave Mercy (LaFevers), 49
  The Walls Around Us (Suma), 105
political corruption
  The Golden Compass (Pullman), 126
  Incarceron (Fisher), 113
  Mortal Engines (Reeve), 115
  The Peculiar (Bachmann), 117
political intrigue
  The Gilded Wolves (Chokshi), 53
  Grave Mercy (LaFevers), 49
  Mark of the Thief (Nielsen), 59
political oppression
  Ghostopolis (TenNapel), 38
  Like Water on Stone (Walrath), 151
  The Mark of the Dragonfly (Johnson), 113
pollution
  The Mark of the Dragonfly (Johnson), 113
  Me and Marvin Gardens (King), 94
postapocalyptic world, 115
post–Civil War era (American), 57
postmodern stories
  The Astonishing Color of After (Pan), 100
  Clockwork, or All Wound Up (Pullman), 125
  The Collected Essex County (Lemire), 34
  Hey, Kiddo (Krosoczka), 33
  Midwinterblood (Sedgwick), 103
  The Nest (Oppel), 99
  Speak: The Graphic Novel (Anderson & Carroll), 30
postwar life, 56

poverty
  American Street (Zoboi), 91
  Audacity (Crowder), 143
  Crenshaw (Applegate), 92
  Illegal (Eoin & Donkin), 31
  Inside Out & Back Again (Lai), 147
  Out of the Dust (Hesse), 146
  The Red Pencil (Pinkney), 149
  Serafina's Promise (Burg), 141
  Under the Mesquite (McCall), 148
princes
  Clockwork, or All Wound Up (Pullman), 125
  Leviathan (Westerfeld), 116
  Mechanica (Cornwell), 120
princesses
  Airman (Colfer), 119
  Dragon's Keep (Carey), 52
prisoners
  Airman (Colfer), 119
  Incarceron (Fisher), 113
prisons/jails, 105
problem solving, 101
prophecies/omens
  Dragon's Keep (Carey), 52
  The Golden Compass (Pullman), 126
psychic ability
  The Diviners (Bray), 51
  The Strange and Beautiful Sorrows of Ava Lavender (Walton), 106
psychological focus
  All the Broken Pieces (Burg), 136
  The Astonishing Color of After (Pan), 100
  Audacity (Crowder), 143
  Bone Gap (Ruby), 90
  The Collected Essex County (Lemire), 34
  Cuckoo Song (Hardinge), 56
  Hey, Kiddo (Krosoczka), 33
  Inside Out & Back Again (Lai), 147
  The Lie Tree (Hardinge), 48
  A Monster Calls (Ness), 89
  The Nest (Oppel), 99
  Out of the Dust (Hesse), 146
  The Red Pencil (Pinkney), 149
  Release (Ness), 98
  Serafina's Promise (Burg), 141

174 SUBJECT/THEME/APPEALS INDEX

psychological focus *(continued)*
    Speak: The Graphic Novel (Anderson &
      Carroll), 30
    Spinning (Walden), 41
    Summer of Salt (Leno), 95
    Unbound (Burg), 142
    When the Moon Was Ours (McLemore),
      96
psychological suspense
    Cuckoo Song (Hardinge), 56
    The Poisoned House (Ford), 54
puppets/puppeteers, 61
purpose in life, 41

Q

Queen Victoria's Diamond Jubilee, 50

R

racial segregation, 153
racism
    All the Broken Pieces (Burg), 136
    Brown Girl Dreaming (Woodson), 153
    Inside Out & Back Again (Lai), 147
    The Lightning Queen (Resau), 103
    New Kid (Craft), 27
    Other Words for Home (Warga), 152
    *Stone Mirrors: The Sculpture and
      Silence of Edmonia Lewis* (Atkins), 139
    Unbound (Burg), 142
    The Walls Around Us (Suma), 105
railway travel, 124
Realistic Fiction
    Bone Gap (Ruby), 90
    Catching a Storyfish (Harrington), 145
    Crenshaw (Applegate), 92
    The Crossover (Alexander), 135
    Garvey's Choice (Grimes), 144
    Home of the Brave (Applegate), 138
    Inside Out & Back Again (Lai), 147
    Long Way Down (Reynolds), 149
    Lucky Strike (Pyron), 101
    Me and Marvin Gardens (King), 94
    New Kid (Craft), 27
    Other Words for Home (Warga), 152
    Out of the Dust (Hesse), 146
    The Red Pencil (Pinkney), 149
    Serafina's Promise (Burg), 141
    Under the Mesquite (McCall), 148
reality. *See* appearance versus reality

reason/scientific thinking, 127
rebellions, 143
reconciliation, 101
refugees
    All the Broken Pieces (Burg), 136
    Home of the Brave (Applegate), 138
    Illegal (Eoin & Donkin), 31
    Inside Out & Back Again (Lai), 147
    The Red Pencil (Pinkney), 149
Regency novels, 58
religious faith
    American Street (Zoboi), 91
    Brown Girl Dreaming (Woodson),
      153
    *The Inquisitor's Tale, or, The Three
      Magical Children and Their Holy Dog*
      (Gidwitz), 55
    The Passion of Dolssa (Berry), 50
    The Red Pencil (Pinkney), 149
    Release (Ness), 99
rescues
    Illegal (Eoin & Donkin), 31
    Larklight (Reeve), 128
    Midwinterblood (Sedgwick), 104
resilience
    El Deafo (Bell), 26
    Hey, Kiddo (Krosoczka), 33
    *The Strange and Beautiful Sorrows of
      Ava Lavender* (Walton), 106
    A Year without Mom (Tolstikova), 39
revenge
    Airman (Colfer), 119
    Long Way Down (Reynolds), 150
    Thornhill (Smy), 37
richly detailed descriptions
    Clockwork Angel (Clare), 118
    Cuckoo Song (Hardinge), 56
    The Diviners (Bray), 51
    The Gilded Wolves (Chokshi), 53
    The Golden Compass (Pullman), 126
    The Lie Tree (Hardinge), 48
    *Stone Mirrors: The Sculpture and
      Silence of Edmonia Lewis* (Atkins), 139
    Stormdancer (Kristoff), 122
    Thornhill (Smy), 37
    When the Moon Was Ours (McLemore),
      96
    Wonderstruck (Selznick), 36
    A Year without Mom (Tolstikova), 39

SUBJECT/THEME/APPEALS INDEX

robbery/thieves
Airman (Colfer), 119
The Book of Boy (Murdock), 98
The Boundless (Oppel), 124
Illegal (Eoin & Donkin), 31
Larklight (Reeve), 128
romance
The Astonishing Color of After (Pan),
100
Belzhar (Wolitzer), 107
Bone Gap (Ruby), 90
Clockwork Angel (Clare), 118
The Crossover (Alexander), 135
Ghostopolis (TenNapel), 38
The Gilded Wolves (Chokshi), 53
Grave Mercy (LaFevers), 49
Honor Girl (Thrash), 38
The Mark of the Dragonfly (Johnson),
113
Mechanica (Cornwell), 120
Midwinterblood (Sedgwick), 103
The Peculiars (McQuerry), 123
The Poet X (Acevedo), 134
The Quest to the Uncharted Lands
(Johnson), 122
Release (Ness), 98
Summer of Salt (Leno), 95
When the Moon Was Ours (McLemore),
96
Romani, 103
runaways, 36
Russia (twentieth century), 39

S

saints
The Book of Boy (Murdock), 98
The Inquisitor's Tale, or, The Three
Magical Children and Their Holy Dog
(Gidwitz), 55
San Francisco, 92
saving and investment
Audacity (Crowder), 143
Crenshaw (Applegate), 92
Inside Out & Back Again (Lai), 147
Serafina's Promise (Burg), 141
Under the Mesquite (McCall), 148
science versus faith, 48
science versus magic
Crenshaw (Applegate), 92

Lucky Strike (Pyron), 101
scientific exploration, 114
scientific inquiry, 123
scientists
Airman (Colfer), 119
The Quest to the Uncharted Lands
(Johnson), 122
sea adventures
Lucky Strike (Pyron), 101
Secrets at Sea (Peck), 50
sea voyages, 50
séances, 54
seaside towns
Lucky Strike (Pyron), 101–102
Pablo and Birdy (McGhee), 88
Seattle, 106
secret codes/clues
American Street (Zoboi), 91
Bone Gap (Ruby), 90
The Walls Around Us (Suma), 104
Wonderstruck (Selznick), 36
secret societies
Clockwork Angel (Clare), 118
The Clockwork Scarab (Gleason), 121
A Great and Terrible Beauty (Bray), 46
secrets
All the Broken Pieces (Burg), 136
American Street (Zoboi), 91
The Astonishing Color of After (Pan),
101
Dragon's Keep (Carey), 52
Leviathan (Westerfeld), 116
The Lie Tree (Hardinge), 48
The Poisoned House (Ford), 54
Release (Ness), 99
Speak: The Graphic Novel (Anderson &
Carroll), 30
Stone Mirrors: The Sculpture and
Silence of Edmonia Lewis (Atkins), 139
Summer of Salt (Leno), 95
The Walls Around Us (Suma), 105
self-esteem
American Born Chinese (Yang), 29
Belzhar (Wolitzer), 107
El Deafo (Bell), 26
Garvey's Choice (Grimes), 145
Honor Girl (Thrash), 39
Love That Dog (Creech), 137
Lucky Strike (Pyron), 102

176 SUBJECT/THEME/APPEALS INDEX

self-esteem *(continued)*
  The Nest (Oppel), 100
  Smile (Telgemeier), 28
  Summer of Salt (Leno), 95
self-reliance
  Illegal (Eoin & Donkin), 31
  Under the Mesquite (McCall), 148
self-sacrifice
  Ghostopolis (TenNapel), 38
  Illegal (Eoin & Donkin), 31
serfdom, 98
serial killer investigation, 121
serial killers, 51
servants
  Heap House (Carey), 47
  The Poisoned House (Ford), 54
seventeenth-century settings
  Salt: A Story of Friendship in a Time of War (Frost), 144
  Unbound (Burg), 142
sex
  American Street (Zoboi), 91
  Release (Ness), 99
  The Strange and Beautiful Sorrows of Ava Lavender (Walton), 106
  The Walls Around Us (Suma), 105
  When the Moon Was Ours (McLemore), 97
sexual violence
  Bone Gap (Ruby), 90
  Like Water on Stone (Walrath), 151
  Speak: The Graphic Novel (Anderson & Carroll), 30
  Spinning (Walden), 41
  Stone Mirrors: The Sculpture and Silence of Edmonia Lewis (Atkins), 139
  The Strange and Beautiful Sorrows of Ava Lavender (Walton), 106
  Summer of Salt (Leno), 95
shapeshifters, 118
ships, 50
shyness
  Catching a Storyfish (Harrington), 145
  The Strange and Beautiful Sorrows of Ava Lavender (Walton), 106
simplified lifestyles, 102
single-parent families

Pashmina (Nidhi), 35
Roller Girl (Jamieson), 32
sinister atmosphere
  The Charmed Children of Rookskill Castle (Fox), 54
  Clockwork, or All Wound Up (Pullman), 125
  Cuckoo Song (Hardinge), 56
  The Lie Tree (Hardinge), 48
  The Peculiar (Bachmann), 117
sisters
  The Red Pencil (Pinkney), 149
  Summer of Salt (Leno), 95
  When the Moon Was Ours (McLemore), 97
  See also brother-sister relationships
skeletons, 38
slavery/slaves
  Dread Nation (Ireland), 57
  Mark of the Thief (Nielsen), 59
  Unbound (Burg), 142
slums
  Audacity (Crowder), 143
  The Peculiar (Bachmann), 117
small town life. *See* village/small town life
smugglers, 31
snobbery/elitism, 47
socioeconomic differences. *See* class/ socioeconomic differences
soldiers, 144
sons. *See* father-son relationships
space vehicles, 128
spiders, 128
spies/spying
  Airman (Colfer), 119
  The Charmed Children of Rookskill Castle (Fox), 54
  Etiquette & Espionage (Carriger), 112
  Murder, Magic, and What We Wore (Jones), 58
  The Peculiars (McQuerry), 123
sports
  The Collected Essex County (Lemire), 34
  New Kid (Craft), 27
  Roller Girl (Jamieson), 32

SUBJECT/THEME/APPEALS INDEX

stealing
  Crenshaw (Applegate), 92
  Little Cat's Luck (Bauer), 140
  When the Moon Was Ours (McLemore),
    97
steam-driven technology
  The Boundless (Oppel), 124
  Etiquette & Espionage (Carriger), 112
  Leviathan (Westerfeld), 116
  Mechanica (Cornwell), 120
  The Peculiars (McQuerry), 123
stepmothers, 120
stepsisters, 120
stories
  Brown Girl Dreaming (Woodson), 153
  Catching a Storyfish (Harrington), 145
  Clockwork, or All Wound Up (Pullman),
    125
  *The Inquisitor's Tale, or, The Three
    Magical Children and Their Holy Dog*
    (Gidwitz), 55
  A Monster Calls (Ness), 89
storylines. *See* dual intertwined
    storylines; gradually unfolding
    stories; multiple intertwined
    storylines
stowaways, 122
streetwise characters
  Illegal (Eoin & Donkin), 30
  Long Way Down (Reynolds), 150
  Splendors and Glooms (Schlitz), 61
  *Sweep: The Story of a Girl and Her
    Monster* (Auxier), 46
  The Thief Lord (Funke), 93
strong female characters
  Airborn (Oppel), 114
  Catching a Storyfish (Harrington), 145
  The Diviners (Bray), 51
  Dread Nation (Ireland), 57
  Etiquette & Espionage (Carriger), 112
  Hamster Princess: Harriet the Invincible
    (Vernon), 40
  Honor Girl (Thrash), 38
  Mechanica (Cornwell), 120
  Other Words for Home (Warga), 152
  Pashmina (Nidhi), 35
  The Poet X (Acevedo), 134

Roller Girl (Jamieson), 32
Serafina's Promise (Burg), 141
Spinning (Walden), 41
*Stone Mirrors: The Sculpture and
  Silence of Edmonia Lewis* (Atkins), 139
Stormdancer (Kristoff), 122
Under the Mesquite (McCall), 148
suburban settings
  All the Broken Pieces (Burg), 136
  Catching a Storyfish (Harrington), 145
  El Deafo (Bell), 26
  Garvey's Choice (Grimes), 144
  Little Cat's Luck (Bauer), 140
  Me and Marvin Gardens (King), 94
  Smile (Telgemeier), 28
  Swing It, Sunny (Holm & Holm), 31
  Under the Mesquite (McCall), 148
suicide
  The Astonishing Color of After (Pan),
    101
  Thornhill (Smy), 37
supernatural beings
  American Street (Zoboi), 91
  Midwinterblood (Sedgwick), 104
  Release (Ness), 99
supernatural stories
  American Street (Zoboi), 91
  The Book of Boy (Murdock), 97
  Clockwork, or All Wound Up (Pullman),
    125
  Clockwork Angel (Clare), 118
  Ghostopolis (TenNapel), 38
  A Monster Calls (Ness), 89
  Summer of Salt (Leno), 95
  The Walls Around Us (Suma), 104
survival stories
  Airman (Colfer), 119
  American Street (Zoboi), 91
  Bone Gap (Ruby), 90
  Illegal (Eoin & Donkin), 30
  Inside Out & Back Again (Lai), 147
  Larklight (Reeve), 127
  Like Water on Stone (Walrath), 151
  Mark of the Thief (Nielsen), 59
  Mortal Engines (Reeve), 115
  The Passion of Dolssa (Berry), 50
  The Red Pencil (Pinkney), 149

178 SUBJECT/THEME/APPEALS INDEX

survival stories *(continued)*
    Salt: A Story of Friendship in a Time of War (Frost), 144
    Serafina's Promise (Burg), 141
    The Thief Lord (Funke), 93
    Unbound (Burg), 142
suspense. *See* mystery/suspense
Sylvia Plath, 107

T

teachers
    Belzhar (Wolitzer), 107
    The Lightning Queen (Resau), 103
teachers as mentors
    All the Broken Pieces (Burg), 136
    Love That Dog (Creech), 137
    Me and Marvin Gardens (King), 94
    The Poet X (Acevedo), 135
teamwork/cooperation
    All the Broken Pieces (Burg), 136
    The Clockwork Scarab (Gleason), 121
    Leviathan (Westerfeld), 116
    Little Cat's Luck (Bauer), 140
    Lucky Strike (Pyron), 102
testing. *See* competitions/testing
Texas, 148
thieves. *See* robbery/thieves
time travel
    The Clockwork Scarab (Gleason), 121
    Midwinterblood (Sedgwick), 103
toys (dolls and puppets), 37
trains
    The Boundless (Oppel), 124
    The Mark of the Dragonfly (Johnson), 113
traitors, 38
trauma (emotional or physical)
    Belzhar (Wolitzer), 107
    Summer of Salt (Leno), 95
    The Walls Around Us (Suma), 105
    When the Moon Was Ours (McLemore), 97
Turkey, 151
twins
    American Street (Zoboi), 91
    The Crossover (Alexander), 135

Like Water on Stone (Walrath), 151
The Poet X (Acevedo), 135
The Strange and Beautiful Sorrows of Ava Lavender (Walton), 106
Summer of Salt (Leno), 95

U

underground, 113
unexpected plot twists
    Incarceron (Fisher), 112
    Pashmina (Nidhi), 35
    Summer of Salt (Leno), 95
    The Thief Lord (Funke), 93
unusual/unconventional characters, 127
urban settings
    Brown Girl Dreaming (Woodson), 153
    The Poet X (Acevedo), 134

V

vampires/vampire slayers
    Clockwork Angel (Clare), 118
    The Clockwork Scarab (Gleason), 121
Victorian settings
    Etiquette & Espionage (Carriger), 112
    The Lie Tree (Hardinge), 48
    The Peculiar (Bachmann), 117
    Secrets at Sea (Peck), 50
video games/gaming, 27
Vietnam War
    All the Broken Pieces (Burg), 136
    Inside Out & Back Again (Lai), 147
village/small town life
    Bone Gap (Ruby), 90
    The Lightning Queen (Resau), 103
    Lucky Strike (Pyron), 102
    Pablo and Birdy (McGhee), 88
    When the Moon Was Ours (McLemore), 97
violence/abuse
    American Street (Zoboi), 91
    Release (Ness), 99
    Unbound (Burg), 142
    The Walls Around Us (Suma), 105
    When the Moon Was Ours (McLemore), 97
visions, 55

SUBJECT/THEME/APPEALS INDEX

W
War of 1812, 144
war stories
All the Broken Pieces (Burg), 136
Home of the Brave (Applegate), 138
Inside Out & Back Again (Lai), 147
Leviathan (Westerfeld), 116
Like Water on Stone (Walrath), 151
The Red Pencil (Pinkney), 149
Salt: A Story of Friendship in a Time of War (Frost), 144
war veterans
All the Broken Pieces (Burg), 136
The Poisoned House (Ford), 54
warlocks, 118
wars/battles
Leviathan (Westerfeld), 116
Midwinterblood (Sedgwick), 104
The Red Pencil (Pinkney), 149
wars/battles (imaginary), 38
warships, 116
wealthy girls
Airborn (Oppel), 114
Honor Girl (Thrash), 39
The Walls Around Us (Suma), 105
weapons of mass destruction/bombs, 115
witches
The Charmed Children of Rookskill Castle (Fox), 54
Goblin Secrets (Alexander), 117
The Golden Compass (Pullman), 126
Splendors and Glooms (Schlitz), 61
When the Moon Was Ours (McLemore), 97
witty tone
The Book of Boy (Murdock), 97

Crenshaw (Applegate), 92
The Crossover (Alexander), 135
Dread Nation (Ireland), 57
El Deafo (Bell), 26
Etiquette & Espionage (Carriger), 112
Goblin Secrets (Alexander), 117
Hamster Princess: Harriet the Invincible (Vernon), 40
Heap House (Carey), 47
Honor Girl (Thrash), 38
Murder, Magic, and What We Wore (Jones), 58
New Kid (Craft), 27
The Peculiar (Bachmann), 117
Roller Girl (Jamieson), 32
Smile (Telgemeier), 28
wolves, 36
women in business, 106
words (power of)
Brown Girl Dreaming (Woodson), 153
Summer of Salt (Leno), 95
work, 92
World War I
Leviathan (Westerfeld), 116
Like Water on Stone (Walrath), 151
World War II (homefront life), 54
writers (aspiring), 137
wrongfully accused
Salt: A Story of Friendship in a Time of War (Frost), 144
Summer of Salt (Leno), 95
The Walls Around Us (Suma), 105

Z
zombies, 57

Coping with Challenges Index

A

abandonment/desertion
Beyond the Bright Sea (Wolk), 71
Bone Gap (Ruby), 90
The Book of Lost Things (Voigt), 80
The Case of the Missing Marquess (Springer), 78
The Clockwork Scarab (Gleason), 121
Draw the Dark (Bick), 84
Fever Crumb (Reeve), 127
Hey, Kiddo (Krosoczka), 33
Ink, Iron, and Glass (Clare), 129
The Iron Thorn (Kittredge), 129
Nooks & Crannies (Lawson), 83
Palace of Spies (Zettel), 84
The Peculiars (McQuerry), 123
The Star of Kazan (Ibbotson), 74
The Thief Lord (Funke), 93
Thirteen Doorways, Wolves behind Them All (Ruby), 60

absent parent
Bone Gap (Ruby), 90
The Book of Lost Things (Voigt), 80
Brown Girl Dreaming (Woodson), 153
The Case of the Missing Marquess (Springer), 78
The Collected Essex County (Lemire), 34
Draw the Dark (Bick), 84
Elizabeth and Zenobia (Miller), 76
Everland (Spinale), 130
Hell & High Water (Landman), 84
Hey, Kiddo (Krosoczka), 33
Home of the Brave (Applegate), 138
Mark of the Thief (Nielsen), 59
The Mysterious Howling (Wood), 81

Pashmina (Nidhi), 35
The Secret of Nightingale Wood (Strange), 83
Spy Runner (Yelchin), 82
The Star of Kazan (Ibbotson), 74
Venturess (Cornwell), 129
A Year without Mom (Tolstikova), 39

abuse (emotional)
The Dark Unwinding (Cameron), 84
Dread Nation (Ireland), 57
Goblin Secrets (Alexander), 116
Incarceron (Fisher), 112
Larklight (Reeve), 127
The Lie Tree (Hardinge), 48
The Poisoned House (Ford), 54
Thirteen Doorways, Wolves behind Them All (Ruby), 60
When the Moon Was Ours (McLemore), 96

abuse (physical)
Grave Mercy (LaFevers), 49
The Poisoned House (Ford), 54
When the Moon Was Ours (McLemore), 96

adjusting to change
Roller Girl (Jamieson), 32
Swing It, Sunny, 31

adoption
Nooks & Crannies (Lawson), 83
Pablo and Birdy (McGhee), 88

adults
See evil/manipulative adults; secretive adults

ambivalence about romantic feelings
Cadaver & Queen (Kwitney), 130
Clockwork Angel (Clare), 118

182 COPING WITH CHALLENGES INDEX

ambivalence about romantic feelings
(continued)
  Courting Darkness (LaFevers), 62
  The Dark Days Club (Goodman), 62
  Honor Girl (Thrash), 38
  The Inventor's Secret (Cremer), 129
  Legacy of the Clockwork Key (Bailey),
    129
  Summer of Salt (Leno), 95
anti-Semitism
  Draw the Dark (Bick), 84
  First Class Murder (Stevens), 83
  The Girl Is Trouble (Haines), 83
anxiety/fear
  Airborn (Oppel), 114
  Crenshaw (Applegate), 92
  A Monster Calls (Ness), 89
  The Nest (Oppel), 99
  New Kid (Craft), 27
  Roller Girl (Jamieson), 32
  Secrets at Sea (Peck), 50
  Spinning (Walden), 41
  Unbound (Burg), 141
  See also worry/anxiety about a loved
    one
authoritarian figures, 61
autistic loved ones, 84

B
beauty
  See lack of beauty
being a black sheep, 63
being a child prodigy, 62
being a victim of gossip/slander
  Speak: The Graphic Novel (Halse &
    Carroll), 30
  Spy Runner (Yelchin), 82
  The Strange and Beautiful Sorrows of
    Ava Lavender (Walton), 105
  When the Moon Was Ours (McLemore),
    96
being an outsider/misfit
  American Street (Zoboi), 91
  Audacity (Crowder), 142
  Behemoth (Westerfeld), 129
  The Book of Boy (Murdock), 97
  Catching a Storyfish (Harrington), 145

  Clockwork Angel (Clare), 118
  Dragon's Keep (Carey), 52
  Draw the Dark (Bick), 84
  The Falconer's Knot (Hoffman), 84
  Fever Crumb (Reeve), 127
  The Gilded Wolves (Chokshi), 53
  Goliath (Westerfeld), 129
  Honor Girl (Thrash), 38
  The Inquisitor's Tale, or, The Three
    Magical Children and Their Holy Dog
    (Gidwitz), 55
  Inside Out & Back Again (Lai), 147
  Iron Cast (Soria), 63
  Jackaby (Ritter), 63
  The Language of Spells (Weyr), 62
  Leviathan (Westerfeld), 116
  The Lightning Queen (Resau), 102
  Lucky Strike (Pyron), 101
  Murder Is Bad Manners (Stevens), 79
  The Nest (Oppel), 99
  A Northern Light (Donnelly), 68
  The Peculiar (Bachmann), 117
  The Peculiars (McQuerry), 123
  Roller Girl (Jamieson), 32
  A School for Unusual Girls (Baldwin),
    84
  In the Shadow of Blackbirds (Winters),
    63
  Skybreaker (Oppel), 128
  Spinning (Walden), 41
  Stepsister (Donnelly), 62
  The Strange and Beautiful Sorrows of
    Ava Lavender (Walton), 105
  These Shallow Graves (Donnelly), 72
  When the Moon Was Ours (McLemore),
    96
  Wild Beauty (McLemore), 108
being different
  Airborn (Oppel), 114
  American Born Chinese (Yang), 29
  The Book of Boy (Murdock), 97
  Catching a Storyfish (Harrington), 145
  Curtsies & Conspiracies (Carriger), 128
  The Dark Unwinding (Cameron), 84
  El Deafo (Bell), 26
  Etiquette & Espionage (Carriger), 112
  Heap House (Carey), 47

COPING WITH CHALLENGES INDEX

Home of the Brave (Applegate), 138
Honor Girl (Thrash), 38
*The Inquisitor's Tale, or, The Three
    Magical Children and Their Holy Dog*
    (Gidwitz), 55
Larklight (Reeve), 127
The Mark of the Dragonfly (Johnson),
    113
The Mouse with the Question Mark Tail
    (Peck), 61
The Nest (Oppel), 99
Pashmina (Nidhi), 35
The Ruby in the Smoke (Pullman), 77
*The Strange and Beautiful Sorrows of
    Ava Lavender* (Walton), 105
A Web of Air (Reeve), 128
Wonderstruck (Selznick), 36
A Year without Mom (Tolstikova), 39
being gifted
    Ink, Iron, and Glass (Clare), 129
    Lucky Strike (Pyron), 101
    Premeditated Myrtle (Bunce), 83
    Theodosia & the Serpents of Chaos
        (LaFevers), 61
being misunderstood by parents
    The Boundless (Oppel), 124
    Garvey's Choice (Grimes), 144
    The Lie Tree (Hardinge), 48
    Me and Marvin Gardens (King), 94
    The Poet X (Acevedo), 134
    The Red Pencil (Pinkney), 149
    Speak: The Graphic Novel (Halse &
        Carroll), 30
being overweight, 62
being unconventional, 51, 83
being underestimated by others
    Audacity (Crowder), 142
    Cadaver & Queen (Kwitney), 130
    The Case of the Missing Marquess
        (Springer), 78
    First Class Murder (Stevens), 83
    Garvey's Choice (Grimes), 144
    Ghostopolis (TenNapel), 38
    Hamster Princess: Harriet the Invincible
        (Vernon), 40
    Mark of the Thief (Nielsen), 59
    Midnight Magic (Avi), 72

The Mouse with the Question Mark Tail
    (Peck), 61
Murder at Midnight (Avi), 83
Newt's Emerald (Nix), 63
*Scandalous Sisterhood of Prickwillow
    Place* (Berry), 83
Theodosia & the Serpents of Chaos
    (LaFevers), 61
The Thief Lord (Funke), 93
being unloved by parent(s)
    The Clockwork Scarab (Gleason), 121
    Ghostopolis (TenNapel), 38
    Grave Mercy (LaFevers), 49
    Murder at Midnight (Avi), 83
    Nooks & Crannies (Lawson), 83
    Release (Ness), 98
    A School for Unusual Girls (Baldwin),
        84
    *Thirteen Doorways, Wolves behind Them
        All* (Ruby), 60
being wealthy or privileged
    Airborn (Oppel), 114
    Crenshaw (Applegate), 92
    Dreamland Burning (Latham), 76
    Long Way Down (Reynolds), 150
    The Pearl Thief (Wein), 84
    The Thief Lord (Funke), 93
    The Walls Around Us (Suma), 104
being wronged
    Cadaver & Queen (Kwitney), 130
    The Falconer's Knot (Hoffman), 84
    The Gilded Wolves (Chokshi), 53
    Hell & High Water (Landman), 84
    The Poisoned House (Ford), 54
    The Walls Around Us (Suma), 104
betrayal
    Cadaver & Queen (Kwitney), 130
    Clockwork Angel (Clare), 118
    The Golden Compass (Pullman), 126
    The Inventor's Secret (Cremer), 129
    Iron Cast (Soria), 63
    The Iron Thorn (Kittredge), 129
    Midwinterblood (Sedgwick), 103
    Predator's Gold (Reeve), 128
    The Quest to Uncharted Lands
        (Johnson), 122
    Stormdancer (Kristoff), 122

betrayal *(continued)*
The Strange and Beautiful Sorrows of Ava Lavender (Walton), 105
What I Saw and How I Lied (Blundell), 68

betrayal by a friend
The Falconer's Knot (Hoffman), 84
Stone Mirrors: The Sculpture and Silence of Edmonia Lewis (Atkins), 139
The Walls Around Us (Suma), 104

biracialism
All the Broken Pieces (Burg), 136
The Astonishing Color of After (Pan), 100
Dread Nation (Ireland), 57
Dreamland Burning (Latham), 76
The Gilded Wolves (Chokshi), 53
The Parker Inheritance (Johnson), 75
A Spy in the House (Lee), 84
The Steep and Thorny Way (Winters), 81
Unbound (Burg), 141

blame
See self-blame

blended families, 60

body image, 28
See also poor body image

broken friendships/growing apart
The Crossover (Alexander), 135
Lucky Strike (Pyron), 101
Me and Marvin Gardens (King), 94
Please Ignore Vera Dietz (King), 107
Roller Girl (Jamieson), 32
Smile (Telgemeier), 28

bullying
American Born Chinese (Yang), 29
American Street (Zoboi), 91
Bone Gap (Ruby), 90
Draw the Dark (Bick), 84
Everybody Sees the Ants (King), 107
Garvey's Choice (Grimes), 144
A Great and Terrible Beauty (Bray), 46
Heap House (Carey), 47
Honor Girl (Thrash), 38
Inside Out & Back Again (Lai), 147
Larklight (Reeve), 127
Lucky Strike (Pyron), 101

Me and Marvin Gardens (King), 94
New Kid (Craft), 27
The Parker Inheritance (Johnson), 75
Smile (Telgemeier), 28
Speak: The Graphic Novel (Halse & Carroll), 30
Thornhill (Smy), 37
Unbound (Burg), 141
The Walls Around Us (Suma), 104
When the Moon Was Ours (McLemore), 96

C

career path
See finding a career path

change
Airman (Colfer), 119
Belzhar (Wolitzer), 107
Brown Girl Dreaming (Woodson), 153
Catching a Storyfish (Harrington), 145
Crenshaw (Applegate), 92
The Crossover (Alexander), 135
Incarceron (Fisher), 112
Little Cat's Luck (Bauer), 140
Lucky Strike (Pyron), 101
The Quest to Uncharted Lands (Johnson), 122
The Red Pencil (Pinkney), 149
Summer of Salt (Leno), 95
Under the Mesquite (McCall), 148
A Year without Mom (Tolstikova), 39

class/socioeconomic differences, 35

climate change
All the Wind in the World (Mabry), 107
Me and Marvin Gardens (King), 94

cliques
American Street (Zoboi), 91
A Great and Terrible Beauty (Bray), 46
Lucky Strike (Pyron), 101

compliant/docile personality, 141

concern with what others think
American Born Chinese (Yang), 29
Bone Gap (Ruby), 90
Catching a Storyfish (Harrington), 145
El Deafo (Bell), 26
Garvey's Choice (Grimes), 144
Honor Girl (Thrash), 38

COPING WITH CHALLENGES INDEX

Jackaby (Ritter), 63
Love That Dog (Creech), 137
Other Words for Home (Warga), 152
Roller Girl (Jamieson), 32
Smile (Telgemeier), 28
When the Moon Was Ours (McLemore), 96
confidence
 See lack of confidence
control
 See lack of control over events;
   parent/guardian controlling one's
   destiny
corrupt or criminal parent
 An Affair of Poisons (Thorley), 63
 Dragon's Keep (Carey), 52
 Ink, Iron, and Glass (Clare), 129
 Mortal Engines (Reeve), 115
 Out of the Easy (Sepetys), 70
 The Peculiars (McQuerry), 123
 The Star of Kazan (Ibbotson), 74
 What I Saw and How I Lied (Blundell), 68
corrupt or criminal sibling, 118
critical/fault finding parent
 The Astonishing Color of After (Pan), 100
 Scandalous Sisterhood of Prickwillow Place (Berry), 83
 The Thief Lord (Funke), 93
cruelty
 A Great and Terrible Beauty (Bray), 46
 Incarceron (Fisher), 112
 Larklight (Reeve), 127
 Mechanica (Cornwell), 120
 Nooks & Crannies (Lawson), 83
cruelty toward oneself, 30

D

death of a loved one
 The Aviary (O'Dell), 61
 The Blackthorn Key (Sands), 69
 The Collected Essex County (Lemire), 34
 Dragon's Keep (Carey), 52
 In the Shadow of Blackbirds (Winters), 63

Thirteen Doorways, Wolves behind Them All (Ruby), 60
What I Saw and How I Lied (Blundell), 68
Wild Beauty (McLemore), 108
death of a parent
 Airborn (Oppel), 114
 The Astonishing Color of After (Pan), 100
 Brightstorm (Hardy), 128
 The Collected Essex County (Lemire), 34
 The Crossover (Alexander), 135
 Devil and the Bluebird (Mason-Black), 108
 The Girl Is Murder (Haines), 73
 The Girl Is Trouble (Haines), 83
 A Great and Terrible Beauty (Bray), 46
 The Haunting of Falcon House (Yelchin), 62
 Home of the Brave (Applegate), 138
 Legacy of the Clockwork Key (Bailey), 129
 Leviathan (Westerfeld), 116
 The Mark of the Dragonfly (Johnson), 113
 Mechanica (Cornwell), 120
 A Monster Calls (Ness), 89
 The Night Gardener (Auxier), 61
 A Northern Light (Donnelly), 68
 Out of the Dust (Hesse), 146
 The Red Pencil (Pinkney), 149
 The Ruby in the Smoke (Pullman), 77
 The Steep and Thorny Way (Winters), 81
 Thanks for the Trouble (Wallach), 108
 These Shallow Graves (Donnelly), 72
 Under the Mesquite (McCall), 148
 The Wizard of Dark Street (Odyssey), 61
 Wonderstruck (Selznick), 36
death of a sibling
 Cuckoo Song (Hardinge), 56
 The Diviners (Bray), 51
 The Gilded Cage (Gray), 84
 A School for Unusual Girls (Baldwin), 84

death of a sibling *(continued)*
>*The Secret of Nightingale Wood* (Strange), 83
>*Splendors and Glooms* (Schlitz), 61
>*This Monstrous Thing* (Lee), 130
>*Tigers, Not Daughters* (Mabry), 108

death's finality
>*The Astonishing Color of After* (Pan), 100
>*Belzhar* (Wolitzer), 107
>*Ghostopolis* (TenNapel), 38
>*Goblin Secrets* (Alexander), 116
>*Grave Mercy* (LaFevers), 49
>*Love That Dog* (Creech), 137
>*A Monster Calls* (Ness), 89
>*Notes from My Captivity* (Parks), 108
>*Out of the Dust* (Hesse), 146
>*Pablo and Birdy* (McGhee), 88
>*Under the Mesquite* (McCall), 148

deception
>*The Star of Kazan* (Ibbotson), 74
>*Thirteen Doorways, Wolves behind Them All* (Ruby), 60
>*Venturess* (Cornwell), 129

depression
>*Out of the Dust* (Hesse), 146
>*Speak: The Graphic Novel* (Halse & Carroll), 30

desertion
>*See* abandonment/desertion

desire for parental approval, 62

desire to find absent parent
>*All the Broken Pieces* (Burg), 136
>*American Street* (Zoboi), 91
>*Home of the Brave* (Applegate), 138
>*The Peculiars* (McQuerry), 123

desire to find birth parent
>*Beyond the Bright Sea* (Wolk), 71
>*The Clockwork Three* (Kirby), 128, 129
>*Pablo and Birdy* (McGhee), 88
>*The Star of Kazan* (Ibbotson), 74
>*Wonderstruck* (Selznick), 36

destiny
>*See* parent/guardian controlling one's destiny

different
>*See* being different

disability
>*Brightstorm* (Hardy), 128
>*El Deafo* (Bell), 26
>*The Lightning Queen* (Resau), 102
>*The Nest* (Oppel), 99
>*The Night Gardener* (Auxier), 61
>*The Red Pencil* (Pinkney), 149
>*Wonderstruck* (Selznick), 36

disabled loved ones
>*All the Broken Pieces* (Burg), 136
>*The Clockwork Three* (Kirby), 128, 129
>*The Girl Is Murder* (Haines), 73
>*The Nest* (Oppel), 99

disapproval
>*The Diviners* (Bray), 51
>*Garvey's Choice* (Grimes), 144
>*Iron Cast* (Soria), 63

disfigurement
>*Mortal Engines* (Reeve), 115
>*Out of the Dust* (Hesse), 146
>*Predator's Gold* (Reeve), 128
>*A Taste for Monsters* (Kirby), 62

distant/uncommunicative parent
>*Elizabeth and Zenobia* (Miller), 76
>*The Girl Is Murder* (Haines), 73
>*The Girl Is Trouble* (Haines), 83
>*The Lie Tree* (Hardinge), 48
>*The Lightning Queen* (Resau), 102
>*A Northern Light* (Donnelly), 68
>*Out of the Dust* (Hesse), 146
>*The Strange and Beautiful Sorrows of Ava Lavender* (Walton), 105

distrust of others
>*All the Wind in the World* (Mabry), 107
>*The Clockwork Three* (Kirby), 128, 129
>*Courting Darkness* (LaFevers), 62
>*Ink, Iron, and Glass* (Clare), 129

divorced/separated parents, 75

domestic violence
>*Devil and the Bluebird* (Mason-Black), 108
>*Still Life with Tornado* (King), 107
>*Tigers, Not Daughters* (Mabry), 108

domineering friend
>*El Deafo* (Bell), 26
>*Murder Is Bad Manners* (Stevens), 79

COPING WITH CHALLENGES INDEX   **187**

Speak: The Graphic Novel (Halse & Carroll), 30
domineering relatives
    The Dark Days Club (Goodman), 62
    Heap House (Carey), 47
    The Lightning Queen (Resau), 102
    Silver in the Blood (George), 62
doubt
    See self-doubt

E

elitism
    See snobbery/elitism
emotional abuse
    See abuse (emotional)
emotional detachment or avoidance
    All the Broken Pieces (Burg), 136
    All the Wind in the World (Mabry), 107
    Belzhar (Wolitzer), 107
    The Collected Essex County (Lemire), 34
    Everybody Sees the Ants (King), 107
    Fever Crumb (Reeve), 127
    A Monster Calls (Ness), 89
    Thanks for the Trouble (Wallach), 108
    Tigers, Not Daughters (Mabry), 108
    A Web of Air (Reeve), 128
employment
    See finding employment
entanglement in lies
    The Inquisitor's Apprentice (Moriarty), 58
    Scandalous Sisterhood of Prickwillow Place (Berry), 83
entitlement
    See feeling entitled
entrapment in a hopeless situation, 129
entrapment in a way of life
    Out of the Easy (Sepetys), 70
    Sweep: The Story of a Girl and Her Monster (Auxier), 45
epidemic/pandemic threat
    The Book of Boy (Murdock), 97
    Everland (Spinale), 130
    Mark of the Plague (Sands), 83
    In the Shadow of Blackbirds (Winters), 63

evil/manipulative adults
    Airman (Colfer), 119
    Audacity (Crowder), 142
    The Aviary (O'Dell), 61
    Brightstorm (Hardy), 128
    The Charmed Children of Rookskill Castle (Fox), 54
    The Gilded Cage (Gray), 84
    Hell & High Water (Landman), 84
    Legacy of the Clockwork Key (Bailey), 129
    Mark of the Plague (Sands), 83
    Mark of the Thief (Nielsen), 59
    Midnight Magic (Avi), 72
    Midwinterblood (Sedgwick), 103
    The Mysterious Howling (Wood), 81
    The Poisoned House (Ford), 54
    The Quest to Uncharted Lands (Johnson), 122
    Release (Ness), 98
    The Ruby in the Smoke (Pullman), 77
    Silver in the Blood (George), 62
    Splendors and Glooms (Schlitz), 61
    The Star of Kazan (Ibbotson), 74
    Sweep: The Story of a Girl and Her Monster (Auxier), 45
    The Thief Lord (Funke), 93
    Unbound (Burg), 141
    A Web of Air (Reeve), 128
    The Whatnot (Bachmann), 128
exploitation of one's poverty
    All the Wind in the World (Mabry), 107
    Audacity (Crowder), 142
    The Clockwork Three (Kirby), 128, 129
    Out of the Easy (Sepetys), 70
    Sweep: The Story of a Girl and Her Monster (Auxier), 45

F

failing to achieve a goal, 128
failure, 121
faith
    See questioning one's faith
false accusations
    The Girl Who Could Silence the Wind (Medina), 108
    Murder at Midnight (Avi), 83

false accusations *(continued)*
  Poison Is Not Polite (Stevens), 83
  Thornhill (Smy), 37
  The Walls Around Us (Suma), 104
family conflict
  American Street (Zoboi), 91
  The Astonishing Color of After (Pan), 100
  The Collected Essex County (Lemire), 34
  Crenshaw (Applegate), 92
  The Crossover (Alexander), 135
  Everybody Sees the Ants (King), 107
  Hey, Kiddo (Krosoczka), 33
  Midwinterblood (Sedgwick), 103
  Pashmina (Nidhi), 35
  The Poet X (Acevedo), 134
  The Red Pencil (Pinkney), 149
  Speak: The Graphic Novel (Halse & Carroll), 30
  Still Life with Tornado (King), 107
  Tigers, Not Daughters (Mabry), 108
  Wild Beauty (McLemore), 108
father
  See parents; strained relationship with a father
favoritism
  The Diviners (Bray), 51
  Etiquette & Espionage (Carriger), 112
  The Kingdom of Back (Lu), 62
  Mechanica (Cornwell), 120
  Splendors and Glooms (Schlitz), 61
  Thornhill (Smy), 37
fear
  See anxiety/fear
fear of a hereditary disease, 129
fear of facing one's past
  Belzhar (Wolitzer), 107
  Clockwork Angel (Clare), 118
fear of inheriting parental depravity, 62
feeling ashamed of family
  Hey, Kiddo (Krosoczka), 33
  The Inquisitor's Apprentice (Moriarty), 58
  Please Ignore Vera Dietz (King), 107
feeling entitled
  American Born Chinese (Yang), 29

Behemoth (Westerfeld), 129
Goliath (Westerfeld), 129
Home of the Brave (Applegate), 138
Leviathan (Westerfeld), 116
Long Way Down (Reynolds), 150
New Kid (Craft), 27
Salt: A Story of Friendship in a Time of War (Frost), 143
Splendors and Glooms (Schlitz), 61
feeling unprepared for roles/responsibilities
  Everland (Spinale), 130
  Grayling's Song (Cushman), 61
  The Inquisitor's Apprentice (Moriarty), 58
  A Spy in the House (Lee), 84
  Steeplejack (Hartley), 129
females in unconventional roles/occupations, 120
financial loss of parents
  Brightstorm (Hardy), 128
  The Clockwork Three (Kirby), 128, 129
  Crenshaw (Applegate), 92
  The Girl Is Murder (Haines), 73
  Legacy of the Clockwork Key (Bailey), 129
  Magic under Glass (Dolamore), 129
  Murder, Magic, and What We Wore (Jones), 57
  The Pearl Thief (Wein), 84
  Serafina's Promise (Burg), 140
finding a career path
  Dreamland Burning (Latham), 76
  Jackaby (Ritter), 63
  The Wizard of Dark Street (Odyssey), 61
finding a purpose/direction in life
  Courting Darkness (LaFevers), 62
  Devil and the Bluebird (Mason-Black), 108
  Dreamland Burning (Latham), 76
  Leviathan (Westerfeld), 116
  Thanks for the Trouble (Wallach), 108
  These Shallow Graves (Donnelly), 72
finding employment
  All the Wind in the World (Mabry), 107
  The Book of Lost Things (Voigt), 80

COPING WITH CHALLENGES INDEX 189

Serafina's Promise (Burg), 140
flirtatious mothers, 48
forgiving others
    Ghostopolis (TenNapel), 38
    The Lightning Queen (Resau), 102
    Midwinterblood (Sedgwick), 103
    Notes from My Captivity (Parks), 108
foster families, 53
friends
    See betrayal by a friend; broken
    friendships/growing apart;
    domineering friend; lack of friends

G

gay parent, 75
gender identity
    Hamster Princess: Harriet the Invincible
    (Vernon), 40
    When the Moon Was Ours (McLemore),
    96
gender inequality
    Airborn (Oppel), 114
    Behemoth (Westerfeld), 129
    Cadaver & Queen (Kwitney), 130
    The Case of the Missing Marquess
    (Springer), 78
    The Clockwork Scarab (Gleason), 121
    Etiquette & Espionage (Carriger), 112
    The Falconer's Knot (Hoffman), 84
    The Girl Who Could Silence the Wind
    (Medina), 108
    Glow (Bryant), 84
    Goliath (Westerfeld), 129
    A Great and Terrible Beauty (Bray), 46
    Hamster Princess: Harriet the Invincible
    (Vernon), 40
    Jackaby (Ritter), 63
    The Kingdom of Back (Lu), 62
    Leviathan (Westerfeld), 116
    The Lie Tree (Hardinge), 48
    Murder, Magic, and What We Wore
    (Jones), 57
    Newt's Emerald (Nix), 63
    A Northern Light (Donnelly), 68
    Palace of Spies (Zettel), 84
    The Poet X (Acevedo), 134
    Premeditated Myrtle (Bunce), 83

A School for Unusual Girls (Baldwin),
    84
In the Shadow of Blackbirds (Winters),
    63
A Skinful of Shadows (Hardinge), 62
Skybreaker (Oppel), 128
A Spy in the House (Lee), 84
Theodosia & the Serpents of Chaos
    (LaFevers), 61
These Shallow Graves (Donnelly),
    72
gifted
    See being gifted
gossip
    See being a victim of gossip/slander
grief, 63
grieving parent
    The Astonishing Color of After (Pan),
    100
    Cuckoo Song (Hardinge), 56
    The Lightning Queen (Resau), 102
    Out of the Dust (Hesse), 146
    Splendors and Glooms (Schlitz), 61
    Under the Mesquite (McCall), 148
guilt
    An Affair of Poisons (Thorley), 63
    The Book of Boy (Murdock), 97
    Dragon's Keep (Carey), 52
    The Girl Who Could Silence the Wind
    (Medina), 108
    Goliath (Westerfeld), 129
    Home of the Brave (Applegate), 138
    How I Became a Spy (Hopkinson), 83
    The Light Between Worlds (Weymouth),
    63
    A Monster Calls (Ness), 89
    Out of the Dust (Hesse), 146
    Pashmina (Nidhi), 35
    Please Ignore Vera Dietz (King), 107
    The Secret of Nightingale Wood
    (Strange), 83
    Serafina's Promise (Burg), 140
    A Skinful of Shadows (Hardinge), 62
    This Monstrous Thing (Lee), 130

H

hereditary traits, 62

COPING WITH CHALLENGES INDEX

homelessness
  Crenshaw (Applegate), 92
  Devil and the Bluebird (Mason-Black), 108
  The Red Pencil (Pinkney), 149
  Sweep: The Story of a Girl and Her Monster (Auxier), 45
  The Thief Lord (Funke), 93
homesickness
  American Street (Zoboi), 91
  Brown Girl Dreaming (Woodson), 153
  Catching a Storyfish (Harrington), 145
  Home of the Brave (Applegate), 138
  Little Cat's Luck (Bauer), 140
  Other Words for Home (Warga), 152
  Unbound (Burg), 141
homophobia
  The Parker Inheritance (Johnson), 75
  Release (Ness), 98
  Spinning (Walden), 41
  The Steep and Thorny Way (Winters), 81
hopelessness, 146
hostility, 61

I

identity formation
  The Book of Boy (Murdock), 97
  The Mouse with the Question Mark Tail (Peck), 61
  When the Moon Was Ours (McLemore), 96
idolized or famous parents, 121
idolized or famous relatives
  The Case of the Missing Marquess (Springer), 78
  The Haunting of Falcon House (Yelchin), 62
  What I Saw and How I Lied (Blundell), 68
(the) immigrant experience
  American Born Chinese (Yang), 29
  American Street (Zoboi), 91
  Home of the Brave (Applegate), 138
  Illegal (Colfer & Donkin), 30
  Inside Out & Back Again (Lai), 147
  Like Water on Stone (Walrath), 151

  Murder Is Bad Manners (Stevens), 79
  Other Words for Home (Warga), 152
  Pablo and Birdy (McGhee), 88
  Pashmina (Nidhi), 35
  Wild Beauty (McLemore), 108
inability to cooperate/work with others
  The Clockwork Scarab (Gleason), 121
  Ink, Iron, and Glass (Clare), 129
  Little Cat's Luck (Bauer), 140
  The Quest to Uncharted Lands (Johnson), 122
infatuation
  American Born Chinese (Yang), 29
  Smile (Telgemeier), 28
inferiority
  See sense of inferiority
injustice/unfairness
  Airborn (Oppel), 114
  Airman (Colfer), 119
  Brightstorm (Hardy), 128
  Illegal (Colfer & Donkin), 30
  Inside Out & Back Again (Lai), 147
  Long Way Down (Reynolds), 150
  Me and Marvin Gardens (King), 94
  Mechanica (Cornwell), 120
  The Passion of Dolssa (Berry), 50
  Stone Mirrors: The Sculpture and Silence of Edmonia Lewis (Atkins), 139
  Stormdancer (Kristoff), 122
  Unbound (Burg), 141
instincts
  See trusting instincts

J

jealousy
  Airborn (Oppel), 114
  The Astonishing Color of After (Pan), 100
  Brown Girl Dreaming (Woodson), 153
  The Crossover (Alexander), 135
  Devil and the Bluebird (Mason-Black), 108
  Glow (Bryant), 84
  The Kingdom of Back (Lu), 62
  Little Cat's Luck (Bauer), 140
  Predator's Gold (Reeve), 128

COPING WITH CHALLENGES INDEX   **191**

Serafina's Promise (Burg), 140
Skybreaker (Oppel), 128
Starclimber (Oppel), 128
Stepsister (Donnelly), 62
The Strange and Beautiful Sorrows of Ava Lavender (Walton), 105
Tigers, Not Daughters (Mabry), 108

L

lack of beauty
 A Northern Light (Donnelly), 68
 Stepsister (Donnelly), 62
 A Taste for Monsters (Kirby), 62
lack of confidence
 The Book of Boy (Murdock), 97
 Catching a Storyfish (Harrington), 145
 Garvey's Choice (Grimes), 144
 How I Became a Spy (Hopkinson), 83
 Other Words for Home (Warga), 152
 Roller Girl (Jamieson), 32
 Smile (Telgemeier), 28
 Steeplejack (Hartley), 129
 Stepsister (Donnelly), 62
 A Taste for Monsters (Kirby), 62
 The Whatnot (Bachmann), 128
 When the Moon Was Ours (McLemore), 96
lack of control over events
 The Blackthorn Key (Sands), 69
 Crenshaw (Applegate), 92
 Heap House (Carey), 47
 The Language of Spells (Weyr), 62
 Like Water on Stone (Walrath), 151
 Mark of the Thief (Nielsen), 59
 Serafina's Promise (Burg), 140
 Thirteen Doorways, Wolves behind Them All (Ruby), 60
lack of friends
 Crenshaw (Applegate), 92
 The Language of Spells (Weyr), 62
 Lucky Strike (Pyron), 101
 Nooks & Crannies (Lawson), 83
 Thanks for the Trouble (Wallach), 108
 Thornhill (Smy), 37
lack of parental guidance
 The Charmed Children of Rookskill Castle (Fox), 54

Mark of the Plague (Sands), 83
Sweep: The Story of a Girl and Her Monster (Auxier), 45
living up to high expectations, 121
loneliness
 American Street (Zoboi), 91
 The Aviary (O'Dell), 61
 The Case of the Missing Marquess (Springer), 78
 The Collected Essex County (Lemire), 34
 Curtsies & Conspiracies (Carriger), 128
 The Girl Is Murder (Haines), 73
 Home of the Brave (Applegate), 138
 Illegal (Colfer & Donkin), 30
 Inside Out & Back Again (Lai), 147
 Mechanica (Cornwell), 120
 Midwinterblood (Sedgwick), 103
 A Monster Calls (Ness), 89
 Out of the Dust (Hesse), 146
 Speak: The Graphic Novel (Halse & Carroll), 30
 Stone Mirrors: The Sculpture and Silence of Edmonia Lewis (Atkins), 139
 Thornhill (Smy), 37
 Wild Beauty (McLemore), 108
 A Year without Mom (Tolstikova), 39
loved ones
 See death of a loved one; disabled loved ones; worry/anxiety about a loved one
loved ones with a physical disability, 92

M

manipulation
 See evil/manipulative adults
memories
 See traumatic memories
mentally ill family member
 The Astonishing Color of After (Pan), 100
 The Iron Thorn (Kittredge), 129
 The Lightning Queen (Resau), 102
misfit
 See being an outsider/misfit

misunderstanding
See being misunderstood by parents

moral dilemmas
Audacity (Crowder), 142
Behemoth (Westerfeld), 129
Courting Darkness (LaFevers), 62
Glow (Bryant), 84
Grave Mercy (LaFevers), 49
Leviathan (Westerfeld), 116
The Mark of the Dragonfly (Johnson), 113
Midwinterblood (Sedgwick), 103
Mortal Engines (Reeve), 115
A Northern Light (Donnelly), 68
Out of the Easy (Sepetys), 70
Pablo and Birdy (McGhee), 88
The Peculiars (McQuerry), 123
The Poet X (Acevedo), 134
The Red Pencil (Pinkney), 149
Salt: A Story of Friendship in a Time of War (Frost), 143
Serafina's Promise (Burg), 140
The Star of Kazan (Ibbotson), 74
This Monstrous Thing (Lee), 130
Unbound (Burg), 141

mother
See parents; troubled relationship with a mother

moving to a new school
Murder Is Bad Manners (Stevens), 79
New Kid (Craft), 27

moving/relocating
American Street (Zoboi), 91
Brown Girl Dreaming (Woodson), 153
Catching a Storyfish (Harrington), 145
Elizabeth and Zenobia (Miller), 76
The Gilded Cage (Gray), 84
The Girl Is Murder (Haines), 73
Home of the Brave (Applegate), 138
The Parker Inheritance (Johnson), 75
The Secret of Nightingale Wood (Strange), 83
Stone Mirrors: The Sculpture and Silence of Edmonia Lewis (Atkins), 139
A Year without Mom (Tolstikova), 39

murder of a loved one, 72

N

needing to prove oneself
Behemoth (Westerfeld), 129
Goliath (Westerfeld), 129
Leviathan (Westerfeld), 116
Murder, Magic, and What We Wore (Jones), 57
Murder at Midnight (Avi), 83
Release (Ness), 98
Roller Girl (Jamieson), 32

neglect
See parental neglect

O

obsessions, 84

orphanhood
The Blackthorn Key (Sands), 69
Clockwork Angel (Clare), 118
The Diamond of Drury Lane (Golding), 83
Everland (Spinale), 130
The Gilded Cage (Gray), 84
The Gilded Wolves (Chokshi), 53
The Mark of the Dragonfly (Johnson), 113
The Passion of Dolssa (Berry), 50
The Poisoned House (Ford), 54
The Ruby in the Smoke (Pullman), 77
Sweep: The Story of a Girl and Her Monster (Auxier), 45

ostracism/rejection
Beyond the Bright Sea (Wolk), 71
The Book of Boy (Murdock), 97
Curtsies & Conspiracies (Carriger), 128
Fever Crumb (Reeve), 127
Spy Runner (Yelchin), 82
The Steep and Thorny Way (Winters), 81
Still Life with Tornado (King), 107
When the Moon Was Ours (McLemore), 96

outsider
See being an outsider/misfit

overly critical view of self
American Born Chinese (Yang), 29
Courting Darkness (LaFevers), 62
The Lie Tree (Hardinge), 48

COPING WITH CHALLENGES INDEX

overprotective parent
The Aviary (O'Dell), 61
Cuckoo Song (Hardinge), 56
The Girl Is Trouble (Haines), 83
These Shallow Graves (Donnelly), 72

P

panic attacks, 99
parent with post-traumatic stress
disorder, 83
parental affair, 83
parental disapproval
An Affair of Poisons (Thorley), 63
Audacity (Crowder), 142
The Boundless (Oppel), 124
The Diviners (Bray), 51
The Red Pencil (Pinkney), 149
Release (Ness), 98
Stepsister (Donnelly), 62
parental guidance
See lack of parental guidance
parental neglect
The Golden Compass (Pullman), 126
Hey, Kiddo (Krosoczka), 33
Nooks & Crannies (Lawson), 83
Out of the Easy (Sepetys), 70
Spinning (Walden), 41
The Thief Lord (Funke), 93
Thornhill (Smy), 37
Tigers, Not Daughters (Mabry), 108
parent/guardian controlling one's
destiny
An Affair of Poisons (Thorley), 63
The Dark Days Club (Goodman), 62
The Falconer's Knot (Hoffman), 84
Heap House (Carey), 47
Release (Ness), 98
Silver in the Blood (George), 62
parents
See absent parent; being
misunderstood by parents; being
unloved by parent(s); corrupt
or criminal parent; critical/fault
finding parent; death of a parent;
desire to find absent parent;
desire to find birth parent; distant/
uncommunicative parent; financial

loss of parents; grieving parent;
overprotective parent
past wrongdoing
How I Became a Spy (Hopkinson), 83
Please Ignore Vera Dietz (King), 107
A Taste for Monsters (Kirby), 62
physical abuse
See abuse (physical)
physical violence, 30
poor body image
Bone Gap (Ruby), 90
The Book of Boy (Murdock), 97
Dragon's Keep (Carey), 52
Garvey's Choice (Grimes), 144
Mortal Engines (Reeve), 115
The Peculiar (Bachmann), 117
The Peculiars (McQuerry), 123
Predator's Gold (Reeve), 128
Under the Mesquite (McCall), 148
post-traumatic stress disorder, 63
poverty
Airborn (Oppel), 114
American Street (Zoboi), 91
The Blackthorn Key (Sands), 69
Crenshaw (Applegate), 92
The Dark Unwinding (Cameron), 84
The Diamond of Drury Lane (Golding),
83
Glow (Bryant), 84
Illegal (Colfer & Donkin), 30
The Inquisitor's Apprentice (Moriarty),
58
Inside Out & Back Again (Lai), 147
Legacy of the Clockwork Key (Bailey),
129
The Mark of the Dragonfly (Johnson),
113
The Night Gardener (Auxier), 61
A Northern Light (Donnelly), 68
Skybreaker (Oppel), 128
Splendors and Glooms (Schlitz), 61
Steeplejack (Hartley), 129
Stormdancer (Kristoff), 122
*Sweep: The Story of a Girl and Her
Monster* (Auxier), 45
A Taste for Monsters (Kirby), 62
Under the Mesquite (McCall), 148

poverty *(continued)*
  The Whatnot (Bachmann), 128
  See also exploitation of one's poverty
powerlessness
  Clockwork, or All Wound Up
    (Pullman), 125
  The Dark Unwinding (Cameron), 84
  Devil and the Bluebird (Mason-Black),
    108
  Everybody Sees the Ants (King), 107
  The Gilded Cage (Gray), 84
  Illegal (Colfer & Donkin), 30
  Incarceron (Fisher), 112
  Magic under Glass (Dolamore), 129
  Me and Marvin Gardens (King), 94
  A Monster Calls (Ness), 89
  Newt's Emerald (Nix), 63
  The Peculiar (Bachmann), 117
  The Secret of Nightingale Wood
    (Strange), 83
  A Skinful of Shadows (Hardinge), 62
  Splendors and Glooms (Schlitz), 61
  Still Life with Tornado (King), 107
  *Stone Mirrors: The Sculpture and
    Silence of Edmonia Lewis* (Atkins),
    139
  The Whatnot (Bachmann), 128
prejudice
  The Inquisitor's Apprentice (Moriarty),
    58
  Iron Cast (Soria), 63
  *Stone Mirrors: The Sculpture and
    Silence of Edmonia Lewis* (Atkins),
    139
preoccupied/busy parents
  Everybody Sees the Ants (King), 107
  The Nest (Oppel), 99
  Theodosia & the Serpents of Chaos
    (LaFevers), 61
  Thornhill (Smy), 37
privilege
  See being wealthy or privileged;
    recognizing privilege
proving oneself
  See needing to prove oneself
purpose
  See finding a purpose/direction in life

Q

questioning one's faith
  Courting Darkness (LaFevers), 62
  Grave Mercy (LaFevers), 49
  Notes from My Captivity (Parks), 108
  The Passion of Dolssa (Berry), 50
  The Poet X (Acevedo), 134
  Release (Ness), 98

R

racial prejudice, 68
racial segregation, 91
racism
  American Born Chinese (Yang), 29
  Brown Girl Dreaming (Woodson), 153
  The Diamond of Drury Lane (Golding),
    83
  Dread Nation (Ireland), 57
  Dreamland Burning (Latham), 76
  Fever Crumb (Reeve), 127
  First Class Murder (Stevens), 83
  The Girl Is Trouble (Haines), 83
  Hell & High Water (Landman), 84
  Inside Out & Back Again (Lai), 147
  Larklight (Reeve), 127
  Mechanica (Cornwell), 120
  New Kid (Craft), 27
  The Parker Inheritance (Johnson), 75
  The Pearl Thief (Wein), 84
  The Peculiar (Bachmann), 117
  Skybreaker (Oppel), 128
  The Steep and Thorny Way (Winters),
    81
  Steeplejack (Hartley), 129
  The Whatnot (Bachmann), 128
  When the Moon Was Ours
    (McLemore), 96
recognizing privilege
  Audacity (Crowder), 142
  Brown Girl Dreaming (Woodson), 153
  Home of the Brave (Applegate), 138
  Inside Out & Back Again (Lai), 147
  Long Way Down (Reynolds), 150
  Other Words for Home (Warga), 152
  The Red Pencil (Pinkney), 149
  *Salt: A Story of Friendship in a Time of
    War* (Frost), 143

COPING WITH CHALLENGES INDEX 195

Serafina's Promise (Burg), 140
*Stone Mirrors: The Sculpture and
Silence of Edmonia Lewis* (Atkins),
139
Unbound (Burg), 141
recognizing privilege in oneself
American Street (Zoboi), 91
The Haunting of Falcon House
(Yelchin), 62
The Lightning Queen (Resau), 102
New Kid (Craft), 27
Notes from My Captivity (Parks), 108
The Thief Lord (Funke), 93
The Walls Around Us (Suma), 104
rejection
American Born Chinese (Yang), 29
Belzhar (Wolitzer), 107
See also ostracism/rejection
relatives
See domineering relatives; idolized or
famous relatives
religious intolerance or persecution
*The Inquisitor's Tale, or, The Three
Magical Children and Their Holy Dog*
(Gidwitz), 55
Like Water on Stone (Walrath), 151
religious prejudice, 50
relocating
See moving/relocating
responsibility for younger siblings, 63
revenge (desire for)
The Lie Tree (Hardinge), 48
Long Way Down (Reynolds), 150
*Salt: A Story of Friendship in a Time of
War* (Frost), 143
The Steep and Thorny Way (Winters),
81
Stormdancer (Kristoff), 122
romantic feelings
See ambivalence about romantic
feelings

S

scandal, 48
secretive adults
American Street (Zoboi), 91
Cuckoo Song (Hardinge), 56

Silver in the Blood (George), 62
A Skinful of Shadows (Hardinge), 62
Spy Runner (Yelchin), 82
Venturess (Cornwell), 129
self-blame
All the Broken Pieces (Burg), 136
The Astonishing Color of After (Pan),
100
Draw the Dark (Bick), 84
How I Became a Spy (Hopkinson), 83
Out of the Dust (Hesse), 146
Spinning (Walden), 41
Unbound (Burg), 141
The Wizard of Dark Street (Odyssey),
61
self-doubt
The Book of Boy (Murdock), 97
The Book of Lost Things (Voigt), 80
Curtsies & Conspiracies (Carriger), 128
Goblin Secrets (Alexander), 116
Grayling's Song (Cushman), 61
Love That Dog (Creech), 137
Mortal Engines (Reeve), 115
The Poet X (Acevedo), 134
Serafina's Promise (Burg), 140
Spinning (Walden), 41
Starclimber (Oppel), 128
Still Life with Tornado (King), 107
Thornhill (Smy), 37
self-harm, 63
sense of inferiority
American Born Chinese (Yang), 29
Brown Girl Dreaming (Woodson), 153
Courting Darkness (LaFevers), 62
Goblin Secrets (Alexander), 116
The Lie Tree (Hardinge), 48
Mortal Engines (Reeve), 115
Murder at Midnight (Avi), 83
The Nest (Oppel), 99
Serafina's Promise (Burg), 140
Starclimber (Oppel), 128
*Stone Mirrors: The Sculpture and
Silence of Edmonia Lewis* (Atkins),
139
Summer of Salt (Leno), 95
Thanks for the Trouble (Wallach), 108
Thornhill (Smy), 37

196   COPING WITH CHALLENGES INDEX

separating from parents/leaving home, 63

sexual assault
  Bone Gap (Ruby), 90
  Speak: The Graphic Novel (Halse & Carroll), 30
  Spinning (Walden), 41
  Stone Mirrors: The Sculpture and Silence of Edmonia Lewis (Atkins), 139
  The Strange and Beautiful Sorrows of Ava Lavender (Walton), 105
  Summer of Salt (Leno), 95
  Tigers, Not Daughters (Mabry), 108
  Wild Beauty (McLemore), 108

sexual harassment in the workplace
  The Girl Who Could Silence the Wind (Medina), 108
  Glow (Bryant), 84
  Release (Ness), 98

sexual identity
  The Pearl Thief (Wein), 84
  Spinning (Walden), 41
  When the Moon Was Ours (McLemore), 96

shame
  Belzhar (Wolitzer), 107
  Dragon's Keep (Carey), 52
  The Nest (Oppel), 99
  Summer of Salt (Leno), 95

shyness, 76

sibling issues/rivalry
  The Crossover (Alexander), 135
  Cuckoo Song (Hardinge), 56
  Devil and the Bluebird (Mason-Black), 108
  The Inventor's Secret (Cremer), 129
  The Kingdom of Back (Lu), 62
  Secrets at Sea (Peck), 50
  Summer of Salt (Leno), 95
  Tigers, Not Daughters (Mabry), 108

siblings
  See death of a sibling

single-parent dating, 83

slander
  See being a victim of gossip/slander

snobbery/elitism
  The Girl Is Murder (Haines), 73
  The Haunting of Falcon House (Yelchin), 62
  Other Words for Home (Warga), 152
  Secrets at Sea (Peck), 50
  Serafina's Promise (Burg), 140

stepparents
  The Steep and Thorny Way (Winters), 81
  Thirteen Doorways, Wolves behind Them All (Ruby), 60

strained relationship with a father
  First Class Murder (Stevens), 83
  Like Water on Stone (Walrath), 151
  Me and Marvin Gardens (King), 94
  A Monster Calls (Ness), 89
  Please Ignore Vera Dietz (King), 107
  Tigers, Not Daughters (Mabry), 108

strict/controlling adults, 61

suicide of a loved one
  The Astonishing Color of After (Pan), 100
  The Girl Is Murder (Haines), 73

T

talents
  See underutilizing one's talents

timidity
  See unassertiveness/timidity

traumatic memories
  Belzhar (Wolitzer), 107
  Bone Gap (Ruby), 90
  A Skinful of Shadows (Hardinge), 62
  Still Life with Tornado (King), 107

troubled relationship with a mother
  Out of the Dust (Hesse), 146
  Out of the Easy (Sepetys), 70
  The Poet X (Acevedo), 134
  Venturess (Cornwell), 129

trust
  See distrust of others

trusting instincts
  Bone Gap (Ruby), 90
  Devil and the Bluebird (Mason-Black), 108
  The Nest (Oppel), 99

Notes from My Captivity (Parks), 108

U

unassertiveness/timidity
The Aviary (O'Dell), 61
El Deafo (Bell), 26
Elizabeth and Zenobia (Miller), 76
Grayling's Song (Cushman), 61
Heap House (Carey), 47
Love That Dog (Creech), 137
The Peculiar (Bachmann), 117
Smile (Telgemeier), 28
underestimation
See being underestimated by others
underutilizing one's talents
Love That Dog (Creech), 137
A Web of Air (Reeve), 128
unfairness
See injustice/unfairness
unloved by guardian, 84
unloved by parent
See being unloved by parent(s)
unpopularity
Bone Gap (Ruby), 90
Curtsies & Conspiracies (Carriger), 128
Garvey's Choice (Grimes), 144
A Great and Terrible Beauty (Bray), 46
Premeditated Myrtle (Bunce), 83
unpreparedness
See feeling unprepared for roles/responsibilities

V

village/small-town life
Bone Gap (Ruby), 90
Inside Out & Back Again (Lai), 147
Lucky Strike (Pyron), 101
The Strange and Beautiful Sorrows of Ava Lavender (Walton), 105
Summer of Salt (Leno), 95
Tigers, Not Daughters (Mabry), 108
When the Moon Was Ours (McLemore), 96

W

war trauma
All the Broken Pieces (Burg), 136
Home of the Brave (Applegate), 138
Like Water on Stone (Walrath), 151
The Red Pencil (Pinkney), 149
wealth
See being wealthy or privileged
worry/anxiety about a loved one
Bone Gap (Ruby), 90
The Book of Lost Things (Voigt), 80
Catching a Storyfish (Harrington), 145
Crenshaw (Applegate), 92
Devil and the Bluebird (Mason-Black), 108
The Girl Who Could Silence the Wind (Medina), 108
The Nest (Oppel), 99
Other Words for Home (Warga), 152
Pashmina (Nidhi), 35
Poison Is Not Polite (Stevens), 83
Swing It, Sunny, 31
wrongs
See being wronged

Author/Title Index

A

Abel's Island (Steig), 50
The Absolutely True Diary of a Part-Time Indian (Alexie), 33
The Accidental Genius of Weasel High (Detorie), 29
Acevedo, Elizabeth, 134–135
Adeyemi, Tomi, 57
The Adventures of a Girl Called Bicycle (Uss), 88
Airborn (Oppel), 114, 119
Airman (Colfer), 114, 118–119
Alexander, Joy, 132
Alexander, Kwame, 135
Alexander, William, 116–117
Alexie, Sherman, 33
All American Boys (Kiely), 105
All Our Hidden Gifts (O'Donoghue), 95–96
All the Broken Pieces (Burg), 133, 136
All the Wind in the World (Mabry), 107
Allende, Isabel, 86
Almond, David, 100
Almost American Girl (Ha), 29
American Born Chinese (Yang), 25, 28–29
American Street (Zoboi), 90–91
The Amulet of Samarkand (Stroud), 59
An Affair of Poisons (Thorley), 63
Anderson, Laurie Halse, 29–30
Andrews, Jan, 143
Anya's Ghost (Brosgol), 35
Applegate, Katherine
    Crenshaw, 92
    Home of the Brave, 133, 137–138
Are You Listening? (Walden), 39
Arthur Trilogy (Crossley-Holland), 43

The Astonishing Color of After (Pan)
    matching readers with, 17
    overview of, 100–101
Atkins, Jeannine, 132–133, 138–139
Atwood, Margaret, 67
Audacity (Crowder), 18, 142–143
Auxier, Jonathan
    The Night Gardener, 61
    Peter Nimble and His Fantastic Eyes, 93–94
    Sweep: The Story of a Girl and Her Monster, 45–46, 61
Avi (Edward Irving Wortis)
    City of Orphans, 58–59
    Crispin, 98
    Midnight Magic, 71–72
    Murder at Midnight, 83
    popularity of novels by, 65
The Aviary (O'Dell), 61, 76

B

Bachmann, Stefan
    The Peculiar, 47, 111, 117
    The Whatnot, 128
The Bad Beginning (Snicket), 82
Bailey, Kristin, 77, 129
Baldwin, Kathleen, 84, 112
Bardugo, Leigh, 53
Bauer, Marion Dane, 133, 139–140
Baum, L. Frank, 85
Bawden, Nina, 55
Beard, David, 14
Beatty, Robert, 46
Bechdel, Alison, 24, 30
Behemoth (Westerfeld), 129

Bell, Cece
El Deafo, 24, 26
Graphic Novels by, 25
The Bell Jar (Plath), 106–107
Bellair, John, 125
Belzhar (Wolitzer), 106–107
Berry, Julie
The Passion of Dolssa, 50–51
The Scandalous Sisterhood of Prickwillow Place, 79, 83
Between Shades of Gray (Sepetys), 151
Beyond the Bright Sea (Wolk), 70–71, 88
Bick, Ilsa J., 84
Billet, Julie, 39
The Birchbark House (Erdrich), 144
Birdsall, Jeanne, 74
Black, Holly, 56
Black Girl Unlimited (Brown), 91
The Blackthorn Key (Sands), 65, 69
Blanca & Roja (McLemore), 96
Blankets (Thompson), 34
Block, Francesca Lia
I Was a Teenage Fairy, 106
Love in the Time of Global Warming, 97
Blundell, Judy, 60, 67–68
Bob (Mass & Stead), 92
Bojanowski, Sandra, 6
Bone Gap (Ruby), 89–90, 106
The Book of Boy (Murdock), 55, 97–98
The Book of Lost Things (Voigt), 58, 79–80
Booked (Alexander), 133, 135
The Boundless (Oppel), 124
Bow, Erin, 113
Bowers, Mary Ann, 87
Bracken, Alexandra, 104
Bray, Libba
The Diviners, 51, 73
A Great and Terrible Beauty, 17, 46, 118
in historical fantasy genre, 44
The Breakaways (Johnson), 32
The Bridge Home (Venkatraman), 31
Brightstorm (Hardy), 128
Brosgol, Vera, 35
Brown, Echo, 91
Brown, Nancy, 13–14
Brown Girl Dreaming (Woodson), 133, 152–153
Bryant, Megan E., 70

Bunce, Elizabeth C., 79, 83
Burg, Ann E.
All the Broken Pieces, 133, 136
Serafina's Promise, 18, 140–141
Unbound, 133, 141–142
Verse Novel genre and, 134
Burnett, Frances Hodgson, 36–37

C

Cadaver & Queen (Kwitney), 127, 130
Cameron, Sharon, 84
Carey, Edward
for fans of series novels, 44
Heap House, 47, 117
Carey, Janet Lee, 51–52
Carrie's War (Bawden), 55
Carriger, Gail
Curtsies & Conspiracies, 128
Etiquette & Espionage, 111–112
Finishing School books, 111
Manners & Mutiny, 122
novels in Steampunk genre, 110
Carroll, Emily, 29–30
The Case of the Missing Marquess (Springer), 77–78
Cashores, Kristin, 49
Catching a Storyfish (Harrington), 133, 145
Catherine's War (Billet), 39
The Charmed Children of Rookskill Castle (Fox), 54–55, 61
Chbosky, Stephen, 107
Children of Blood and Bone (Adeyemi), 57
Chokshi, Roshani, 52–53
Cinder (Meyer), 113
Cinderella Liberator (Solnit), 40
Cisneros, Sandra, 135
City of Ember (DuPrau), 113
City of Orphans (Avi), 58–59
Clare, Cassandra, 110, 118
Clare, Gwendolyn, 118, 129
Clockwork, or All Wound Up (Pullman), 111, 124–125
Clockwork Angel (Clare), 118
The Clockwork Scarab (Gleason), 120–121
The Clockwork Three (Kirby)
matching readers with, 128, 129
as read-alike, 55
Code Name Verity (Wein), 116

AUTHOR/TITLE INDEX

Colfer, Eoin
  Airman, 114, 118–119
  Illegal, 30–31
  The Collected Essex County (Lemire), 33–34
Condie, Allie, 127
Confessions of an Imaginary Friend (Cuevas), 92
A Contract with God (Eisner), 24
Cooper, Brenda, 85
Coraline (Gaiman), 56
Cornwell, Betsy
  Mechanica, 119–120
  Venturess, 129
Count Karlstein (Pullman), 43
Courting Darkness (LaFevers), 53, 62
Craft, Jerry
  New Kid, 18, 26–27
  works of, 25
Creech, Sharon
  Love That Dog, 133, 136–137
  Verse Novel genre and, 134
Cremer, Andrea R., 129
Crenshaw (Applegate), 92
Crispin (Avi), 98
Crossley-Holland, Kevin, 43
The Crossover (Alexander), 135
Crowder, Melanie, 18, 142–143
Cuckoo Song (Hardinge), 55–56
Cuevas, Michelle, 92
Cunningham, Hugh, 3
Curtis, Christopher Paul, 142
Curtsies & Conspiracies (Carriger), 128
Cushman, Karen, 61
Cypress, Leah, 48

D

The Dark Days Club (Goodman), 58, 62
The Dark Matter of Mona Starr (Gulledge), 33
The Dark Unwinding (Cameron), 84
Dashner, James, 115
Death Sworn (Cypress), 48
Detorie, Rick, 29
Devil and the Bluebird (Mason-Black), 108
The Diamond of Drury Lane (Golding), 83
DiCamillo, Kate
  The Magician's Elephant, 72

The Tale of Despereaux, 50
Dickinson, Peter, 126
The Disturbed Girl's Dictionary (Ramos), 135
The Diviners (Bray), 51, 73
Dolamore, Jaclyn, 46, 129
Doll Bones (Black), 56
Donkin, Andrew, 30–31
Donnelly, Jennifer
  A Northern Light, 68–69
  Stepsister, 62
  These Shallow Graves, 72–73
Downes, Anne, 7–8
The Downstairs Girl (Lee), 70
The Dragon's Boy (Yolen), 43
Dragon's Gate (Yep), 124
Dragon's Keep (Carey), 51–52
Drama (Telgemeier), 28
Draw the Dark (Bick)
  dark secrets in, 65
  matching readers with, 84
  past/present in, 66
Dread Nation (Ireland), 56–57
Dreamland Burning (Latham)
  dark secrets in, 65
  overview of, 75–76
  past/present in, 66
DuPrau, Jeanne, 113

E

Eagar, Lindsay, 103
Echo (Ryan), 36
Eisner, Will, 24
El Deafo (Bell)
  genre blends in, 24
  graphic art in, 25
  overview of, 26
Elizabeth and Zenobia (Miller), 65, 76
Ella Enchanted (Levine), 112
Enchanted Air: Two Cultures, Two Wings (Engle), 153
The End of the Wild (Helget), 95
Engle, Margarita
  Enchanted Air: Two Cultures, Two Wings, 153
  Jazz Owls, 148
  With a Star in My Hand, 139
English, Karen, 27

202   AUTHOR/TITLE INDEX

Erdrich, Louise, 144
Escape from Mr. Lemoncello's Library
   (Grabenstein), 75
Etiquette & Espionage (Carriger), 111–112
Everland (Spinale), 116, 130
Everybody Sees the Ants (King), 107

F

The Falconer's Knot: A Story of Friars,
   Flirtation and Foul Play (Hoffman),
   50–51, 84
Falling Over Sideways (Sonnenblick), 89
Faris, Wendy B., 86
Faruqi, Reem, 152
Fever Crumb (Reeve), 126–127
Finishing School books (Carriger),
   111–112
First Class Murder (Stevens), 83
The First Rule of Punk (Perez), 32
Fisher, Catherine, 112–113
Fleischman, Sid, 72
Flores, Angel, 85
Ford, Michael, 53–54
Fowler, Olive, 7–8
Fox, Helena, 89
Fox, Janet, 54–55, 61
Frankenstein (Shelley), 109
Frost, Helen, 133, 143–144
Fun Home (Bechdel), 24, 30
Funke, Cornelia
   Inkheart, 125
   The Thief Lord, 93–94

G

Gaiman, Neil
   Coraline, 56
   The Graveyard Book, 38, 117
Garber, Romina, 91
Garfield, Leon, 65
Garvey's Choice (Grimes), 144–145
George, Jessica Day, 62
Ghost (Reynolds), 27
Ghostopolis (TenNapel), 37–38
Ghosts (Telgemeier), 28
Gibbons, Dave, 23
Gidwitz, Adam, 55, 98
Gilbert, Kelly Loy, 101

The Gilded Cage (Gray), 73, 84
The Gilded Wolves (Chokshi), 52–53
The Girl Is Murder (Haines)
   as Historical Mystery, 65
   overview of, 73–74
   as read-alike, 68
The Girl Is Trouble (Haines), 78, 83
The Girl Who Could Silence the Wind
   (Medina), 108
The Glass Sentence (Grove), 126
Gleason, Colleen, 110, 120–121
Glow (Bryant)
   dark secrets in, 65
   past/present in, 66
   as read-alike, 70
Goblin Secrets (Alexander), 116–117
The Golden Compass (Pullman), 125–126
Golding, Julia, 83
Goliath (Westerfeld), 129
Goodman, Alison, 58, 62
Grabenstein, Chris, 75
Graceling (Cashores), 49
Grave Mercy (LaFevers), 48–49
The Graveyard Book (Gaiman), 38, 117
Gray, Lucinda, 73, 84
Grayling's Song (Cushman), 61
A Great and Terrible Beauty (Bray)
   matching readers with, 17
   overview of, 46
   as read-alike, 118
Greenglass House (Milford), 69
Grimes, Nikki
   Garvey's Choice, 144–145
   Words with Wings, 145
Grove, S. E., 126
Gulledge, Laura Lee, 33
Guts (Telgemeier), 28

H

Ha, Robin, 29
Haddix, Margaret Peterson, 120
Haines, Kathryn Miller
   The Girl Is Murder, 68, 73–74
   The Girl Is Trouble, 78, 83
Hale, Shannon, 26
Hamster Princess: Harriet the Invincible
   (Vernon), 40

AUTHOR/TITLE INDEX

Hardinge, Frances
  Cuckoo Song, 55–56
  in historical fantasy genre, 44
  The Lie Tree, 47–48, 54
  A Skinful of Shadows, 62
Hardy, Vashti, 128
Harrington, Janice N., 133, 145
Hartley, A. J., 123, 129
Hartman, Rachel, 52
Hatchet (Paulsen), 124
Hate That Cat (Creech), 137
The Hate U Give (Thomas), 81
Hattie Big Sky (Larson), 69
The Haunting of Falcon House (Yelchin), 62
Heap House (Carey), 47, 117
Heartbeat (Creech), 137
Helget, Nicole Lea, 95
Hell & High Water (Landman), 84
Hesse, Karen
  Out of the Dust, 132, 133, 146
  Stowaway, 122
Hey, Kiddo (Krosoczka), 25, 32–33
Hiassen, Carl, 95
The Higher Power of Lucky (Patron), 102
Hiranandani, Veera, 103
The Hired Girl (Schlitz), 69
His Name Was Walter (Rodda), 36
The Hobbit (Tolkien), 117
Hoffman, Alice
  Incantation, 51
  Practical Magic, 97
Hoffman, Mary, 50–51, 84
Holm, Jennifer L., 31
Holm, Matthew, 31
Home of the Brave (Applegate), 133, 137–138
Honor Girl (Thrash), 38–39, 41
Hoot (Hiassen), 95
Hopkinson, Deborah, 82, 83
Hour of the Bees (Eagar), 103
The House on Mango Street (Cisneros), 135
The House with a Clock in Its Walls (Bellair), 125
House without Walls (Russell), 136, 147
How I Became a Spy (Hopkinson), 82, 83
How It Feels to Float (Fox), 89

The Hundred and One Dalmations (Smith), 140
The Hundred Secret Senses (Tan), 101

I

I Was a Teenage Fairy (Block), 106
Ibbotson, Eva, 71, 74
Illegal (Eoin & Donkin), 30–31
In the Shadow of the Blackbirds (Winters), 63
Incantation (Hoffman), 51
Incarceron (Fisher), 112–113
Ink, Iron, and Glass (Clare), 118, 129
Inkheart (Funke), 125
The Inquisitor's Apprentice (Moriarty), 58–59, 80
The Inquisitor's Tale, or, The Three Magical Children and Their Holy Dog (Gidwitz), 55, 98
Inside Out & Back Again (Lai)
  as immigration story, 133
  overview of, 146–147
  as read-alike, 136
The Invention of Hugo Cabret (Selznick), 80
The Inventor's Secret (Cremer), 129
Ireland, Justina, 44, 56–57
Iron Cast (Soria), 51, 63
The Iron Thorn (Kittredge), 120, 129
Island of the Blue Dolphins (O'Dell), 71
It All Comes Down to This (English), 27
Iyengar, Sheena S., 6

J

Jackaby (Ritter)
  as Historical Fantasy/Historical Mystery, 45
  matching readers with, 63
  as read-alike, 121
Jacob Have I Loved (Paterson), 74
Jake and Lily (Spinelli), 31
Jamieson, Victoria
  Roller Girl, 28, 31–32
  When Stars Are Scattered, 31, 149
Jazz Owls (Engle), 148
Johnson, Cathy G., 32
Johnson, Jaleigh
  The Mark of the Dragonfly, 113

Johnson, Jaleigh *(continued)*
    The Quest to the Uncharted Lands,
      121–122
Johnson, Varian, 74–75
Jones, Kelly, 57–58
The Journey of Little Charlie (Curtis), 142
Just Ella (Haddix), 120

K
Keller, Tae, 35
Kiely, Brendan, 105
King, Amy Sarig
    Everybody Sees the Ants, 107
    Me and Marvin Gardens, 87, 94–95
    Please Ignore Vera Dietz, 107
    Still Life with Tornado, 107
King Arthur Trilogy (Sutcliff), 43
The Kingdom of Back (Lu), 62
Kirby, Matthew J.
    The Clockwork Three, 55, 128, 129
    A Taste for Monsters, 51, 62
Kittredge, Caitlin, 120, 129
Konigsberg, Bill, 99
Krashen, Stephen, 15
Kristoff, Jay, 122–123
Krosoczka, Jarrett, 25, 32–33
Kwiecien, Shelley, 6
Kwitney, Alisa, 127, 130

L
LaFevers, Robin
    Courting Darkness, 53, 62
    Grave Mercy, 48–49
    in historical fantasy genre, 44
    Theodosia & the Serpents of Chaos, 61
Lai, Thanhhà, 133, 136, 146–147
Landman, Tanya, 84
The Language of Spells (Weyr), 62
Larklight (Reeve), 127–128
Larson, Kirby, 69
The Last Voyage of Poe Blythe (Condie),
    127
Latham, Jennifer, 75–76
Law, Ingrid, 102
Lawson, Jessica, 83
Le Guin, Ursula K., 52
Lee, Mackenzi, 130

Lee, Stacey, 70
Lee, Y. S., 77, 84
Legacy of the Clockwork Key (Bailey), 77,
    129
Legend (Lu), 113
Lemire, Jeff, 33–34
Leno, Katrina, 95–96
Lepper, Mark R., 6
Leviathan (Westerfeld), 115–116
Leviathan Trilogy (Westerfeld), 111, 115
Levine, Gail Carson, 112
Lewis, C. S., 85
Liar & Spy (Stead), 82
Library Journal, 9
The Lie Tree (Hardinge), 47–48, 54
The Light Between Worlds (Weymouth),
    46, 63
Light It Up (Magoon), 76
The Lightning Queen (Resau), 102–103
Like Water on Stone (Walrath), 150–151
Lirael (Nix), 123
Listening for Lions (Whelan), 74
Little Cat's Luck (Bauer), 133, 139–140
Little Dog, Lost (Bauer), 140
Lobizona (Garber), 91
Lockhart, E., 107
Long Way Down (Reynolds), 149–150
Love in the Time of Global Warming
    (Block), 97
Love That Dog (Creech), 133, 136–137
Lovejoy, Sharon, 142
Lowry, Lois, 82
Lu, Marie
    The Kingdom of Back, 62
    Legend, 113
Lucky Strike (Pyron), 101–102
Lyddie (Paterson), 54

M
Maas, Sarah J., 49
Mabry, Samantha
    All the Wind in the World, 107
    Tigers, Not Daughters, 108
Magic under Glass (Dolamore), 46, 129
The Magician's Elephant (DiCamillo), 72
Magoon, Kekla, 76
Make Lemonade (Wolff), 132

AUTHOR/TITLE INDEX

Manners & Mutiny (Carriger), 122
The Mark of the Dragonfly (Johnson), 113
Mark of the Plague (Sands), 83
Mark of the Thief (Nielsen), 59
Márquez, Gabriel García, 86
Mason-Black, Jennifer, 108
Mass, Wendy, 92
Maus (Spiegelman), 24
Max and the Midknights (Peirce), 40
The Maze Runner (Dashner), 115
McArdle, Megan M., 4
McBratnie, Sean, 5
McCall, Guadalupe Garcia, 147–148
McGhee, Alison, 87–88
McLemore, Anna-Marie
    Blanca & Roja, 96
    When the Moon Was Ours, 86–87, 90, 96–97
    Wild Beauty, 108
McQuerry, Maureen, 123–124
Me and Marvin Gardens (King), 87, 94–95
Mechanica (Cornwell), 119–120
Medina, Meg, 108
Meyer, Marissa, 113
The Midnight Horse (Fleischman), 72
Midnight Magic (Avi), 71–72
Midwinterblood (Sedgwick), 103–104
Milford, Kate, 69
Miller, Jessica, 76
Mohamed, Omar, 31, 149
Monster (Myers), 105
A Monster Calls (Ness)
    matching readers with, 17
    overview of, 88–89
    as read-alike, 100
Moo (Creech), 137
Moore, Allen, 23
Morgan, Tony, 8
Moriarty, Chris, 58–59, 80
Mortal Engines (Reeve), 114–115
The Mouse with the Question Mark Tail (Peck), 61
Murder, Magic, and What We Wore (Jones), 57–58
Murder at Midnight (Avi), 83
Murder Is Bad Manners (Stevens), 78–79
Murder Most Unladylike series, 65

Murdock, Catherine Gilbert, 55, 97–98
The Music of What Happens (Konigsberg), 99
Myers, Walter Dean, 105
The Mysterious Howling (Wood), 81–82

N

Narnia novels (Lewis), 85
Ness, Patrick
    A Monster Calls, 17, 88–89, 100
    Release, 98–99
The Nest (Oppel), 99–100
New Kid (Craft), 18, 26–27
Newt's Emerald (Nix)
    matching readers with, 63
    as read-alike, 58
    suspense in, 45
Nidhi, Chanani, 24, 34–35
Nielsen, Jennifer A., 44, 59
The Night Diary (Hiranandani), 103
The Night Gardener (Auxier), 61
Ninth Ward (Rhodes), 141
Nix, Garth
    Lirael, 123
    Newt's Emerald, 45, 58, 63
Nooks & Crannies (Lawson), 83
A Northern Light (Donnelly), 68–69
Notes from My Captivity (Parks), 108

O

O'Dell, Kathleen, 61, 76
O'Dell, Scott, 71
O'Donoghue, Caroline, 95–96
Odyssey, Shawn Thomas, 61
Older, Daniel José, 57
Oliver, Mary, 131
Oppel, Kenneth
    Airborn, 114, 119
    The Boundless, 124
    The Nest, 99–100
    novels in Steampunk genre, 110
    Skybreaker, 128
    Starclimber, 128
Other Words for Home (Warga)
    overview of, 151–152
    as read-alike, 138, 147

Out of the Dust (Hesse)
  as breakout title, 132
  music in, 133
  overview of, 146
Out of the Easy (Sepetys), 68, 69–70
Out Stealing Horses (Petterson), 34

P

Pablo and Birdy (McGhee), 87–88
Palace of Spies (Zettel), 84
Pan, Emily X. R., 17, 100–101
The Parker Inheritance (Johnson), 74–75
Parks, Kathy, 108
Pashmina (Nidhi), 24, 34–35
Passenger (Bracken), 104
The Passion of Dolssa (Berry), 50–51
Paterson, Katherine
  on characters, 66
  Jacob Have I Loved, 74
  Lyddie, 54
Patron, Susan, 102
Paulsen, Gary, 124
The Pearl Thief (Wein), 84
Peck, Richard
  The Mouse with the Question Mark Tail,
    61
  The River Between Us, 81
  Secrets at Sea, 49–50
The Peculiar (Bachmann), 47, 111, 117
The Peculiars (McQuerry), 123–124
Peirce, Lincoln, 40
The Penderwicks (Birdsall), 74
Pène du Bois, William, 43, 119
Perez, Celia, 32
The Perilous Guard (Pope), 43
The Perks of Being a Wallflower (Chbosky),
    107
Persepolis (Satrapi), 24
Peter Nimble and His Fantastic Eyes
    (Auxier), 93–94
Petterson, Per, 34
Picture Us in the Light (Gilbert), 101
Pinkney, Andrea Davis, 148–149
Plath, Sylvia, 106–107
Please Ignore Vera Dietz (King), 107
The Poet X (Acevedo), 133, 134–135
The Poison Diaries (Wood), 48

Poison Is Not Polite (Stevens), 83
The Poisoned House (Ford), 53–54
Pope, Elizabeth Marie, 43
Practical Magic (Hoffman), 97
Pratchett, Teri, 47
Predator's Gold (Reeve), 123, 128
Premeditated Myrtle (Bunce), 79, 83
Prince, Liz, 41
Pullman, Philip
  Clockwork, or All Wound Up, 111,
    124–125
  Count Karlstein, 43
  The Golden Compass, 125–126
  popularity of novels by, 65
  The Ruby in the Smoke, 77, 78
  Sally Lockart series, 121
  series by, 67
Punching the Air (Zoboi & Salaam), 150
Pyron, Bobbie, 101–102

Q

The Quest to the Uncharted Lands
    (Johnson), 121–122

R

Ramos, NoNieqa, 135
Raskin, Ellen, 75
Readers' Advisory Service in the Public
    Library (Saricks & Brown), 13–14
Real Friends (Hale), 26
Rebound (Alexander), 135
The Red Pencil (Pinkney), 133, 148–149
Reeve, Philip
  Fever Crumb, 126–127
  Larklight, 127–128
  Mortal Engines, 114–115
  novels in Steampunk genre, 110
  Predator's Gold, 123, 128
  A Web of Air, 114, 128
Release (Ness), 98–99
Resau, Laura, 102–103
Reynolds, Jason
  Ghost, 27
  Long Way Down, 149–150
Rhodes, Jewell Parker, 141
Rigano, Giovanni, 30
Ritter, William, 63, 121

AUTHOR/TITLE INDEX

The River Between Us (Peck), 81
Rodda, Emily, 36
Roh, Franz, 85
Roller Girl (Jamieson), 28, 31–32
Rooftoppers (Rundell), 93
A Room away from the Wolves (Suma), 60
The Ropemaker (Dickinson), 126
Ross, Catherine Sheldrick, 16–17
Ruby, Laura
 Bone Gap, 89–90, 106
 Thirteen Doorways, Wolves behind Them
  All, 59–60, 74
 York: The Shadow Cipher, 69
The Ruby in the Smoke (Pullman), 77, 78
Rundell, Katherine, 93
Running Out of Night (Lovejoy), 142
Russell, Ching Yeung, 136, 147
Ryan, Pam Muñoz, 36

S

Salaam, Yusef, 150
Sally Lockart series (Pullman), 65, 121
Salt: A Story of Friendship in a Time of War
 (Frost), 133, 143–144
Sands, Kevin
 The Blackthorn Key, 69
 Mark of the Plague, 83
 series by, 67
Saricks, Joyce, 13–14
Satrapi, Marjane, 24
Savvy (Law), 102
The Scandalous Sisterhood of Prickwillow
 Place (Berry), 79, 83
Schlitz, Laura Amy
 The Hired Girl, 69
 Splendors and Glooms, 60–61, 117
A School for Unusual Girls (Baldwin), 84,
 112
The Scorpion Rules (Bow), 113
The Secret Garden (Burnett), 36–37
The Secret of Nightingale Wood (Strange),
 76, 83
Secrets at Sea (Peck), 49–50
Sedgwick, Marcus, 103–104
Selznick, Brian
 The Invention of Hugo Cabret, 80
 Wonderstruck, 26, 35–36

Sepetys, Ruta
 Out of the Easy, 68, 69–70
 Between Shades of Gray, 151
Serafina and the Black Cloak (Beatty), 46
Serafina's Promise (Burg), 18, 140–141
Seraphina (Hartman), 52
Shadowshaper (Older), 57
Shelley, Mary, 109
Silver in the Blood (George), 62
Silvera, Adam, 99
Sisters (Telgemeier), 28
Six of Crows (Bardugo), 53
Skellig (Almond), 100
A Skinful of Shadows (Hardinge), 62
Skybreaker (Oppel), 128
Smile (Telgemeier), 27–28
Smith, Dodie, 140
Smy, Pam, 36–37
Snicket, Lemony, 82
Solnit, Rebecca, 40
Sonnenblick, Jordan, 89
Soria, Destiny, 51, 63
Speak: The Graphic Novel (Anderson &
 Carroll), 29–30
Spiegelman, Art, 24
Spinale, Wendy, 116, 130
Spinelli, Eileen, 145
Spinelli, Jerry, 31
Spinning (Walden), 30, 41
Splendors and Glooms (Schlitz), 60–61, 117
Springer, Nancy, 67, 77–78
A Spy in the House (Lee), 77, 84
Spy Runner (Yelchin), 82
The Star of Kazan (Ibbotson), 71, 74
Starclimber (Oppel), 128
Stead, Rebecca
 Bob, 92
 Liar & Spy, 82
The Steep and Thorny Way (Winters), 76,
 80–81
Steeplejack (Hartley), 123, 129
Steig, William, 50
Stepsister (Donnelly), 62
Stevens, Robin
 First Class Murder, 83
 Murder Is Bad Manners, 78–79
 Poison Is Not Polite, 83

Stevens, Robin *(continued)*
  series by, 67
Still Life with Tornado (King), 107
Stone Mirrors: The Sculpture and Silence of Edmonia Lewis (Atkins), 132–133, 138–139
Stormdancer (Kristoff), 122–123
Stowaway (Hesse), 122
Strange, Lucy, 76, 83
The Strange and Beautiful Sorrows of Ava Lavender (Walton), 104, 105–106
Stroud, Jonathan, 59
Suma, Nova Ren
  A Room away from the Wolves, 60
  The Walls Around Us, 104–105
Summer of Salt (Leno), 95–96
Sutcliff, Rosemary, 43
Sweep: The Story of a Girl and Her Monster (Auxier), 45–46, 61
The Sweetest Sound (Winston), 145
Swing It, Sunny (Holm & Holm), 31

T

The Tale of Despereaux (DiCamillo), 50
Tamaki, Mariko, 39
Tan, Amy, 101
A Taste for Monsters (Kirby), 51, 62
Telgemeier, Raina
  Graphic Novels by, 25
  Smile, 27–28
TenNapel, Doug, 37–38
Thanks for the Trouble (Wallach), 108
Theodosia & the Serpents of Chaos (LaFevers), 61
These Shallow Graves (Donnelly), 72–73
They Both Die at the End (Silvera), 99
Thi-Beard, Kate Vo, 14
The Thief (Turner), 59
The Thief Lord (Funke), 93–94
Thirteen Doorways, Wolves behind Them All (Ruby), 59–60, 74
This Monstrous Thing (Lee), 130
This One Summer (Tamaki), 39
Thomas, Angie, 81
Thompson, Craig, 34
Thorley, Addie, 63
Thornhill (Smy), 36–37

Thrash, Maggie, 38–39, 41
Throne of Glass (Maas), 49
Tigers, Not Daughters (Mabry), 108
The Time Machine (Wells), 109
To See the Stars (Andrews), 143
Tolkien, J. R. R., 117
Tolstikova, Dasha, 39
Tomboy: A Graphic Memoir (Prince), 41
The Tombs of Atuan (Le Guin), 52
Trent, Tiffany, 123–124
Truckers (Pratchett), 47
Turner, Megan Whalen, 59
Twenty Thousand Leagues under the Sea (Verne), 109
The Twenty-One Balloons (Pène du Bois), 43, 119

U

Unbound (Burg), 133, 141–142
Under the Mesquite (McCall), 133, 147–148
The Unnaturalists (Trent), 123–124
Unsettled (Faruqi), 152
Uss, Christina, 88

V

Van Riel, Rachel, 7–8
Venkatraman, Padma, 31
Venturess (Cornwell), 129
Verne, Jules, 109
Vernon, Ursula, 40
Voigt, Cynthia, 58, 79–80

W

Walden, Tillie
  Are You Listening? 39
  Spinning, 30, 41
Wallach, Tommy, 108
The Walls Around Us (Suma), 104–105
Walrath, Dana, 150–151
Walton, Leslye, 104, 105–106
Warga, Jasmine, 138, 147, 151–152
Watchmen (Moore & Gibbons), 23
We Were Liars (Lockhart), 107
A Web of Air (Reeve), 114, 128
Wein, Elizabeth
  Code Name Verity, 116
  The Pearl Thief, 84

AUTHOR/TITLE INDEX

Wells, H. G., 109
Westerfeld, Scott
  Behemoth, 129
  Goliath, 129
  Leviathan, 115–116
  Leviathan Trilogy, 111, 115
  novels in Steampunk genre, 110
The Westing Game (Raskin), 75
Weymouth, Laura E., 46, 63
Weyr, Garret, 62
Whaley, John Corey, 90
What I Saw and How I Lied (Blundell), 60,
  67–68
The Whatnot (Bachmann), 128
Whelan, Gloria, 74
When Stars Are Scattered (Jamieson &
  Mohamed), 31, 149
When the Moon Was Ours (McLemore)
  magic in Magical Realism, 86–87
  overview of, 96–97
  as read-alike, 90
When You Trap a Tiger (Keller), 35
Where I Live (Spinelli), 145
Where Things Comes Back (Whaley), 90
Wild Beauty (McLemore), 108
The Willoughbys (Lowry), 82
Winston, Sherri, 145
Winters, Cat
  In the Shadow of the Blackbirds, 63
  The Steep and Thorny Way, 76, 80–81
With a Star in My Hand (Engle), 139
Witness (Hesse), 146
The Wizard of Dark Street (Odyssey), 45,
  61

The Wizard of Oz (Baum), 85
Wolf Hollow (Wolk), 46
Wolff, Virginia Euwer, 132
Wolitzer, Meg, 106–107
Wolk, Lauren
  Beyond the Bright Sea, 70–71, 88
  Wolf Hollow, 46
Wonderstruck (Selznick)
  overview of, 35–36
  as read-alike, 26, 37
Wood, Maryrose
  The Mysterious Howling, 81–82
  The Poison Diaries, 48
  series by, 67
Woodson, Jacqueline, 133, 152–153
Words with Wings (Grimes), 145
Worth, Sarah E., 5

Y

Yang, Gene Luen, 25, 28–29
A Year without Mom (Tolstikova), 39
Yelchin, Eugene
  The Haunting of Falcon House, 62
  Spy Runner, 82
Yep, Laurence, 124
Yolen, Jane, 43
York: The Shadow Cipher (Ruby), 69

Z

Zettel, Sarah, 84
Zoboi, Ibi
  American Street, 90–91
  Punching the Air, 150